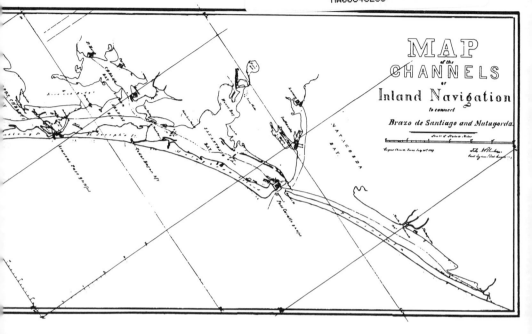

The map on inside covers, prepared in 1867 by Felix A. Blucher, shows the coastline during the 1860s. The line down the center of the bays is Blucher's proposed location of an intracoastal canal. (Corpus Christi State University, Special Collections Section)

TEXAS FORGOTTEN PORTS

Mid-Gulf Coast Ports from Corpus Christi to Matagorda Bay

Keith Guthrie

Illustrated by Iris Guthrie

EAKIN PRESS ★ Austin, Texas

FIRST EDITION

Copyright © 1988
By Keith Guthrie

Published in the United States of America
By Eakin Press, P.O. Box 90159, Austin, Texas 78709

ISBN 0-89015-661-1

34567890

LIBRARY OF CONGRESS
Library of Congress Cataloging-in-Publication Data

Guthrie, Keith.
     Texas' forgotten ports / by Keith Guthrie
        p.   cm.
     Bibliography: p.
     Includes index.
     ISBN 0-89015-661-1 : $22.95
     1. Gulf Coast (U.S.) — History. 2. Texas — History, Local. 3. Harbors —
Texas — History. 4. Harbors — Gulf Coast (U.S.) — History. I. Title.
F392.G9G87   1988
976.4'1 - dc19   88-16504
                                                                                                CIP

*It is with pride that this book is dedicated to our grandchildren —
Alan, Janey, and Carol Thomas; Jessica and Patrick Houser;
and Sara, Douglas, and Matthew Guthrie.*

Contents

Preface

There are many rewards that come from writing a book. The biggest is meeting and talking to people who are interested in their local history. The stories about the old port cities of the mid-Texas coast are unique, since they tell a side of Texas history too often forgotten. The men who founded these ancient port cities had a lot in common. They were adventurers who knew they were involved in making history. At the same time, they were astute businessmen who had dreams of making a fortune. The real estate boom of the 1830s, 1840s, and 1850s brought out the best, and worst, of these men as they all sought to establish the dreamed-of Gateway to the West port city.

A great number of these cities boomed and died during the post-Texas Republic days. Several are still prosperous cities with thriving coastal port trade. Only one, Corpus Christi, was able to bring her dreams to full fruition and become a deepwater port.

As my wife and I traveled throughout the area, folks were most generous in helping us. Mr. and Mrs. Abel Pierce of Blessing took us out to view the old site of Tidehaven, despite the fact that rain had somewhat of a dampening effect on the river safari. Roy Traylor of Matagorda took time out to visit with us about olden times. Margaret Pickel of Bay City allowed us to browse through the stacks and stacks of notes made by her brother, James Yeamans, Sr., who had devoted a lifetime to writing about Matagorda. He had hoped to publish a book, but died before doing so. I trust that he would approve of the way we have used some of his original material. A number of other people furnished us letters, family histories, and other stories which dealt with the old port cities. Mrs. Fred Mires of Taft not only furnished us information about Lamar, but went with us to Live Oak Point to show us where her pioneer ancestors, the McRaes and Brundretts, settled in the Texas Republic days.

We especially want to thank the people in the libraries who helped us gather material. Donna Hutchins of the Taft Public Library fed our requests for books into the South Texas Library System, which did a wonderful job of sending us material from all over the state. Margaret Rose of the Corpus Christi Public Library took time out to dig out material which only librarians know about. Lucy Swanger of the Victoria Public Library helped us along the way. Paul Medley, research librarian at Corpus Christi State University, assisted our work in the Kilgore Collection. Frances Parker of the Bay City Public Library took time out to give us invaluable insights into the history of Matagorda County. The libraries at Port Lavaca and Rockport also gave us assistance.

George Fred Rhodes of Port Lavaca provided more than help — he furnished us a number of back issues of his weekly column, "Historically Speaking," which deals with the history of Calhoun County. His interest was very helpful. Dr. John Tunnell opened his large Texana library to our use and even dug into books to aid in our search for little-known happenings.

In the time that I have been delving into early history of South Texas, I have developed a sincere admiration for historian Hobart Huson. His two-volume work on the history of Refugio County serves as a guide for any historical work of the area. My only regret is that I put off too long to visit personally with the greatest historian South Texas ever produced.

My wife Iris and I hope that you enjoy the book as much as we enjoyed putting it together.

Corpus Christi Bay/ Aransas Bay

(Copano Bay, St. Charles Bay, Mission Bay, Red Fish Bay)

Sparkling sand, clear blue water, and an abundance of freshwater rivers and creeks greeted early explorers as they sailed into Corpus Christi and Aransas bays of Texas. No doubt literally hundreds of early expeditions pushed into these bays and river basins as explorer-adventurers sought to experience the amazingly beautiful South Texas coast.

Who came first? No one will ever know exactly, but Alonzo Álvarez de Piñeda had to be one of the first. He brought a four-ship convoy to the Gulf Coast under orders from the Spanish king to explore and map the coastline from Florida to Vera Cruz. The maps that this explorer made were said to have been in the possession of Panfilo de Narvaez when he headed the expedition in 1527 of the famous Alvar Nuñez Cabeza de Vaca.[1]

Probably no diary has been studied more by Southwestern historians than that which Cabeza de Vaca made in his six-year odyssey of wandering along the Texas coast. Shipwrecked, and eventually washed ashore on Galveston Island, Cabeza de Vaca gave us graphic descriptions of the pristine land and its native Indians. Narvaez and Cabeza de Vaca started their expedition in 1527, and

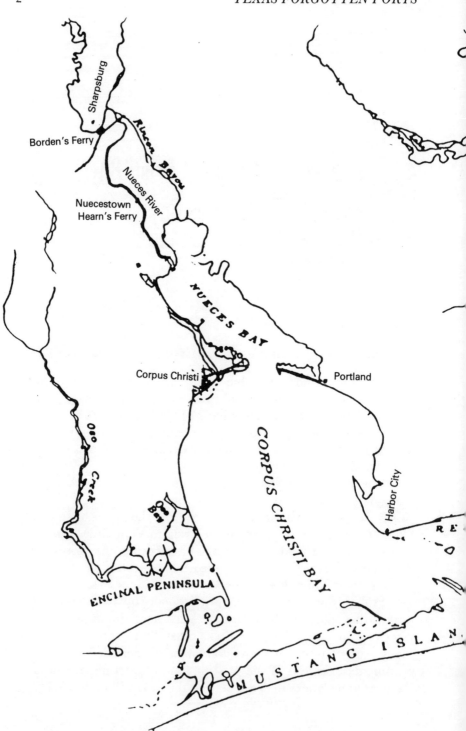

*CORPUS CHRISTI AND ARANSAS BAYS — A great deal of traffic passed
over the bar between Mustang and St. Joseph islands during the pre-Texas Republic
and postwar days. About eight to eleven feet of water flowed over the bar, depending
upon the condition of the tide, but many boats broke up after missing the pass. The earliest port founded in these bays was El Copano.*

for the latter the adventure lasted more than six years. Cabeza de Vaca's wanderings brought him into the Coastal Bend area, and many historians place his adventures in the Aransas Bay area.

René Robert Cavelier, Sieur de La Salle, brought the French influence to the Texas coast in 1685 when he landed in Matagorda Bay. La Salle, who had been aiming for the mouth of the Mississippi, made the best of a bad situation and set out to map the entire Texas coast. His map clearly shows the bays and rivers in this area, giving credence to the belief that he worked through Aransas and Corpus Christi bays.[2]

Alonso de León's 1689 expedition came by land from Mexico to find La Salle. Since he made several expeditions between 1689 and 1691, it is considered probable by historians that he probed as far as Corpus Christi Bay.[3]

In December of 1686 two barks were authorized by the Spanish to be built, equipped with oars and sails, of a shallow draft, in order to investigate all of the bays and rivers along the Texas coast. These crafts were skippered by Capt. Martín de Rivas and Capt. Antonio de Iriarte. The expedition took so long that the authorities sent out another party to look for the first. As a result, two reports were filed.[4]

The trip of Jean Béranger into Aransas Bay in 1720 offers a number of important facts about the local Indians and surroundings. His maps clearly identify Harbor Island, and his descriptions of the Karankawa Indians are some of the best in existence.[5]

A party of Frenchmen came ashore on St. Joseph Island in 1712 and were murdered by the natives. Another group of Frenchmen landed in 1718 on the same island and were unharmed. In 1721 Barnard de la Harpe, with the explorer Semars de Bellisle, landed at Matagorda Bay and built a fort.[6]

The influence of José de Escandón was great, since his maps and field notes exhibit a high degree of accuracy. Commissioned by the Spanish government, he conducted his explorations to the Texas coast between 1745 and 1747. Escandón remained active in colonial affairs and was still busy making detailed investigations on Padre, Mustang, and St. Joseph islands in 1766.[7]

Ortíz Parrilla was also instrumental in advancing knowledge of the area. In 1766 he headed an expedition that left the Rio Grande and crossed the Nueces River near Mathis, probably at the La Fruta crossing, and then explored the river to its mouth. He explored the Nueces River Valley and San Patricio County as far as Ingleside. Part of his recommendation was that two forts be founded in the area. The old Spanish fort of Aranzaza on Live Oak Point is thought to be a direct result of his comments. The other was probably at Mesquite Landing.[8]

During the period of 1766 to 1785, the Spanish government was active in the exploration of South Texas and the coastline. It was during this period that the mission system was started, with supply lines from the coast to supply the churches. The old port of El Copano was known to have been used to supply Goliad and Bexar. San Bernardo Landing is also mentioned in early Spanish papers as having been used as an off-loading port to supply missions. San Bernardo was near the later community of Matagorda. In fact, Matagorda Bay was known as San Bernardo Bay during this early period.[9]

In 1785 the Spanish government commissioned Don José de Evia to prepare charts of the Texas coast. The method was unique. Mapping was conducted from the ships the *Grande* and *Chica Besana* and from a land party headed by de Evia. He had to use several pirogues to be able to get through the many marshes which dotted the coast.[10]

Fresh water was always a primary consideration of old sailing vessels, with limited capacity to carry drinking water. The bays of this region had an abundance of rivers and creeks that flowed pure water. In some instances the rivers proved navigable many miles upstream. The Nueces River was the largest stream to enter Corpus Christi Bay; however, Oso Creek did furnish some water. Streams emptying into Copano Bay included the Mission River, Chiltipin Creek, Aransas River, and Copano Creek. Several small creeks fed St. Charles Bay.

Sailing ships, particularly the smaller ones, had flat bottoms and could be eased in close to the sandy beaches. Some beaches were better suited as unloading places for explorers, and these locations became known as "landings." In many cases, landings turned into early port cities.

One thing that explorers of this region shared was their delight in the beauty of the Texas coast.

El Copano
First Texas Seaport

It was a good life at the *Paraje de los Copanes* (Place of the Copanes) that had been unchanged for countless years.[1] The Copano
Indians, one of the branches of the Karankawa Nation,[2] kept coming back year after year to the banks of Copano Bay because everything was to their liking: They had campsites on high ground, game
was plentiful on the prairies and along the creeks that snaked their
way into Mission Bay, and, above all, oysters and fish abounded in
the clear waters of Copano Bay. "The Big Field," their burial
ground, was nearby, keeping them close to their ancestors.

The love that the Copanoes had for their native habitat was
evidenced in the 1790s. Father Manuel Julio Silva was directed by
the Catholic church to inspect existing missions and to encourage
the missionaries in their apostolic labors. At that time there were
eight missions in Texas: five in San Antonio, Espiritu Santo and
Rosario in Goliad, and one in Nacogdoches.[3] The *padres* had an especially hard time keeping the Karankawas and Copanoes in the
Mission Rosario, chiefly because the Indians loved their old hunting grounds and returned there at every opportunity. Probably
they were also better able to find food on the shores of Copano Bay
than at Mission Rosario, where the standard fare was corn, beans,
chili, watermelons, cantaloupes, pumpkins, and garden produce
garnered by the sweat of the Indians. Finding food on the banks of
Copano Bay was fun for the Indians and did not involve blisters or
the sweat of the brow.

When Father Silva consulted the Copanoes as to why they had
left Mission Rosario, he got this reply from Chief Llano Grande: "If
you want to, put a mission here on the coast for us. We will gather
in it, all of us who are Christians, and we will bring with us all the
heathens who are on this coast from the mouth of the Nueces to the
Colorado River." [4] Thus the idea of a new mission was born —
Mission de Nuestra Señora del Refugio.

Actually, church politics entered into the picture and the mission was finally located, according to author Carlos E. Castañeda,
on an islet formed by the mouths of the Guadalupe River.[5] It was
known as *Muelle Viejo*, or the Old Wharf (later known as Mesquite
Landing). The swampy location proved to be a disaster, totally un-
suited for a mission settlement.

In February 1793 the mission was moved to a location in present-day Calhoun County. The site is at the confluence of the Guadalupe and San Antonio rivers on a high bank of Goff Bayou, about a half mile from the present town of Long Mott. Hard times, and trouble with Karankawa Chief Fresada Pinto, eventually caused the mission to be moved to a site easier to protect called the Rancho de los Mosquitos. It was located on Los Mosquitos Creek, a small stream on the south side of the Guadalupe River about halfway between the juncture of the San Antonio and Guadalupe rivers in what is now Refugio County.[6]

The new site did not prove to be satisfactory, and, with the backing of Father Silva, the mission was moved once again, this time to Rancho de Santa Gertrudis, or present-day Refugio.

It is at this point that historians disagree.[7] Persistent oral tradition tells that at one time the old church was actually located on Mission Bay, or on Copano Bay (then Aranzazu Bay). Hobart Huson tells the story:

> At the present time the ruins of several large shell-concrete buildings can still be discerned at Hynes Spring, which is near the north side of Mission Lake and below the mouth of Melon Creek. This site is situated near the toe of the slope of a high bluff, about 20 feet above sea level. Hynes Spring was formerly a perennial fresh water spring. It is now dry, probably because of debris filling it. As it now appears, the spring is a perfectly circular hole about 10 feet in diameter and about nine feet deep to the debris which now encumbers it. Its appearance would indicate an artificial enlargement and improvement of the natural spring.[8]

George C. Martin, archaeologist and historian of Rockport, had this to say:

> For some unknown reason, the site of the Mission of Refugio in Calhoun County proved unsatisfactory, so about two years after its founding the mission was removed to a site near the Port of Copano, in the country occupied by the Copanes. It is probable that the protection afforded by the garrison at the port had something to do with the removal.[9]

Dr. Herbert E. Bolton, an authority on Texas missions, adds more proof:

> The site of the mission was near the mouth of the Mission River flowing into Aransas Bay. The actual site to which the mission

was removed was on the north side of the stream close to the junction of what are now known as Mission Lake and Mission Bay. In recent times the ground on which the mission stood has yielded sherds of pottery of Indian manufacture, sherds of such as were made at the missions under Spanish instruction, and crosses chiseled out of sheets of lead.[10]

An ancient map, in the possession of Earl Albrecht of Austin, actually shows a mission symbol on Mission Bay — thus, he says, the name "Mission Bay."

Life was first breathed into the Port of El Copano when Don José Galvez was viceroy and decreed that a port be opened for trade and small commerce.[11] Little was known about Aranzazu Bay (Copano Bay) in the last part of the 1700s until Don José de Evia charted it in 1785,[12] despite the fact that a number of Spanish and French explorers had sailed up and down the Texas coast and poked into its bays. On May 15, 1785, Evia set out from Florida with two schooners, the *Grande* and the *Chica Besana*. His instructions were to chart the Texas coast from Barataria (Jean Lafitte's refuge) to the Rio Bravo. Later the plan was amended to cover the territory from the Bay of San Bernardo (Matagorda) and work his way south.[13]

The work was accomplished by putting Capt. Don Elias de Castro in charge of a land party making readings while other sightings were made from the ship. When the land party reached a boggy area, they used pirogues to skirt the area. The maps produced by this expedition were reduced to one by Juan de Langara in 1799 and is known today as the Langara map.[14] As an outgrowth of this expedition, as well as other compelling reasons, the first port of Texas, El Copano, was established by Galvez's vice-regal decree in 1785. It is generally agreed by historians that Copano Bay had been used as a place to offload supplies destined for La Bahía and Bexar as early as 1750.[15]

Today the old port is a forgotten memory. Its shell-crete buildings that sheltered countless early settlers to South Texas are now crumbled mounds overgrown with weeds and running mesquite. The shores that saw both the Mexican army and volunteers for the Texas War for Independence land their men and supplies are now eroded by the constant wave action. The piers that were the lifeline of the early settlers, for both imports and exports, are all gone. The giant crescent-shaped oyster shell reef that outlined the protected

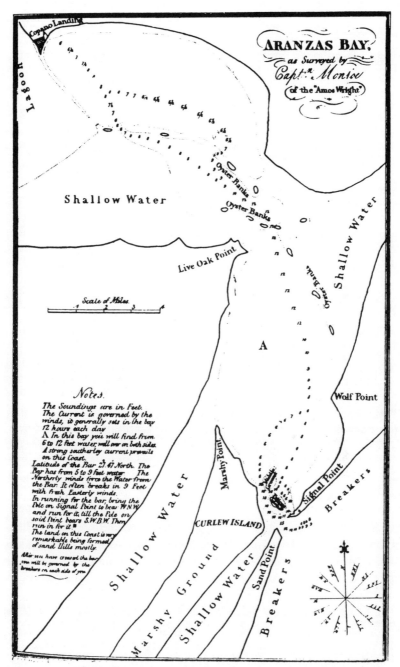

CAPT. I. MUNROE brought the Amos Wright *into Copano Bay in 1833 and provided future ship captains with this amazingly accurate chart, complete with soundings, of the channel from Aransas Pass into El Copano, or Copano Landing. (First published in Kennedy's* Texas *in 1841)*

harbor is no more, probably dredged out to pave roads in the area.
The natural channel that the sharp-eyed sailing skippers could
trace due to its dark blue hue is gone. The site is still picturesque,
but hardly up to Hobart Huson's stirring description:

> No land boasts a more beautiful inland coast than Texas. Mere
> words are inadequate to describe its superlative charm. No can-
> vas can ever recreate its glories. No score can ever perpetuate its
> divine rhapsodies. One of its most ornate jewels is the now aban-
> doned and almost forgotten port of El Copano, in Refugio
> County.[16]

No doubt the port of El Copano was used by the Spanish, and
later the Mexicans, in getting supplies to Goliad and Bexar. But
early in its history the port got a name as a haven for smugglers.
Records reveal that one of the main reasons that the Spanish
wanted to establish a mission west of the Guadalupe was that Copano Bay had been for some time one of the principal landings for
vessels engaged in smuggling.[17] This also gives credence to the idea
that the Refugio Mission, with its accompanying soldiers, was at
one time located on the banks of Mission Bay just a few miles from
the Port of El Copano. Perhaps the seclusion of this port made it a
haven for illicit trade, or it could be that the deep inland bay protected shallow-draft vessels from heavy waves. Nevertheless, smuggling became so great that a garrison was stationed at Aranzazu on
Live Oak Point and another was kept either at the Paraje de los Copanes or near Mission Bay.[18] Aranzazu later became the site of Aransas City. Despite smugglers and unfriendly Indians, trade
through El Copano did exist.

In 1824 a company of Bordeaux merchants landed at El Copano with a large quantity of goods destined for Santa Fe. They
conveyed the goods some distance beyond San Antonio on pack animals until the animals were stolen by the Comanches. The merchants were able to get oxen and carts from San Antonio and eventually reached Santa Fe.[19]

No proof of pirate Jean Lafitte's presence in Copano Bay exists, but old legends persist that he frequently branched out from
his known headquarters in the Cedar Bayou area to the other secluded inland bays such as Copano.

It was during this period that an honest-to-goodness treasure
story "landed" at Copano Bay. Old Spanish records reveal that a
barkentine, laden with specie to pay the military, was blown ashore

in a storm and wrecked in Copano Bay. The Karankawa Indians are said to have plundered the wrecked ship and taken all of the gold, which they fashioned into points for their arrows. The Fagan family in 1829 salvaged a great deal of decking and iron out of the wreck and used it in their home on the San Antonio River.[20]

Through the years illegal trade evidently flourished and did not lessen with the coming of the Americans. In 1830 Gen. Anastacio Bustamente issued a decree regulating trade. To enforce the prohibition against the Americans, he sent troops to Texas and opened customshouses at Bexar, Nacogdoches, Anahuac, Copano, and the mouth of the Brazos, where duties were collected to support the Mexican army of occupation.[21]

El Copano was the focal point of immigration during the empresario days in South Texas. In 1828 James McGloin and John McMullen received a grant from the Mexican government to bring 200 Irish families into Texas. The *New Packet,* loaded with settlers, crossed the bar in late October of 1829 at Aransas Pass. Capt. Jonan Harris unloaded at El Copano the first of many families who were destined to settle in San Patricio and later Refugio.[22] In the next six years El Copano was a busy port, as more and more families braved the unknown to make new homes in the virgin land. James Power and Dr. James Hewetson landed hundreds of families at El Copano during the early 1830s as they developed their colonization grant that ran from the Nueces River to the Guadalupe. Some of the more famous names in South Texas history who arrived through the port were Col. James Grant, Col. Francis W. Johnson, Col. James W. Fannin, the Welders and O'Briens, John J. Linn, and Peter Fagan.

Not all ship arrivals at El Copano were without incident. Quite a few were lost either crossing the bar at Aransas Pass or within the bays. The schooners *Wildcat,* commanded by Captain Ramsdale, and *Sea Lion,* skippered by Captain Living, were wrecked on a reef off Live Oak Point, within sight of their destination. Living became one of the signers of the Goliad Declaration of Independence and served in the Texas navy.[23]

The often-told story of Mrs. Ann Burke depicts the landing of settlers in 1829 at El Copano. To make the story even more poignant, it must be told that her husband had died from cholera while en route and was buried at sea.

Upon landing at El Copano, the colonists' bedding, clothing, foodstuffs, cooking utensils, arms, ammunition, axes, spades and farming equipment were stacked in individual piles on land high enough above the water's edge to protect the property from the tides.

One hour after Mrs. Ann Burke landed at El Copano, labor pains started paving the way for the entrance of a child who was destined to become one of Bee County's prominent ranchmen — and Patrick Burke, Jr., was born.

After reaching mature years, this man, who was the first child born to any of the Irish colonists, wrote a brief autobiography, which was published in the *Galveston News*. His story describes many of the hardships that were experienced by the first settlers and is a historical gem that should be preserved.

"My birth occurred about one hour after my mother set foot on Texas soil and before she had gone the one mile from the shore where she and the other colonists were landed. Her breasts rose and she was unable to nurse me. This section of the country was uninhabited, and it was out of the question to obtain milk or nourishment suitable for an infant.

"But Providence, in His kindness and mysterious way, provided the relief. At this juncture an Indian squaw, who had left her babe with her tribe, entered the camp of the colonists, and, her heart no doubt being touched by my cries, came to my mother's bed, took me and nursed me. Thus, as God sent the ravens to feed Elijah at the brook Cherith, so did He send this uncouth and uncivilized Indian squaw to nurse and furnish me, a starving infant, with nourishment in the wilderness of Texas. She carried me to her tribe and cared for me until my sick and bereaved mother was able to take care of me.

"Each day she brought me back for my mother to see me. Her manner of handling me was in striking contrast with that of my own mother. She would pitch and sling me about like I was a pup or a bundle of dry goods.

"During all the time the colonists remained in the camp this woman was the only Indian who came about us, or even came in sight of any one of the colonists. If others of the tribe ever came near they kept themselves perfectly secreted." [24]

During this period of colonization Captain Monroe, skipper of the schooner *Amos Wright*, brought the Beale and Grant Rio Grande Colony to Texas and landed them at Copano. Captain Monroe was something of a mapmaker and produced a map of Aranzas Bay. On early maps Copano Bay was then part of Aransas (Aranzaso, Aranzazo, Aranzas) Bay and is shown on his map with Live Oak Point as a divider. Previous to this and the Langara map, about the only other map to show Copano Bay was the one attributed to La Salle in 1684–85.

As more and more settlers came through Copano, other ships arrived with lumber and other materials that the people needed to start their homes in a land devoid of any source of supplies closer than New Orleans. El Copano, situated at the end of a long, tortuous channel, was hard to reach by sailing ships. However, a substantial number of ships moved through the old port because it was closer to final destinations than other landings nearer to Aransas Pass. At that time the Mexicans maintained the customs office in Goliad, making it necessary for word to be sent to Goliad that a customs official was needed at El Copano to inspect the cargo of each ship. Messengers used an ancient road, which connected El Copano with the Refugio Mission, and on to Goliad. The road was known as the "Old Saddle Road," indicating that it was suitable for only foot and horseback traffic. Later, a longer and more traveled road known as the "Old Copano Road" was laid out. This road left El Copano along the bluff to the north, crossed Melon Creek, and then proceeded west to Refugio.[25]

During this period of activity at El Copano, frequent mention is made of a customs building that served as a shelter and a place to store goods. Some accounts remembered it as a wooden frame building and others as a brick building. A definite shell-crete type of building did exist later, according to records. In the 1833–34 period a Mexican coast guard unit was stationed at El Copano. Dr. John Charles Beale, in his diary, reported the presence of Mexican officials:

> The master of the schooner [Mr. Monroe] went ashore and brought off the captain of the Mexican coast-guard and all his force, consisting of a corporal and two soldiers. Had at supper the pleasure of the officer's company who went ashore at 7 o'clock, completely intoxicated . . . . There was a small half-finished frame-house on the beach, usually uninhabited, but occupied, when there was any vessel in the bay, by the captain of the coast-guard . . . . Today (Dec. 15, 1833) the much-expected collector of the customs, Don Jose Maria Cosio, made his appearance; and as our vessel *[Amos Wright]* is the largest that has entered this port, he brought with him his wife and another lady, as well as an In-

dian . . . . The Indian amused the people very much by his skill in shooting with bow and arrow. I sent him out to shoot game, and he returned in a short time with a very fine deer, for which I paid him half a dollar.[26]

The schooner *Santa Pia* was purchased by the Mexicans in New Orleans and fitted out as a revenue boat for use in Copano Bay. It was one of many actions through which the Mexican government hoped to control the rapid spread of the Anglo influence on Texas.

Worried by the growth of Texas in 1834, the Mexican government sent Gen. Juan N. Almonte to Texas to report back to General Santa Anna. Part of his report dealt with El Copano:

> Copano seems to be the deepest port in Texas, according to information which I have been able to gather in Bexar. It has from fifteen to eighteen feet of water at the bar and ten or twelve throughout the Bay of Aransas. Ships of small draught can anchor within a few yards of land. The port of Copano is admirably situated for a maritime custom house. There are two roads from this port to Goliad, one over which vehicles may travel, and another suitable only for horse travel. This department has also two other ports: that of Corpus Christi, to the south of Copano, and that of Sabinito, which is to the north in Matagorda Bay.[27]

Almonte also recommended that the port of Copano be fortified. This was never carried out.

Accompanying Almonte on this inspection was Edward Gritton, who was afterwards collector of the port of El Copano in 1835–36. Gritton's closeness to Almonte caused a quarrel in 1836 between Governor Smith and the council.[28]

As Texans began to think more and more of controlling their own destiny, the importance of the old port of El Copano began to take on an even greater significance. Historian Henry Stuart Foote, who wrote his *Texas and the Texans* in 1841, clearly pinpointed the port's importance:

> There are two points on the western frontier of what in 1835 was considered Texas, which may be well called "the Keys" of the country: San Antonio de Bexar, and Goliad, or LaBahia . . . . Both San Antonio and Goliad were, at the period now under review, strongly fortified places, and were, moreover, occupied by Mexican garrisons. Goliad, is distant from Copano, or the head of Aransas Bay, only fifteen leagues, and the interjacent surface be-

tween these two positions is exceedingly level . . . . Copano was famous as a commercial "entrepot" among the Spaniards, more than 50 years ago, and has been at one time a place of deposit for immense quantities of merchandise for the supply of the Mexican population to the west and northwest, who are, unfortunately, destitute of any maritime emporium.[29]

Clearly, it was recognized that El Copano had become the principal port for Goliad and Bexar. A Mexican army advancing from the Rio Grande must draw its supplies by mule train from the Mexican interior, unless El Copano and Aransas Pass, its gulf entrance, were Mexican controlled.[30] The Mexicans recognized this fact and the Texans knew it from experience. Probably few ports in history have been used by two opposing armies on more-or-less an alternating basis.

The year of 1835 may have been one of the busiest in the old port's history. Gen. Martín Perfecto de Cos, son-in-law of General Santa Anna, was commissioned to head an army to crush the rising rebellion in Texas. He moved to Matamoros, where he stayed for several months gathering supplies and troops, getting ready to move his army to Texas. He evidently had many problems, as seen by numerous dispatches. One sent on May 27, 1835, to de la Aduna, administrator at Matagorda, detailed that he was still in Matamoros and ordered Aduna to make every effort to pay expenses of moving troops from El Copano to Bexar.[31]

Messages flew back and forth between the council and the port as everyone anxiously awaited Cos's arrival. John J. Linn, merchant, adventurer, and later mayor of Victoria and author, was sent September 7, 1835, to Copano to provide information on Cos. He sent this message to James Kerr at LaBaca (Lavaca, or now Port Lavaca): "Cos troops arriving. It is possible that I may go to Matagorda and will determine when the carts come back if the whiskey is anything like the other barrel [I will] bring one more." [32] Evidently, Trader Linn was active as well as Spy Linn.

Cos actually landed over 400 troops and munitions at Copano in August of 1835 and proceeded at a leisurely pace to round up carts to transport his supplies to Goliad. The army apparently cleared out of Copano by October, as Philip Dimmitt sent this message to Austin on October 17, 1835: "No hostile forces at Copano." [33]

Once General Cos left El Copano, the Texans moved in and

took charge. Gen. Sam Houston sent a message to Barrett instructing him to station his army to command Port Copano and Refugio Mission. Houston sent another message to Bowie reminding him of the importance of Copano. But Houston also realized the dual role forced on Copano and so advised MacComb on December 18, 1835, to arm his ship, and "in the event the port is not in our possession" to return to Matagorda. Houston sent a message to Allen on December 19 instructing him to proceed with his command to Copano and command the port and protect stores.

Messages went out regularly from Houston to different commanders, advising them to proceed to Copano. Finally, on December 27, Houston sent out this message: "I now recommend that all volunteers come by sea and land at Copano, Coxes Point or Matagorda." The general followed this up on December 30 with: "All volunteers arriving on the shores of Texas will forthwith report to headquarters by express and proceed to Copano where I designate they be stationed — Tents will be necessary at Copano or Refugio." [34]

Col. James Fannin sent a message to James W. Robinson on January 28, 1836, telling him that he had arrived at Aransas Bay aboard the schooner *Columbus*. With Fannin was Major Ward's Georgia Battalion. The schooner *Flora* was also involved. The contingent included four pieces of artillery, two six- and two four-pounders,[35] and the Lone Star flag made by Joanna Troutman, presented by her to Ward's Georgia Company at Columbus, Georgia.[36] The following week it was noted that Fannin's command was scouring the countryside for carts to move supplies toward Refugio.

An eyewitness to the landing of Fannin's men made a note about the physical appearance of the old port: "A lonely, one-story, wooden building, which had formerly served as a warehouse for the goods of the people moving to San Antonio, stood on this immensely beautiful shore." [37]

The strategic importance of the old port was underlined in Houston's letter on February 18 to George Collinsworth. He recommended fortifying Live Oak Point on Copano Bay (ships had to pass this point to get to the port of Copano). A month later Santa Anna sent a dispatch to Gen. Vicente Filisola ordering him to build fortifications at Copano.[38]

With both armies using Copano as a port, unusual things were bound to happen.

The Mexican army moved into Copano on March 16, 1836, when Gen. José de Urrea sent Col. Rafael de la Vara to Texas with sixty men to garrison the old port. The mission at Refugio was converted into a hospital and military supply depot, while El Copano was opened as a supply point for all material earmarked for the Mexican armies in Texas. Texans who had been captured by the Mexican army and not executed were sent through El Copano to Matamoros for confinement. Santa Anna was so sure that he would quickly polish off the Texas army that he ordered a ship to El Copano to pick him up.[39]

Unfortunately, on March 21 a ship entered the bay carrying Maj. William P. Miller and his Nashville Company of about eighty-six volunteers for the Texas army. Not knowing that the port was held by the Mexicans, the ship dropped anchor several hundred yards off the shore. The men, who had been confined to the ship for several weeks, took advantage of the arrival by shucking their clothes and plunging into the cooling water. Their swim was interrupted when the Mexican troops appeared. Caught with "their pants down," the men surrendered and were eventually taken to Goliad and imprisoned along with Fannin's men, who had surrendered after being bested in battle. When Fannin's men were taken out and shot in cold blood, Miller's men were spared because "they had entered Texas without arms in their hands." [40]

The coin had two sides. On May 29, 1836, Maj. Isaac Burton, with a company of twenty mounted Rangers, was ordered to scour the coastline from the Guadalupe River to Mission Bay and report any enemy activity. On June 2 they were informed that a vessel was seen approaching Copano Bay. The Rangers got to Copano and found the vessel anchored just offshore. They waited until morning and signaled the ship to send a boat ashore. The Mexicans fell into the trap. The soldiers were taken as prisoners, and the Rangers manned the small boat and approached the ship. Evidently putting on a bluff, they secured the surrender of the ship (the *Watchman*).

Burton made preparations to take his prize ship and her supplies, destined for the Mexican army, to Velasco but was delayed due to bad weather. On June 17 two other Mexican vessels, the *Comanche* and the *Fanny Butler*, laden with more supplies for the Mexican army, sailed into the bay. Burton immediately caused the Mexican flag to be run up on the *Watchman* and the two unsuspecting ships sailed up to the shore, furled their sails, and dropped anchor.

Burton now had three prize ships and a new nickname for his troop of Rangers — the "Horse Marines." Goods taken from these three ships played a big part in supplying the Texas army.[41]

During the period of Mexican occupation of Copano, Santa Anna appointed Juan Davis Bradburn as collector at the port. Bradburn was an American who was considered by Texans as a turncoat. This arrangement was good for Bradburn so long as the Yucatan detachment of Mexican troops was on hand to back him up. Conditions changed rapidly when Santa Anna surrendered on April 21, 1836, and ordered all Mexican armies to leave Texas. In his retreat, Filisola came through Copano in May of 1836 and picked up the Yucatan detachment. For some reason (some historians say he was left behind by the Mexican army to warn the *Watchman*) Bradburn elected to stay at Copano until a detachment of Texans took over the port. He was lucky not to have been shot as a conspirator; instead he was given a small skiff and told to leave. He made his way to Padre Island, where he was later picked up by a Mexican vessel.[42]

While the struggle for Texas independence was far from over, the port of El Copano was getting its due recognition. The general council of San Felipe on December 12, 1835, searching for a means of raising money, created customs districts and recommended the appointment of Edward Gritton as the first collector at El Copano, but he was rejected. Governor Smith addressed a note to the council on December 17 pointing out that Mrs. Gritton was an avowed spy. She was English by birth and a Mexican by adoption. Actually, it was not until July 17, 1837, that a workable customs service found its way into Copano Bay, when Thomas M. Duke was appointed collector of customs for the District of Aransas. In August of 1837 President Houston authorized the establishment of a military post at Copano for the protection of revenue, but there is no record of this ever being accomplished. The inaccessibility of El Copano, along with real estate politics, caused Duke to select Live Oak Point as the place for the new customs office rather than the old port. For the next ten years, Copano would have to play second fiddle to new ports being pushed by a series of old soldiers, frontier leaders, and politicians.[43]

The first entry found in customs records involves the schooner *Southern* that arrived at Live Oak Point on September 11, 1837, with an interesting cargo consisting of "2 bbls. brandy, 2 bbls. rum, 1 bbl. sugar, 2 sacks coffee, 10 bbls. flour, 421 bales tobacco, 15

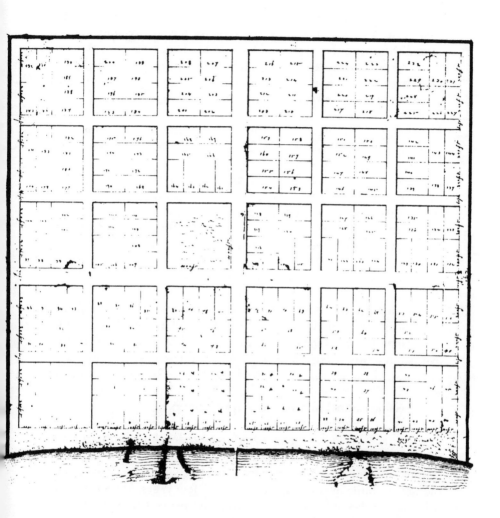

EL COPANO — As early as the 1750s, the Spanish used Copano Landing as the port to supply missions in South Texas. Used by the Texas and Mexican armies during the War for Independence, a community grew up there shortly after the fight and a townsite was laid out.

boxes soap, 5 kegs lard, 6 boxes claret (1 doz. each), 1 sack of salt, 7 boxes tea, 1 cask crackers, 1 box lemons, 1 keg rice and 1 grindstone." Shortly after this, on October 11, Duke wrote to the state treasurer and complained that only one ship had entered the port since he took office. He also announced that he was ill and would have to resign. The treasurer accepted his resignation and named Alvin White, Duke's deputy, to take charge of the office at a pay of $1 per day. Later Smith advised Duke to abandon the port until business got better and to dismiss White. Evidently, Duke's resignation was held in abeyance for some time.[44]

Col. George W. Fulton was appointed to the job on June 18, 1838, and was instructed to rent an office and hire clerks and officials. Fulton later helped organize the Coleman-Fulton Pasture Company and served as its head until his death in 1893. Samuel Hewes was appointed collector to replace Fulton on January 17, 1839.

Local politics raised its head when Hewes recommended moving the customs office from Aransas City (Live Oak Point) to Lamar, a new city that had started directly across Aransas Bay on Lookout Point. The recommendation was not accepted, and for the time being the customs office remained in Aransas City. A dispute over salary fills several letters in the old records. Hewes appeared to be the winner, but he received no cash, only credit, to his account.[45]

Joseph Elton Plummer was appointed collector of customs at Aransas and confirmed by the Senate on January 20, 1840. Plummer, a surveyor, would be involved in land development in the area until his death in 1859. He built the first home in the "new" city of Copano in 1840. It was constructed out of shell-crete, as were all of the homes built in this area for the next few years. When the land title on which his home was constructed proved to be faulty, the family moved down the beach and built another shell-crete home.[46]

Joseph's son, Samuel A. Plummer, was also an eminent force in the shaping of Copano. He was probably one of President Mirabeau B. Lamar's closest friends and business associates. Plummer, an attorney, came to South Texas with the hope of promoting a city on a survey patented by Lamar on the north bank of Copano Bay (the northeast side of Copano Creek). Several letters in the papers of Mirabeau Lamar detail the close bond between the two men. On March 12, 1839, Plummer wrote to Lamar: "Since my arrival here [New Orleans] I have been most earnestly striving to raise some money, but so far, have failed . . . . Gen. Foot has promised to raise forty thousand for me." On May 17, 1840, he wrote from Victoria: "Within a short time past, there have been a great many very respectable persons visiting that section of country and all that have seen Copano Bay are desirous of getting a foot holt there." [47] While Lamar and Samuel A. Plummer were never able to get their city of Copano off the drawing boards, Plummer continued to be a big influence in local politics at Aransas City. He was a captain in the cavalry in the Republic of Texas Army in 1839 (appointed by Lamar) and was also active in the group of Texans who backed the Federalist cause in Mexico.

Customs records of the Republic of Texas do not list a single vessel arriving or departing from Copano during the period of 1836 to 1845. More than likely there was a limited amount of trade, but it was never logged in or out of the customshouse in Aransas City.

A slow growth was experienced along the coast until 1849, when Henry Dearborn Norton came to Copano and built a large two-story shell-crete store building, outbuildings, and a large underground water cistern. His business prospered (he opened another store in Refugio and later purchased a San Antonio firm) and a large home was built across the street for his family. Since there was no local source for fresh water, it was necessary for every home to have its own cistern. The nearest fresh water was Melon Creek and Hynes Spring, both about three to four miles distant.

After Norton completed his store at Copano, he built a 900-foot pier into the bay, supported by native mesquite posts. These posts were still in evidence as late as the 1940s, and perhaps even now the bottoms could be located, buried in the shell-mud of the bottom. A large shed at the pier was used to store lumber and other materials, as well as to house goods coming in and out of the port.

Norton was a merchant of a large scale. He was a forwarding agent for cities as far west as Uvalde and received goods for export from all over the area. Cotton, hides, tallow, pelts, and salt were the main exports. When Norton opened his company, other businessmen also made their way to the growing port city.

Patrick Shelly purchased the Norton stores in Refugio and Copano in about 1860. He finally closed the Copano store during the Civil War due to lack of goods. It closed permanently in 1867, when Henry D. Norton died.

Despite the fact that records do not show any ships using Copano during this period, evidently a number of ships did call at the old port. Late in 1836 Colonel Power established a mercantile business at his home on Live Oak Point and was known to have used the old Mexican customshouse at Copano as a storage point for his business. Since there was an existing road out of Copano to the Mission Refugio, and hence on to Goliad and Bexar, it is likely that a lot of Power business funneled through Copano. Power is known to have had a large importing and forwarding business, handling large amounts of such items as tobacco and manufactured goods. On September 11, 1837, the schooner *Southern* checked in at the customshouse at Live Oak Point from Galveston, and among other things had 421 bales of tobacco on board.[48] It is probable that this cargo was offloaded at Copano, then made its way by ox-cart train to the interior of Texas through the Power Trading Company.[49]

Philip Power, in his memoirs, has this to say about Copano before the wharf was built: "Wagons were driven out into the bay as far as they could be safely taken and cargoes lightered to the vessels riding at anchor in the bay." [50]

The extent of the business in and out of Copano can be seen from a letter written by Marcellus Turner in 1852, from his ranch at Alguna (near the juncture of Chiltipin Creek and the Aransas River) to his sister in Lavaca County. He wrote about conditions at the ranch and in the area. Evidently, the fall of 1852 was wet, as he wrote: "Heavy rains up the country, 'copious tears' of the Irish settlers, flooded the streams, but with no loss in stock . . . . There was considerable hustle on the Copano, a cargo of fifty to sixty thousand feet of lumber was sold in sixty days." Lumber for the growing countryside must have been funneled through the port of Copano.[51]

In 1850 Power, who had maintained his residence on Live Oak Point since founding the Power-Hewetson Colony in the early 1830s, moved his residence to Copano and built a two-story shell-crete home on Power's Point. This new home was just in front of the first Plummer home, which Plummer was forced to abandon when it was proved that he did not own the land. The Power mansion incorporated the old Plummer home as the dining room. Power died at his home on Live Oak Point on August 15, 1852, before the new home was finished. However, the Power family lived in the home for the next several decades, turning it into a hospitality center of the area. In fact, the residents of Copano were largely made up of kin of the Power family.[52]

The Refugio County Commissioners Court recognized the growth of Copano in the early 1840s with mention about the Copano Road. On December 10, 1846, the court approved a bridge over Melon Creek on the road between Copano and the town of Refugio. Edward St. John, Patrick O'Boyle, and Michael Fox were appointed commissioners to oversee the construction of the bridge.[53] In July of 1855 the court voted to upgrade and establish Copano Road from Thomas O'Connor's corner crossing on Melon Creek to Crescent Village on Hynes Bay.

Judge W. L. Rea of Refugio was a student of Copano and shared his memories years ago with Hobart Huson. According to Judge Rea, Copano did a thriving business during the Civil War. As in earlier days, the secluded bay was an excellent place to load blockade runners unobserved by the Yankees on patrol in the gulf. The ships then slipped out to sea. Cotton and salt were exported to Matamoros and paid for in Mexican silver. The judge remembers that Mexican money was in vogue in Refugio County during, and for a long time after, the Civil War.

Aransas City bowed out as a port city in about 1846 as Copano grew into a village with twenty to thirty residences and several businesses. Most of the houses were along the rim of the bluff. As Aransas City started to fade, Power became more interested in the development of Copano as a port. Historian Huson gives probably the best description of the old town at this point:

> Empresario Power's home was the dominant building. Next north was that of William Wilson, who married Eliza Power, daughter of the Empresario; next to the north of the Wilson home was that of Judge Walter Lambert, who married Tomasita C. Power, another daughter of Col. Power; across the street from it was the two-story store of Walter Lambert; next to the north of Judge Lambert's home was that of another Lambert, probably Nicholas Lambert. Next in sequence were two more houses facing the bay, one being the home of Christopher Smith, then another, facing north, which was the Norton residence; then came the large store building of the Norton Brothers, which was situated at a point where the bluff sloped more gradually to the beach. Between the store building and the bay was a large warehouse, or lumber shed, and from it extended the Norton's wharf. Next north of the Norton store was the Adams residence, and finally, beyond it was the home of Moses Simpson, in front of which was another wharf into Copano Bay. Back from the bluff, and behind the Adams residence, was a small building used as a school, which lasted until 1874. Southwest of the Power home is the village graveyard. Although most of the inhabitants were devout

Catholics, no church was ever built at Copano. Circuit riding priests would come periodically to the village, and services would be held at the Power home.

About three-quarters of a mile up the bay was the Plummer home, and a wharf in front of it. A post office was maintained at Copano from the days of the Republic until about 1880. Walter Lambert, Charles G. Norton and James Power, Jr., were some, if not all of the postmasters. Walter Lambert also had a store at Copano at one time and was a wharf agent.[54]

Throughout the history of Copano, a great deal of its trade was contraband. When the Federalists were battling the Centralists in Mexico immediately after the end of the War for Independence, a number of men in the area profited greatly in the trade with Mexico. Men whose names were connected with Texas history were in the forefront, including Col. Henry L. Kinney, Col. James Power, Philip Dimmitt, and John J. Linn and his brother Edward. Locals who played a part in profitable trade included William P. Aubrey, James H. Morris, Thomas Thatcher, Edwin Belden, Richard Pearse, John C. Pearse, Steward Newell, Samuel W. Wybrants, James Upton, and James A. Gourlay, Jr.

During the Civil War the old port, as noted previously, did a thriving export business because of its secluded position. The activities brought a federal gunboat into the bay in 1864. When the gunboat anchored offshore, after bombarding Lamar, the people took to the brush; however, no troops came ashore and life returned to normal after the ship left.[55]

No self-respecting port in those days was complete without talk about a railroad. Copano was on the cutting edge of plenty of talk, but no rails. Col. Pryor Lea's railroad dream envisioned a line from Goliad to the coast. In 1846 Power, the Mississippi Walkers, and Robert Hughes projected the Copano townsite, and Lea joined the group. Robert Hughes and Thomas M. League undertook in 1850 the organization of a railroad from a Copano Bay terminus to San Antonio. Lea and others still favored Lamar as a terminus, but actually neither idea got out of the planning stage. Later the men joined a like-minded group from Corpus Christi to promote the Texas Western Railroad Company to build a railroad from the Copano area through Corpus Christi to the Rio Grande Valley. Power, the biggest supporter of the project, died in 1852, and despite dedicated efforts of Judge Milford P. Norton and Gen. Duff Green, the project died aborning. The port of Copano was shifted into the Saluria Customs District and usually had a surveyor, inspector, or wharf agent acting locally. Walter Lambert and Moses Simpson were two who served.[56]

Judge Rea, who probably furnished historians the best first-hand glimpse of the old port in its declining days, had these remarks as an epitaph for Copano:

> I first visited Copano in 1870. At that time it was quite a settlement. There were about a dozen shell-concrete buildings. The old two-story shell-lime store building in which Henry D. and Charles G. Norton had their store, was standing, but not in use.
>
> A number of houses were vacant in 1870. Each house had about a half-acre of land. None of the lots were fenced.
>
> The widow of the old Empresario [Power] lived in her two-story shell-lime house near the reef. With her lived her children, Phil, Mary, Agnes and Mrs. Wilson.
>
> Mrs. Tomasita Lambert [widow of Judge Walter Lambert] lived in a home of her own, with her children, James, Philip, Lolla and Allie.
>
> There was another widow Lambert living there in a house of her own [widow of James Lambert]. She was the mother of Nicholas, Pat, Walter and Mary.
>
> Moses Simpson lived at the north end of the settlement. I always stayed at his house when I went to Copano.
>
> Vessels came within about 300 yards of the shore. At that time the wharfs were not used. The hides were lightered from shore to the ships. Moses Simpson floated barrels of tallow on the water to the boats.
>
> The hardest problem with which the people of Copano had to contend was that of drinking water. No one seems to have considered boring artesian wells, and rain water captured in the cisterns and water hauled from Hynes Spring and Melon Creek were the sole means of supply. Women of the village had community washdays. They would load the washing into ox-carts and drive to the creek several miles above the town and spend the day.
>
> At the time I was there there was a thriving shipping business. Three-masted schooners came into port, and there was a prosperous business in shipping tallow and hides, which were prepared at the packery about six miles below Refugio on Mission River. These products were shipped by vessel from Copano to New Orleans. All of the young men of Copano were engaged in loading boats.[57]

The packery business grew to be one of the largest on the coast. One of the most elaborate plants was at Packery Flat, near the mouth of Mission River and just a few miles from Copano. This packery was owned by James McCarthy of St. Mary's, who also operated a ferry across the Mission River between Mission Lake and Mission Bay. There were large ovens, or vats, which were used for rendering the tallow. Cattle were skinned by starting at the hind end, hitching a mule to the hide and pulling the hide off the carcass, which was then dumped into the boiling vat. The tallow was drawn off and put up in barrels for shipment. At times part of the choice meat was saved and packed with salt into barrels.[58] J. Frank Dobie tells about cattle being driven to this packery and sold for seven dollars per head, payment to be made as soon as a certain ship carrying a cargo of salt beef should return. Frequently the ships did not return, which caused the coining of the refrain, "the ship that never returned." The hides were salted and rolled for shipment.[59]

Many things caused the final death of the oldest port in Texas. The lack of adequate fresh water was a contributing cause, as was the fact that the channel from the pass was long and crooked. The main cause was the rise of the new port of Rockport, located closer to the pass and easier to reach.

In its time, at the center of history in the Gulf Coast, El Copano stood watch as the explorers first disturbed the routine of the Copano Indians at their Paraje de los Copanes home. Then the pioneers brought their families, the armies brought their cannons, and finally the real estate promoters of the 1840s introduced an era of growth in other ports. For El Copano the end finally came in the 1880s as the last families moved away, leaving the once solid shell-crete homes to silently melt away as the years passed. Ranchers ran barbed wire across the old roads that had been packed by thousands of feet, and Copano was no more.

Aransas City
Long Forgotten Star

A meteor makes a brilliant light as it flashes across the sky, only to burn out and fall into oblivion.

Aransas City, a long-forgotten community of the post-Republic days, had its meteoric brilliance and burnout from about 1838 to the early 1850s. The brainchild of Empresario James Power, the city was located on Live Oak Point at a spot that made it look attractive as the dreamed-about western port that would funnel people and supplies into the Far West.

Live Oak Peninsula was a beauty spot of the coast. Its clean beaches sloped up to a coastline that was uncluttered for several hundred yards inland. Oak trees formed a majestic setting that captivated everyone who landed on the beach. Sweet bay trees, or laurels, provided still another touch of natural beauty. The beautiful beaches not only attracted the early settlers, but the Indians for countless years used Live Oak Peninsula as campgrounds when they visited the coast on fishing expeditions.

Live Oak Peninsula was part of the land that Power had purchased from the Mexican government. Early in the 1830s he built his family home on Live Oak Point, where his children were born. In 1832 Power married Dolores Portilla, the daughter of Felipe Roque de la Portilla and Maria Ignacia de la Garza, respected residents of Matamoros. Don Felipe was an empresario under the Spanish regime.[1]

During the War for Independence, all of the settlers in that part of the state had to flee ahead of the invading Mexicans. Refugio and San Patricio counties were declared "depopulated" areas.[2] After the Mexican armies left Texas, Mrs. Power and the children returned to Live Oak Point, but Power, who was in ill health, went to New Orleans to seek medical treatment. While he was absent from home in 1836, his wife died in childbirth of stillborn twins. It was months before the news reached him. In May of 1837 Power brought his father-in-law, Don Felipe, and his two children to New Orleans to live with him. When his sister-in-law Tomasita visited in August, Power married her.[3]

Always full of plans, Power conceived the idea of a new town at Live Oak Point while he was still in New Orleans. He entered into a partnership agreement with Robert J. Walker to build a town to be called "Aransas City" at Live Oak Point near his home. Evidently, Walker did not have much luck in promoting the new town, because in 1838 Power entered into another contract with Governor Henry Smith, also a resident on Live Oak Peninsula, to work on the development. Power and Smith had been staunch friends ever since Power offered his unwavering support for Smith when he was impeached as governor of Texas.[4]

Although the new town was slow in getting started, it did not stop Power from organizing a trading company near his home, probably in late 1836 and 1837. As an adjunct to his headquarters on Live Oak Point, Power used the old Mexican customshouse at the port of Copano to store his goods. Copano was also connected with roads that reached to Refugio, Goliad, and on to Bexar. He had his own fleet of ox carts to carry the goods into the interior. The new city is said to have been laid out on the site of the old Mexican fort known as Aranzaso or Aranzazu.[5]

Probably no other new city attracted the caliber of men that flocked to Aransas City. Each, no doubt, had the same vision — a port city that would offer unlimited opportunities for trade of all types. And where there was trade, there was the hope of making a fortune. Power, of course, wanted to market the vast land domain that he and Empresario James Hewetson had purchased from the Mexican government when they secured a grant to settle colonists in Texas. Col. H. L. Kinney, later founder of Corpus Christi, an opportunist who knew the secret to wealth and power vested in ports and trade, was in Aransas City from 1837 to 1838. Governor Smith and his nephew, Joseph F. Smith, joined the cast of speculators early, as did Lieutenant Governor James W. Robinson, who was sworn in as governor when Smith was impeached. Col. George W. Fulton, who later organized the famous Coleman-Fulton Pasture Co., was on hand and was named collector of customs in 1838; and John Henry Brown, author of *History of Texas* and *Life and Times of Henry Smith*, wrote both books while living on Live Oak Peninsula.[6]

The fact that Aransas City figured into the land battle that was shaping up can be seen in the fact that at least nine attorneys and seven surveyors opened offices in this community of perhaps 200. Lawyer Robinson was joined in his office by Edward Fitzgerald, the latter being a retired district judge. Willard Richardson, Samuel A. White, James C. Allen, Col. Samuel A. Plummer, Benjamin F. Neal, Maj. Stuart Perry, and Henry Smith rounded out the contingent of attorneys. Joseph E. Plummer, Sr., was one of the leading surveyors, with others being Reuben H. Roberts, James B. Collinsworth, Joel T. Case (also a Presbyterian minister and adventurer), Willard Richardson, Victor Loupe, and Samuel Addison White.[7]

When the State of Texas organized customs districts by the act of June 12, 1837, the District of Aransas was created. The boundaries ran from the Rio Grande to the mouth of the San Antonio

River, which included Corpus Christi, Aransas, Espiritu Santo, and Copano bays. The provisional government of Texas had previously created the revenue district of Aransas and made Copano the port of entry. Smith appointed Edward Gritton to the post, but the council refused to confirm him.[8] Evidently, the post never functioned.

According to customs records, Thomas M. Duke was appointed to the job of collector of customs on July 17, 1837, and at the same time President Sam Houston authorized the establishment of a military post for the protection of the district. This action was taken, of course, at the urging of Power and his associates. Duke was empowered to select a site for the customshouse, passing over the old port of Copano to select Live Oak Point.[9] A letter dated September 11, 1837, instructed Duke to rent a building as "soon as possible" in order to prevent so much smuggling.

On September 11, the schooner *Southern* became the first official ship to pass through customs. Its manifest listed "2 bbls. brandy, 2 bbls. rum, 1 bbl. sugar, 2 sacks coffee, 10 bbl. flour, 421 bales tobacco, 15 boxes soap, 5 kegs lard, 6 boxes claret (1 doz. each), 1 sack of salt, 7 boxes tea, 1 cask crackers, 1 box lemons, 1 keg rice, 1 grind stone." [10]

Most of the ships which crossed over the bar at Aransas Pass must have landed either at Copano or some other landing, without going through customs. On October 11, 1837, Duke wrote to his boss that "only one vessel has entered the port since I took office." He also complained about being ill and the lack of enough income to pay expenses, requesting permission to resign. His resignation was accepted on January 28, 1838, with Alvin White put in charge. However, before Duke finally left he was instructed to discharge White and abandon the port.[11]

The promoters of Aransas City got busy and on June 18, 1838, Col. George W. Fulton was made collector of customs at Live Oak Point. He was to rent an office and employ as many people as necessary to carry out the job. Since smuggling was deemed top priority, he was to send small boats into adjacent bays to put a stop to the illicit entry of goods. In his report dated December 31, 1838, Fulton said that he had sold confiscated goods amounting to $692.37, less expenses amounting to $563.53. Reports in the following months showed $2,699 in whiskey seized. Evidently, Fulton was stopping part of the smuggling trade.

Mexican trade through Aransas City was heightened during this period by the outbreak of trouble with the Federalists in northern Mexico and the so-called "Pastry War" with France. French ships attempted to blockade Mexican ports, and, as a result, Mexico tried to land supplies between Corpus Christi Bay and Brazos Santiago. Texas viewed this commerce as contraband, or smuggling, and tried to put a stop to it. Flour Bluff got its name when a cargo of contraband flour was seized there in 1838 by customs officers operating out of Aransas City.[12]

Samuel Hewes was appointed collector at Live Oak Point to replace Fulton on January 17, 1839. In May of that year, Hewes stirred up a swirl of political turmoil when he wrote to "His Excellency, Gen. M. B. Lamar, President of the Republic of Texas" and recommended the moving of the customshouse from Aransas City to Lamar. The new town of Lamar had been laid out in 1837 across the bay on Lookout Point by a group of livewire promoters headed by Capt. James W. Byrne. Hewes added that Byrne had offered a 100 x 140-foot lot on which they had promised to erect a 16 x 26 frame building for the customshouse. He reasoned that "the proprietors of Aransas City have made no offer, and since there were twelve houses and thirty people at Aransas City and twenty houses and sixty people at Lamar, the best location would be Lamar." [13]

On June 15 the citizens of Aransas City convened a meeting in the council house to protest to President Lamar. A committee consisting of Col. James Power, George W. Fulton, Edward Fitzgerald, Joel T. Case, R. C. Jackson, and H. L. Kinney was appointed to draft a series of resolutions protesting the removal of the customshouse. The resolution pointed out that "Lamar was a place unapproachable by vessels drawing seven feet of water within three quarters of a mile of the shore." Aransas City was pictured as an "excellent harbour and anchorage sheltered from the force of the winds in every direction with seven feet of water within one hundred yards of shore." [14]

Despite this moving resolution, President Lamar favored the town bearing his name. The customshouse was moved and a lighthouse was built at Lamar during his administration. However, the Aransas City promoters had enough clout in the Texas Congress to get a law passed making Aransas City the port of entry for the customs district of Aransas.[15] An unsuccessful attempt was made in

1842 to again move the office to Lamar, but it failed and the office remained in Aransas City until the end of the Republic.

Joseph Elton Plummer was appointed to the customs job on January 20, 1840, and served until Samuel W. Wybrants took over on May 1, 1843. Wybrants was replaced by Henry Redmond on October 1, 1843; William Mann took over in May 1844 and served until George Collinsworth's appointment in January of 1845, lasting until the end of the Republic.[16]

Shipping in and out of the Aransas District was never great; however, in 1839 a total of thirty ships came into the port with slightly greater numbers in following years. A number of passengers also came through the port, but few were listed. In the quarter ending September of 1839, passengers arriving were: Patrick Lawler, 45, from New Orleans; A. P. Howe, 40, New Orleans; W. H. Beardslea, 30; James Power, 50, Texas; P. T. Phillips, 25, New Orleans; Bunill Betts, 32, Texas; S. Mauzny, 35, New Orleans; W. S. Thornburg, 32, preacher; Mrs. Thornburg and child, 25; Mrs. Sara Cox and child, 25, Texas; E. Hart, 40, Texas; Mrs. Ryal and child, 25; Henry Ryal, 33; James Reed, 35; Jos. McLaughlin, 30; and James McGohan, 30.[17]

Life in Aransas City was not dull. Since the Indians, mainly Lipans, Karankawas, and Comanches, had frequented Live Oak Peninsula for centuries, President Sam Houston sought to make peace with them. He deputized Colonel Power to meet with the Lipans to try and bring an end to their attacks on the peaceful settlers of Texas. On January 18, 1838, Chief Cuelgas de Castro and a party of Indian braves met with Power in his home. It was a solemn occasion, with the Indians in full ceremonial dress and observing all of the formalities of the tribal customs. A treaty was signed, but early in 1840 the Lipans raided the coast and drove away a lot of cattle belonging to the settlers. A group under Capt. John Scott followed the Indians all the way to the Rio Grande, where they were ambushed by the Indians. Scott and several others were killed, and ten-year-old Henry Scott was taken prisoner. He was later rescued.[18]

The Lipans were a constant threat. Samuel Hewes, early customs officer at Live Oak Point, reported the discovery of the bodies of nine dead Mexicans, one of them a woman, between Live Oak Point and the Nueces. He attributed their deaths to the Lipans because the "victims' horses were seen in the Lipan Camp." He also observed that "no faith is to be put in Castro." [19]

Indians and Mexican cutthroats were a constant menace to the people on Live Oak Peninsula. In March of 1838 Aransas City was attacked by the Mexican bandit De Los Santos and forty-five of his gang. After terrorizing Power and his family, they seized all that they could carry of Power's trading goods and took Power prisoner. Shortly after Santos left, another band of Mexican bandits forced entry into the Power home and kept Mrs. Power and her children in a state of fear for three days. Finally, they induced the robbers to take twenty-three bales of tobacco, which the first group could not carry.

Santos took Power to Matamoros, where he was kept prisoner for five months. He was finally turned loose when Gen. Adrian Woll was influenced by Power's relatives and friends at Matamoros to release him.[20]

During this time the Comanches raided other parts of Refugio County, massacring the William Gilliland family and raiding other ranches. President Sam Houston, fearful that the Mexicans might mount an invasion of the coast, ordered an expedition to Copano under Lt. John Wade. He was instructed to patrol the entire coast area and examine every vessel that appeared suspect.[21]

Texas customs officials took a dim view of the Mexican government trying to smuggle goods into Texas, but it was looked on as a good business venture when the goods came into the port of Aransas City and were taken overland by one of the growing number of traders. Goods brought into Texas by Texas smugglers also seemed to have an official blessing. During this period, trade with Mexico was lucrative.

The Texian Congress passed a law on January 26, 1839, authorizing the president to give support and encouragement to trade between western ports and Mexican settlements on the Rio Grande. President Lamar issued a proclamation on February 21, 1839, specifying the military post of Casa Blanca on the Nueces as the point of clearance of all Mexican traders desiring to enter Texas. From Casa Blanca, traders had to go to Goliad or Bexar. Aransas City was left out since President Lamar was at political odds with the promoters of the city. This did not stop the trade from Aransas City, which continued to prosper. The big stumbling block to all trade with Mexico was the organized gangs of robbers

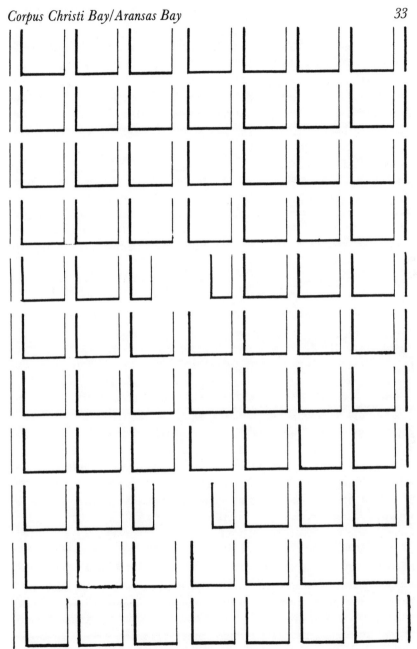

ARANSAS CITY — Empresario James Power had big dreams when he laid out Aransas City on Live Oak Point in the days immediately after San Jacinto. For a few years the city boomed, but then the action moved to other places and the beach was deserted within a few years.

and Indians who waylaid and plundered the caravans.[22] They recognized no power other than that backed with murder and stealing.

A dissertation on the Federalist Wars in the northern Mexican states is not in order at this point. However, how they affected the growth of Aransas City is important. Suffice it to say that the people in these northern Mexican states were extremely conservative in political philosophy and were high-class citizens. In fact, a number of prominent Texans, like Col. James Power, Philip Dimmitt, James Cummings, and William G. Cooke, married into these old *grandee* families. When Santa Anna rose to power and did away with the political principles set out in the Mexican Constitution of 1824, these Mexican people rose up in arms. Santa Anna and his Centralist government crushed all of the uprisings, except in the northern states.

In 1838 the Federalist cause broke out anew under the direction of Canales, Urrea, Anaya, Lemos, Carbajal, and Zapata.[23] Texans, who had supported the Federalist cause before the Revolution, now aligned themselves with these Mexican leaders who had stirred them before. Ewen Cameron, captain in a Refugio County ranger company, gathered up about sixty-five men in the area who were supportive of the Federalist cause and left immediately for Mexico. The action taken by these men and other Texans has been fully covered in several books, but in great detail in Hobart Huson's *Iron Men*.

The Federalist cause was mowing down the Centralist forces until the Federalist generals began bickering among themselves. As a result, most of the Federalist troops, except those commanded by Gen. Antonio Canales, assisted by General Zapata, were vanquished. Canales saved his army by retreating north of the Rio Grande to Ft. Lipantitlan (about five miles across the Nueces River from San Patricio). While there, Canales solicited support from his friends, and a Texian Auxiliary Corps, officered by Texans, was formed. Prominent in gathering Texians to the Federalist cause was Col. Samuel A. Plummer, a trusted friend of President Lamar, who probably was responsible for the enlistment of Capt. Reuben Ross of Victoria and his entire ranger force. When the Federalist army finally left Lipantitlan in September of 1839, about 300 Texans were in the battle group.

Once again, with victory at hand, Canales was routed due to desertions in his army. His forces fell back to the Rio Grande and

were reorganized under the Republic of the Rio Grande, with headquarters in Laredo. Once again the army was defeated, retreating
this time to Lipantitlan, with the officials of the Republic of the Rio
Grande. The shattered forces arrived at their Nueces redoubt in
March of 1840.

Freedom-loving Texans rallied around the Federalist forces
and the officials of the Republic of the Rio Grande. This support
was highlighted with a banquet in Victoria, the wellhead of Texas
private and public support.

Part of the Texan leadership dropped out of the new Federalist
force being put together on the Nueces, but others, like Captains
Ewen Cameron, John T. Price, and Thomas Newcomb, brought together a band of Texans to fight again.

Even as the army began its march south in July of 1840, secret
negotiations were under way between General Canales and the
Mexican government to solve their differences. The Texans were
not told of these developments. The final treachery perpetrated by
the Mexicans against Captain Jordan and his men came after the
forces moved deep into Mexico. The Mexican army suddenly
crossed over to the enemy as a battle opened, leaving the Texans
double-crossed in a foreign land. History tells us that these Texans
fought some of the greatest battles of the times as they worked their
way back to the border over mountains, against seemingly insurmountable odds. Remnants of Captain Jordan's force finally
reached the Rio Grande.

In the midst of the fighting, the Federalists needed arms and
supplies of all kinds. Since their own coast was blockaded by the
French navy, their only hope of supplies was from the United
States through Texas. The Texas government was sympathetic; the
only problem was getting the supplies overland to Mexico. It was
necessary to have a port of entry as close to the Rio Grande as possible. That was where Aransas City fitted into the picture. The
men who flocked to Aransas City in 1838–40 had one thing in
common: they wanted to make a fast buck, and trade with the Federalists was an exciting and profitable prospect.

Henry L. Kinney was drawn to the new city and quickly fell in
with Colonel Power and other locals such as William P. Aubrey,
Martin Power, Philip Dimmitt, Edward Linn (brother and partner
of John J. Linn), James H. Morris, Thomas Thatcher, Edwin Belden, Richard Pearse, John C. Pearse, Stewart Newell, Samuel W.

Wybrants, James Upton, and James A. Gourlay, Jr. Out-of-area firms, such as Black & Schoolfield of Bastrop, Francis Dietrich of Austin, James P. McKinney & Co. of Velasco-Quintana, J. W. Pitkin and Daniel Donahoe of Liberty County were large shippers to Aransas City. Capt. J. P. Black, of Black and Schoolfield, had two schooners, the *Louisiana* and the *Olympus,* which landed cargoes regularly at Live Oak Point, or Aransas City. Republic customs records show these ships making several "official" calls at the port.[24] There is no record of their unofficial calls.

For a brief period in 1837 and 1838, it appeared that the bulk of the population of Refugio County could be found either in Aransas City or at the Carlos Ranch (located on the San Antonio River at Carlos Crossing). When Chief Justice Allen was elected in Refugio County in 1838, he found practically all of the official business being transacted in Aransas City, since most of the county officials made their home in the new city or at Lamar. Allen tried to reestablish Refugio as the "county seat" but evidently failed. When Chief Justice Neal came on the scene in 1840, he set up his office in Refugio and apparently convinced other officials to return to Refugio. At that time Neal was living in Aransas City, as were the district clerk, sheriff, and surveyor. An entry in the commissioners court minutes dated October 12, 1840, ordered the sheriff to take possession of the Stone Church and that "said building hereafter be known as the courthouse of Refugio County." [25] During Neal's term of office, the county officials had to flee due to raiding Mexicans and take refuge at the Carlos Ranch or Aransas City.

Kinney pulled out of Aransas City business ventures sometime in 1839 and in September moved to Corpus Christi Bay, where he opened his own trading company which was still closer to Mexico.

Aransas City never did grow the way promoters had envisioned it would. The town was laid out with about seventy-five lots. Old notes refer to a street by the name of Washington and another as Market. Colonel Power's store, established in 1836, was the biggest in the community. Gideon R. Jacques operated a tavern, or barrel house, so called because the liquors were shipped in barrels. The barrel houses became the gathering places for men who could purchase liquor by quarts or gallons, as well as buy crackers or canned meats. Power donated 100 acres to the Catholic church for educational and religious purposes, but no records tell of any church being built in Aransas City.

A wharf reached out from Power's store several hundred yards to where the shallow-draft ships could tie up and unload their goods. About seven feet of water was available at the wharf. Usually, most ships using Aransas City were of the smaller variety of twenty to thirty gross tons.

Aransas City was officially incorporated as a town by an act of Congress on January 28, 1839. The first and only mayor was Colonel Power.[26]

What happened to Aransas City and its meteoric ascent into the ranks of port cities? Probably several things. Colonel Power, perhaps fearing the loss of his land through court action, transferred his allegiance to Copano. A new city, Lamar, started up just across the bay on Lookout Point and took part of the would-be settlers. Kinney opened the rival port of Corpus Christi and seemed to have an inside track on how to get things done. Residents were exposed to roving bands of unfriendly Indians and were at the mercy of Mexicans who plied their trade in the area.

The new city just didn't catch on. Within fifteen years after its founding, Aransas City was a deserted beach. The old homes were either torn down or fell into disrepair. Today most of the modern dwellers along this secluded beach probably do not know that a city was once planned where their barbecue pits now stand.

St. Mary's of Aransas

The great American dream usually has a pot of gold at the end of the rainbow.

The founding of the city of St. Mary's of Aransas on the northwest bank of Copano Bay represented the dreams of many men, but above all it was the dream of Joseph F. Smith, nephew of Governor Henry Smith, provisional governor of Texas during the War for Independence. This dream encompassed many other men as co-conspirators, or partners, as well as many others who would feel bitter disillusionment when their dreams — plus blood and sweat — turned into gall as the master scheme finally fell into place.

But everything has its beginning and so does the saga of the founding of St. Mary's of Aransas. Actually, there were two deep and fundamental causes of the turmoil that set the stage for probably one of the biggest land grabs in the history of modern real estate.

Unwittingly, the first players on the stage were members of

the legislative body in Mexico when the colonization law of 1821 went on the books. Under the terms of this new and liberalized law, empresarios were allowed to negotiate grants from the Mexican government to bring colonists into Texas. For their part in organizing expeditions, the empresarios were given headrights and premium lands. This looked like a good thing to two young, ambitious men who were familiar with the workings of the Mexican mind, since both had been actively engaged in business at Matamoros. Later the law was amended, making certain transactions subject to the supreme Mexican authorities (as opposed to the states, which were given power to negotiate the contracts).

Thus, Col. James Power and Dr. James Hewetson entered into negotiations with the Mexican government and received a grant to colonize ten littoral leagues with as many as 400 families. These settlers were to be half Irish-Catholic and the other half Mexican. In addition to their headrights and premium lands, the young promoters had visions of great fortunes to be made from Texas land. They purchased twenty-two more leagues of land, to be located within the limits of their concession. This acquisition covered most of the choice coastal land and bayfronts, including the shores of Copano and Aransas bays; Live Oak, Lookout, and St. Charles peninsulas; and Mustang, Harbor, Hog, St. Joseph, and Matagorda islands. What these young empresarios were foreseeing was that he who controlled the new port cities would be able to control the sale of land to new colonists. However, there was one big snag that the promoters overlooked. Mexican law provided that special permission for such land purchases must be obtained from the supreme executive of Mexico. The empresarios assumed that such permission was not necessary since all land was located within their grant. This view would probably never have been contested, had it not been for one other happening.

During the dark days of the War for Independence, the provisional government of Texas struggled to scrape together enough money to buy needed supplies for the army to fight the Mexicans. Since Texas's population was small, and relatively poor, the state fathers had to look elsewhere for the needed money. They came up with what is known as the First Texian Loan. These 1835 bonds were bought chiefly in the United States, usually at bargain rates. In 1836 a committee representing the holders of a large amount of these Texian bonds, and members of the Texas government, met in

Harrisburg to put their financial house in order. The plan that evolved was to issue land scrip certificates, redeemable in sections of 640 acres on land which might still be open to location.

A land certificate was worthless unless a piece of land could be found that had not been filed on. Once an unencumbered piece of land was found, a holder of a certificate could have the land surveyed and could seek a patent, or title, on the land. Naturally, everyone wanted land that had potential; no one was interested in the vast expanse of West Texas that was controlled by the Indians. Certificate-holders wanted to locate in areas along the sea coast, especially spots which were suitable for new ports, since it was proven that the growth would be in these areas.

A man by the name of Thomas Green ended up with eighty of these land certificates, which he unloaded on Thomas Taylor Williamson, a land promoter in Louisiana, who in turn assigned the instruments to his wife, Tirzah Ann Williamson. Eventually, Williamson came to Texas and the General Land Office to locate his eighty certificates. Just how Williamson and Joseph F. Smith got together is not known, except that Smith was an attorney who had become an expert land title lawyer. Smith not only had a deep knowledge about the land office and land titles; he is credited with helping write legislation that applied to Texas land law.

Governor Henry Smith and his family were the possessors of a number of land certificates. But they were not the only ones seeking land. President Mirabeau B. Lamar and his trusted friend, Samuel A. Plummer, had dreams of a real estate development involving a port located in the Copano or Aransas Bay area. Similar thoughts were nurtured by Stuart Perry (Port Preston), George Armstrong, Cyrus W. Egery (Egery Island or Black Point), James W. Byrne (Lamar and Lookout peninsulas), G. R. Hull, George Armstrong, and others. These people had surveys made and applied for junior patents to be affixed on top of the empresario purchases of Colonel Power. In most instances these individuals took possession of the land which they coveted, after having filed a junior claim.

Colonel Power also had land certificates, and it is possible that this drew him to consult with Joseph Smith. In fact, Power is reputed to have retained Smith as his attorney. Records indicate that the two were business associates for several years.

Evidently, Joseph F. Smith, recognized as an authority of Mexican land titles, soon became aware of the fact that Colonel

Power had never obtained the consent of the federal executive to his private transaction involving twenty-two leagues of land. It was on this point that Smith and others were now challenging the legality of the land titles held by Power on this vast expanse of coastal land and islands.

Smith's first challenge to Power's land titles failed, as the commissioner of the General Land Office held that the lands had already been lawfully granted to Power and Hewetson. This did not faze Smith. His next ploy was to go to the state legislature and lobby successfully for the passage of a bill that said: "All persons owning lands in the counties of Refugio and San Patricio, by titles from the Mexican government or government of Coahuila and Texas, the lines of which have not been correctly and permanently marked and designated, shall within two years from the passage of this act, cause the same to be resurveyed at their own expense." This act became law February 1, 1845. Probably Smith should be given the title of the first lobbyist in Texas.

With this law on the books, Smith sat back and waited, confident in his belief that eventually the courts would rule in his favor and the hundreds of land certificates that he and his associates had filed over the Power titles would prevail. The process was long, but Smith's view finally prevailed in 1856 after several appeals, public meetings, and countless trials.[1]

The town of St. Mary's had first been conceived by Williamson and Smith in 1839, at which time an actual survey was made and the site selected (at present-day Bayside). With the litigation under way, plans for the new port were put aside and not brought out again until 1856, when a new plat was laid out and surveyed by Lyman H. Ward. Smith engaged Capt. Frederick Augustine with his boat *Waterloo* to make soundings in the bay to determine the best port site. As a result of these findings, the actual site of the new port was moved two miles east of Bayside, or about six miles west of Mission Bay and El Copano.[2] While located on a bluff, the site was not quite as commanding as Bayside, but afforded deeper water close to shore. The site picked did prove to be ideal, as it provided a view of the entire bay, with Lookout Peninsula on the left and Live Oak Point on the right.

The importance of the new port is evidenced in the action taken by the Refugio commissioners court on January 3, 1858, when it ordered a new road from St. Mary's to Refugio and also a

Liquor in the days of the Texas Republic was shipped in wooden barrels so that any grocery store or hardware store could have several barrels of spirits, which they would sell by the pint or gallon. The term "barrel houses" was applied to those drink-it-here or take-it-home stores. St. Mary's of Aransas had several famous barrel houses.

direct road from St. Mary's to the San Patricio crossing on the Aransas River near Aldrete. Joseph F. Smith, J. R. McCarty, C. E. Dugat, J. M. Crandall, and T. M. Dorsett were appointed road commissioners.[3]

The town was laid off in seven tiers of thirteen blocks each, fronting on the shoreline of the bay with intervening streets. The town proper fronted 2,102 yards on the bay, and in the fifth tier two public squares were provided. Smith reserved Block IV for his own use and built a two-story shell-crete house for his residence and office.[4]

Sales were confined to the first tier of lots that fronted on the bay, and Refugio records show that a total of 212 lots were either sold or given away by Smith. It appears that Smith had a policy of giving lots to those who would actually build and live in the new town. This was especially true when he was attempting to attract an artisan or needed businessman. Some of these settlers included Dr. Rufus Abram Nott, who built a two-story drug store and doctor's office; and James M. Crandall, who sold his wharf on St. Joseph Island and moved to Lamar, but switched to St. Mary's (he first planned a wharf but finally built a two-story opera house as well as a home).[5]

Just as soon as the work of laying out the town was completed, Smith negotiated a contract with Thomas Taylor Williamson to build a warehouse and wharf in front of the town on the southeast corner of Block No. 7. Smith gave Williamson the land for the warehouse and wharf as well as a block of lots. Work started immediately, and by 1858 the wharf and warehouse were completed.

Shortly after completion, Williamson conveyed half interest in the project to John Vineyard, who had arrived in South Texas in the early 1850s and settled in the Ingleside area. He evidently was a man of means and acquired business interests in San Patricio and Refugio counties. He was also credited with lending money to one of the first companies seeking to deepen Aransas Pass. Later Vineyard and his son Samuel opened a lumber yard in St. Mary's and operated a 275-ton schooner between Florida and St. Mary's to bring in lumber.[6]

Williamson and Vineyard operated this first wharf until October 1, 1867, at which time they incorporated and interested others in the business. It then was known as St. Mary's Wharf and Warehouse Company. The name of Capt. Charles F. Bailey was associated with the business, and later the Cottingham family appears to have acquired the property. At that time the wharf was extended out into the bay to reach the depth necessary for "schooners from Florida to tie up and unload their lumber cargoes." [7]

From the very beginning, St. Mary's became the import center for lumber destined for most of South and West Texas. The pine forests of East Texas had not been "discovered" yet, and most of the long-leaf pine lumber was being brought in from Florida in schooners built especially for the lumber trade. As a result, some extremely large lumber yards sprang up in the area. In addition to the yard operated by Vineyard and his son, J. I. Cottingham established a yard which grew into one of the biggest. Other yards opened until St. Mary's probably had more lumber yards than any city in South Texas. With all of the lumber being brought into St. Mary's, it was natural that the ships did not leave empty. During this period, a small export business involving cattle was built up. The other principal exports were cotton, hides, tallow, and salt, the latter being produced by William Brightman and James R. McCarty at Mission Lake, in connection with McCarty's Packery, or by McCarty on the outskirts of the city. Cattle to be shipped by sea were driven by the cowboys into the pens near the wharfs and then loaded aboard the steamers.

As the ships continued to bring in lumber and manufactured goods, the traffic out of St. Mary's increased. Trains of carts or wagons left regularly from the coast for interior cities. Minutes of the commissioners court reflect that a well-traveled road between St. Mary's and Corpus Christi was improved. The old road between Black Point and Refugio also was improved, and a ferry was opened by Thomas B. Kimball on the Mission River crossing below the mouth of Saus Creek. In 1859 the road from St. Mary's to Refugio was opened, and the road from St. Mary's to the town of San Patricio was designated as first-class. In 1862 the people of St. Mary's petitioned the court for a road to Refugio by way of McCarty's ferry on the Mission River.[8] The court records show that St. Mary's was developing as the hub of roads in Refugio County, with an increasing traffic of carts and wagons loaded with merchandise slowly making their way across the prairies.

Smith appeared to be the driving force in increasing the trade in and out of St. Mary's. In 1858 he closed a deal with Vineyard to build an additional wharf and warehouse on the southwest side of

the town. In 1860 Smith contracted with Gilbert B. Willett to build
a warehouse "suitable for doing a founding and commission business." This later became the St. Mary's Wharf and Warehouse
Company.[9]

To help the port grow, Smith reached out and made deals to
bring passenger and freight boats into St. Mary's on a regular
basis. In 1857–58 he made a deal with Captains Peter and Theodore Johnson to make regular calls with their two schooners.[10] The
Johnsons operated a unique service involving both the land and
sea. Passengers, mail, and express were carried by boat from Indianola to Saluria. From Saluria they went overland by stage to St.
Joseph, which was opposite present Rockport. Freight, mail, and
passengers were then loaded on boats to Lamar, Copano, St.
Mary's, Aransas City, and Corpus Christi.[11]

In 1860 Capt. Elisha Leonard of Bondin, Maine, moved to St.
Mary's, at Smith's invitation, to run a schooner between Copano
and Pensacola. Capt. E. L. Snow operated a barge up and down
the coast, catering short hauls, while Capt. Marion Seward and
Capt. Frederick Augustine operated ships in and out of the port.[12]

As the town grew commercially, it also grew in other ways.
Historian Hobart Huson offers a good description of the growth,
giving credit to Sallie J. Burmeister and Charles A. Russell:

> The townsite began to be built up with store buildings and
> residences, a few of them quite pretentious. Smith donated a
> building lot to each important religious denomination of that pe-
> riod, but only one — the Presbyterian — ever erected a church ed-
> ifice. It was also used for schoolhouse purposes. The Methodists
> eventually built a two story building at Well Mott, which was
> used principally as a public school. Post & Hobby and Samuel S.
> Maples each built two-story wooden store buildings. The upstairs
> of the Hobby building was used by the Masonic Lodge (Black
> Point Lodge No. 250, A.F.&A.M., founded May 16, 1860). Loftin
> & Ellis, William D. Campbell and John Low were original mer-
> chants of the town. Sherman conducted what was known as a
> "barrel house," a combination grocery and liquor establishment.
> A two-story wooden hotel, the Neel house, was the first hostelry
> in the new town. It was built by P. M. Neel and later operated by
> his wife, Mrs. Isabella Neel. A second hotel was built by Francis
> M. Ellis, who later replaced it with the famed three-story Ellis
> Hotel, which, after the decline of St. Mary's, was moved to Bee-

ville. A portion of the Neel House is still standing at St. Mary's, being the home of the Brightman boys.

The building activity naturally attracted contractors, builders and artisans to the new town. Archibald McNeill was, perhaps, the principal general contractor. T. P. McNeill established a brick yard. Capt. John Low was a carpenter-contractor. Patrick Reynolds and Conde Sweeney were brick, stone and shell-concrete masons. Bellowes established the first blacksmith shop in the town.

The first lawyers were Joseph F. Smith, Cornelius K. Stribling and Gen. T. T. Williamson.[13]

St. Mary's was also noted for its wide open gambling. Mrs. Burmeister tells about the wild and wooly days in her *Recollections:*

> Arthur Haynes and Joe Morgan ran a gambling house in the old Pecard store building. Morgan, who was from Kentucky, handled the saloon end of it, and Haynes managed the gambling part. The place was renovated with new fixtures and mirrors installed. Church people shunned it like Hell. Haynes and Morgan were both perfect gentlemen. Morgan boarded with our family for two years. Morgan was well liked and organized an orchestra composed of local young men known as the "Happy Eight." The orchestra also played for dances at Ellis Hotel.
>
> Many professional gamblers came from other places for "sittings" at Morgan and Haynes. One of them named Bell lived at Rockport. One time a woman gambler (Sally Scull) came to town and gambled with the men. John Wesley Hardin and Ben and Bill Thompson gambled at St. Mary's. In about 1875 the place closed and moved to Rockport.[14]

Marcellus Turner, who operated a ranch near Black Point (Alguna) tells of seeing Sally Scull in St. Mary's on a rather regular basis as she carried on her business of buying and selling horses and cattle.[15]

Even though St. Mary's was officially established in 1857, settlers long before began building homes in the Black Point area and a school was founded there in 1854, with Miss Sarah E. Ellis as a teacher in 1855. (The school was moved to St. Mary's as soon as the town got under way, and by 1860 it was a three-teacher school.) Cyrus W. Egery was appointed as election judge. An early road between Refugio Mission and Corpus Christi came through Black Point, and the appointment of Festus Doyle as overseer of this road is noted in volume one of the commissioners court minutes.[16] As St.

Mary's grew, more and more people from Black Point moved to the new town. Black Point was an early landing point for ships.

Lest the new port be cast into too much of a glowing light, a quote from a letter written in 1859 by Lizzie Ellis, a young lady in St. Mary's, to Marcellus Turner, a young man who was a nearby rancher, puts the town in perspective:

> As usual, times have been very dull in this part of the country .... At the present time our town is at a stand, no business is being carried on (excepting the lumber yard) and the proprietors all appear to be waiting for the town to build itself. Occasionally we see a small sail boat land at the wharf and once in a great while a schooner loaded with lumber for Mr. Vineyard is all the demonstrations we have of there being a town near us.[17]

As the Civil War drew closer, the sentiments ran high in favor of the Confederacy; however, some of the leading citizens of the area stayed loyal to the Union. In April and May of 1861, five home guard units were organized in the county, with one being Capt. William T. Townsend's Home Guards of St. Mary's. Later, still another unit was organized in St. Mary's known as Capt. John Low's Rough and Ready Home Guards.

In December of 1861, when the Texas legislature began putting the country on a war footing, the state was divided into thirty-three brigade districts. Ten counties (Refugio, San Patricio, Nueces, Goliad, Bee, Live Oak, Karnes, McMullen, La Salle, and Dimmitt) made up the 29th Brigade District. Hamilton Bee of Goliad was appointed brigadier general.

Alfred Marmaduke Hobby was probably one of St. Mary's most illustrious soldiers. Hobby moved to St. Mary's in 1857 with his widowed mother and two brothers, Edwin and Barney. He started a mercantile business and became a community leader, being elected delegate to the secession convention at Austin. His brilliant service in this body probably won him his high military rank. He was a member of Townsend's Home Guard, but sought service in the regular army and attained the rank of colonel. He organized a battalion and fought in the Battle of Corpus Christi in 1862, and later guided a regiment.[18] Ex-Governor William P. Hobby, as well as his son, Lieutenant Governor Bill Hobby, are descendants of the Hobby family of St. Mary's. Members of the Hobby family are buried in Old St. Mary's Cemetery.

Conditions in St. Mary's were bad during the war. Food was

scarce, primarily due to lack of men to work the fields or haul grain in from other areas. The commissioners court issued an appeal to the military to release a few older St. Mary's residents to assist in the effort. It is thought that the appeal was granted.[19]

Records indicate that the residents of St. Mary's suffered all sorts of hardships during the Civil War, especially the women and children whose husbands and fathers were serving in the Confederate army. Minutes of the commissioners court on January 2, 1864, pointed out that there were eleven families of soldiers who had no one left to butcher their supply of meat. The court appointed John Martin to do the butchering. Families of soldiers left without support were given a dole by the county, including beef.

War in its real sense came to St. Mary's in July of 1862, when the Federal fleet, under Capt. J. W. Kittredge, entered Copano Bay, landed at Lamar, and captured a blockade runner loaded with 300 bales of cotton. The fleet moved up the bay to Copano, where they anchored for a few hours. The natives hid in the brush and the ships moved on without coming ashore. Next they pulled in at St. Mary's and sent a landing party ashore. Several wounded Confederate soldiers who were at home were taken to the brush to avoid capture. The troops quickly spread out all over town.

Mrs. Clara Dugat (whose descendants still live in the area at Portland) tells one amusing story:

> Shortly after the Yankees had landed, a horseman rode into town from the peninsula to warn the people that the federal fleet was headed for St. Mary's. Not knowing that it had already arrived, he dashed up to the home of Dr. Carpenter and shouted: "The Yankees are coming." At that particular moment a raiding party was searching the Carpenter home and it came out and took the horseman prisoner.
>
> One of the raiding parties went down to Major Wood's home at Black Point, a mile or so below St. Mary's. The fences around the Wood place at that time were palisades, that is logs set upright in the ground. In the enclosure were some cattle moving around. This raiding party, from a distance, conceived the palisades to be men and soldiers and hurried back to St. Mary's with the information that there was a huge body of men coming from Black Point to attack the federals.
>
> At this instant one of the federals climbed to the roof of the school house to take observations. Standing on the roof he was a good target. It so happened that Peyton McNeill was hiding in

the brush thicket near the school. He had a gun and took a shot at the soldier on the roof.[20]

Shortly afterwards, the Federals left hurriedly.

The founders of St. Mary's returned after the war to take up land speculation where they left off. A notable example was Joseph F. Smith, one of the founders, who chose to leave Texas and the United States rather than take the oath of allegiance to the Union. He bought a plantation near Tuxpan, Mexico, where he died.

St. Mary's had a newspaper, the *Vaquero,* for a brief period. Capt. Charles F. Bailey and Geraldo Alonzo Beeman were the owners, and Beeman was the editor. Beeman arrived at St. Mary's with his father-in-law, David M. Rupe, in the fall of 1867, after having fought in a number of Civil War battles. He left his home in Bell County because of poverty, but upon arriving in St. Mary's he wrote: "We found this section was even more destitute than the one we had left. There was no agriculture, no development, nothing but cattle in all the country, and the cattle was worth nothing." [21]

The only known issue of the newspaper is No. 6, dated Saturday, December 11, 1869. An item in the paper gave the establishment date as October 15, 1868, indicating lapses in publication. The paper is thought to have lasted about one and a half years. A number of items of interest were gleaned from that single issue.[22]

The business directory noted the following: Ellis & Wood, dry goods and general mdse.; Ratchford and Vineyard, wholesale and retail grocery; C. A. Russell, dry goods, groceries; R. A. Nott, dry goods and medicines; Martin and Co., livery stable on Main St.; Thomas & McKenny, blacksmith and wheelwright; S. S. Maples, notary public; F. M. Ellis, dealing in cornmeal and flour; J. I. Cottingham, lumber; C. A. Russell, attorney. Firms in Rockport: J. A. Matthews, commission agent for Morgan Lines; D. D. Scrivner, dry goods.

According to the *Vaquero,* mail from Victoria arrived at 8:00 A.M. on Tuesday and departed at 8:00 A.M. on Wednesday. S. S. Maples was listed as the postmaster. For those seeking education, Concrete College in Concrete, DeWitt County, ran an ad, as did the Coletto Seminary at Clinton, also in DeWitt County.

Doing a bit of promotion for St. Mary's, the editor bragged: "Wharfage — Examine the rules of wharfage and storage as advertised in our paper and see if you do not pronounce them more reasonable than at any other point on the coast. The wharf is being put through repairs."

The editor was having publication problems, as noted in a small line on the front page: "Typo sick this week is our apology for being behind time" (typo meaning person who sets type). As an inducement to subscribers, the editor offered: "For every subscriber to the *Vaquero* we will publish one brand." The paper carried a list of brands and earmarks of local cattlemen.

Conditions in St. Mary's immediately after the Civil War corresponded to those all over the South — poverty and hardships. But St. Mary's had a number of things that helped the city snap out of the postwar slump, namely, the fact that it was a port city that was being used more and more. Oddly enough, as St. Mary's prospered, the old port of Copano began to decline, with some families moving from Copano to the new city.

After the war, the wharfs that had fallen into disrepair were put in good order and within a short time the sea-going schooners began calling at St. Mary's. When the Morgan Steamship Line put St. Mary's on its "call" list, the future of the port was assured. The forwarding agents reestablished themselves, and the trains of ox carts and wagons began leaving St. Mary's by the hundreds, headed for San Antonio and points west, as well as the immediate area. Capt. Allen C. Jones established himself as one of the largest wagon train operators out of Beeville and made St. Mary's his primary destination. Capt. William E. McCampbell and his brother T. P. opened a mercantile business in Refugio and St. Mary's with their own fleet of wagons.

A number of veterans returned home, built homes, and opened small businesses, namely, a tin shop and a grist mill. Sextus Garrett opened a large hotel on Second Street to back up the Ellis House and the Neel House, as well as a number of small hotels and boardinghouses.

Education started in 1855 in St. Mary's when the school in Black Point was moved to the new town. Joseph Smith realized the value of higher education and interested the Methodist church in building a church and college at St. Mary's. The deal was made in 1859, but due to the Civil War, construction was postponed. St. Mary's Institute was incorporated by the legislature on November 25, 1871, to create a "permanent establishment and endowment of a purely literary, scientific and moral institution of learning of high degree for the better education of the youth of the land." The first board of curators was W. J. Morris, Joseph F. Smith, W. G. Roark, and John H. Wood.[23] The buildings eventually became the public school and were destroyed by the storm of 1896.

The Western Texas Institute, a school for both male and female students, was the brainchild of John Howard Allen. Listed in the *Texas Almanac* of 1867, it drew a large group of students and lasted for a number of years. The Presbyterians had the only church building in town and it was also used for public school purposes.[24] The two-story Presbyterian church and school was blown flat by the storm of 1869. Mrs. L. B. Randolph had opened a private school in the Joe Dugat house, the roof of which was blown away in the storm.

In 1871 a telegraph line was strung from Indianola to Corpus Christi and on to Brownsville. Coming through St. Mary's, the line brought the outside world a lot closer to the new city. Actually, the line was established to assist the scheduling of steamer traffic up and down the coast. At St. Mary's the company maintained an office that had a combination operator, manager, and repairman. When John R. Martin, the first operator, wasn't in the office, he could be found on horseback riding the line to spot trouble. The job paid $75 per month, with a $15 per month allowance for horse feed. Later Rockport was tied into the line between St. Mary's and Corpus Christi.[25]

With the influx of new people and businesses into St. Mary's after the war, it was soon apparent that the bulk of the county's population lived in the new city. Agitation was rampant to move the county seat from Refugio to St. Mary's. In 1869 a constitutional convention, by a simple ordinance, moved the seat of government from the old mission town of Refugio to St. Mary's. The entrenched county officials chose to ignore the evident wish of the majority of the people, and somehow a proper petition asking for the change was never made. The county seat remained in Refugio until a few years later, when the rising star of Rockport caused the seat of government to officially move to the coast.[26]

During the decade following the Civil War, St. Mary's boomed. New people moved to town, steamers and schooners made regular calls, bringing in more and more lumber and all types of manufactured goods. Cotton and cattle were the principal exports, with lesser amounts of hides and tallow. A number of the people who built new homes in the port were farmers and ranchers from the surrounding area. At its zenith, the town actually encompassed the rim of Copano Bay all the way from the Wood home at Black Point to the outskirts of St. Mary's on the west — a distance of about four miles.

The heart of the new city was in the shipping business. Some of the largest lumber dealers in South Texas were located at the port, namely J. I. Cottingham, Ratchford & Vineyard, and McCampbell Brothers. In later years Coffin Brothers and Kohler & Heldenfels opened substantial yards. The St. Mary's Wharf and Warehouse Company maintained a wharf that reached out in the bay to deep water. Rails on the wharf allowed freight to be moved from the ships to the large warehouses on shore. They also had extensive cattle pens, covering a full block of land, where cattle could be held for shipment. The Morgan Steamship Line provided the big-time regular service that put the port over the top. However, they were not the only ships which called regularly. The *Frances,* with Theodore Johnson as captain, and the *Hannah,* with John Thomas as skipper, were probably some of the first schooners to start using St. Mary's as a port and continued to call long after the large ships left the scene.

A number of smaller vessels, involved in the coastal trade between Matagorda Bay and Corpus Christi Bay, called regularly at St. Mary's, including: the *Alfred* and *Sammy,* Capt. Charles Hughes and Alexander Lemore, mate; *Annie Catherine,* Capt. Osborne Bailey; freight barge, Capt. E. L. Snow; and the *Paul Jones,* Capt. Stephen Peters. In addition to these regulars, the big ocean-going schooners which brought in the loads of Florida yellow pine pulled into St. Mary's on a regular basis.

Getting the merchandise away from the port employed the majority of the men who lived in the city. Any number of local people maintained from one to six wagons or carts, including John H. M. Ryals, S. D. Ezell, R. A. Ezell, John Shoemaker, Louis Unsworth, Mick McGuill, A. J. Heard, Holmes Heard, T. C. Heard, David J. Kelley, Robert A. Rigby, Joseph T. Mahavier, and John Dugat. But to move the bulk of the merchandise, the large merchants, such as A. C. Jones and George McClanahan of Beeville and the McCampbell Brothers of Refugio and St. Mary's, maintained fleets of wagons and carts that ran into the hundreds.[27]

Despite the fact that a tremendous amount of freight was

moved in and out of the old port, a stagecoach line never made a stop at St. Mary's. Most people used the daily mail hack operated by C. F. Leisering to Refugio as a means to make connections with the stage. A post office was opened in the old port in 1857, with Cyrus W. Egery as the first postmaster. The last was William B. Gray, who served until the office was closed in 1907.

Churches represented in St. Mary's included Presbyterian, Methodist, Baptist, Disciples of Christ, and Episcopal. Two of the Methodist ministers were Berry Merchant and C. R. Gillet. Dr. W. J. Morris and Benjamin F. Stribling were Baptist preachers. William Baxter represented the Disciples of Christ. The Episcopalians did not have a church or resident rector; however, Col. John H. Allen and Capt. F. Bailey were lay readers. John N. McCain was a Presbyterian minister, and Mrs. Elenoir N. Campbell was the Sunday School superintendent.[28]

Many things contributed to the final demise of the city which at one time attained a population of over 6,000. The storm of 1875 demolished a large part of the town. The wharf and most of the businesses and homes were rebuilt. At about that time the new city of Rockport appeared to have an even brighter future, and businesses and families began to make the shift. Another storm in 1886 hastened the departure of some of the die-hards. The telegraph office faded into history with the resignation of Frank B. Rooke, who married Roberta Driscoll, daughter of Jeremiah O. Driscoll, and devoted his time to managing his wife's extensive ranching interests. The Rooke Foundation of today is an outgrowth of this family which still lives in the county.

Backers of St. Mary's had always hoped for a railroad to bolster their fading community. When the San Antonio and Aransas Pass Railroad started moving south to the coast, promoters in Refugio and Goliad sought to get the road to come through Refugio County, and possibly to the coast at St. Mary's. When the line finally went to Corpus Christi and eventually Aransas Pass and Rockport, the end of the dream was at hand.

Hobart Huson detailed the last days:

> The last remaining families included John H. Wood, Jeremiah O. Driscoll, Welder, Dugat, William Brightman, John Gray, Foster, Edwin Peets, Charles F. Leisering, Maton, Dorsett, Carpenter, Frank B. Rooke, Jirou, Kelley, Wm. Tedford, Foss, Folsom, Richter, Linney, and McRae.

The business district dwindled to the John H. Wood & Sons store, John Gray store, William Tedford store, Richter gin, John Foss Blacksmith shop and the wooden school building. The Wood store burned in about 1890. John Foss sold his smithy. Richter sold the gin and moved to San Antonio. The Tedford store was the last merchantile establishment at St. Mary's, operating until about 1900, when it moved to Rockport.

The last of the residents living in the old townsite in 1944 were the Brightman brothers, Andrew, Mortimer and Harvey. They occupied what was formerly the Neel Hotel. The only other original building then remaining was the Dugat home.[29]

The modern town of Bayside is about two miles down the bay from the almost forgotten city of St. Mary's.

Memories of St. Mary's live on in the Old St. Mary's Cemetery, where some of the people who made the old town come to life are buried: Maj. Cyrus W. Egery, Texian veteran and Indian fighter, and a son; Gen. Thomas T. Williamson and his daughter, Tirzah Ann McWillie; and Mr. and Mrs. John C. Maton, parents of Tom Maton. The historical marker tells it all:

> Joseph F. Smith, nephew of Texas' provisional Gov. Henry Smith, founded the town of St. Mary's in 1857. Ten acres were set aside for this burial ground, in which the earliest marked grave is dated 1860. The cemetery served the thriving community until an 1886 storm destroyed businesses and homes, causing residents to move away. In 1909, with the return of land development to the area, the cemetery was again used. The burial site of war veterans and pioneer area settlers, the cemetery serves as a reminder of the important early coastal town of St. Mary's.[30]

The storm of 1886 struck a fatal blow to the port city. Buildings which were not destroyed were dismantled and moved to other towns; businesses remained until only a few souls lingered. Probably the final year of the town could be logged as 1907, when the post office was closed.

Lamar
On Lookout Point

Capt. James W. Byrne was a man of action. A well-educated individual, he earned his title of captain in the Battle of Coleto as part of Fraser's militia. He escaped the firing squad when Capt.

Carlos de la Garza managed to save Byrne and several others at Goliad. Undaunted by this close encounter with death, he joined Ewen Cameron's Spy Company Rangers, which was organized at Live Oak Point, and served with distinction for the remainder of the war.[1]

Byrne was an astute businessman who capitalized on the availability of unlocated land certificates. These certificates could be bought for a pittance from soldiers or their heirs. He secured several certificates in late 1836 or 1837 from William Lewis[2] and located a survey on 1,428 acres on Lookout Peninsula. The big catch was that the survey was on lands which had been purchased from the Mexican government by Empresarios Power and Hewetson. Due to fast footwork on the part of some politicians, mainly Joseph F. Smith, these old Mexican titles were under a cloud and land-grabbers were flocking to the Aransas Bay area to squat on part of the Power land. Byrne was associated with George Robert Hull and George Armstrong in this project.[3]

Like the promoters of St. Mary's of Aransas, Aransas City, and Copano, Byrne was planning to build a port city that would bring him a fortune in trade with Mexico and western Texas. Byrne planned his city on Lookout Peninsula and named it Lamar, for his friend President Mirabeau B. Lamar. Within a short time survey-ors had laid out the town on Lookout Point. The new town was al-most directly across the neck of Aransas Bay that divided Lookout Point from Live Oak Point, where the rival city of Aransas City had been established just a few months earlier.

Possibly the first settler in this area was Seth Ballou and his family. He had retired from the sea and operated a steam ferry be-tween Lookout Point and Live Oak Point. Other early settlers that Byrne convinced to move into his new town included James Upton, John R. Talley, George Armstrong, James Gourlay, Jr., Israel Can-field, Jr., John Chain, Frederick Gunderman, Wm. J. Hay, S. L. Lynch, William Lewis, Joseph Magaratt, Joseph Meekers, Archi-bald McRae, Leonard Pickens, Alvin E. White, Isaac E. Robert-son, and George R. Hull.[4]

Competition was intense between the promoters of Aransas City and Lamar to lure settlers and businessmen to their new cities. Byrne built a wharf, with accompanying warehouses, and started making inroads into business at Aransas City. On June 12, 1837, the Congress of the Republic passed an act setting up the Customs

LOOKOUT POINT — Lamar was the port city conceived and built by Capt. James W. Byrne at the mouth of Copano Bay. Plans for this old port called for Pryor Lea to bring his railroad from Goliad to Lamar, thus making the port the entry city to the West. The customshouse was located here for a short time.

District of Aransas to take in the territory from the Rio Grande to the San Antonio River.[5] On July 17, 1837, Thomas M. Duke was appointed the collector of customs and authorized to select a site for the customshouse. He selected Live Oak Point (Aransas City) and was instructed to rent suitable quarters.[6]

The presence of the official customshouse in any port city was tantamount to making it the main port. Byrne set about to get it moved to Lamar from Aransas City, soliciting the aid of President Lamar. Since Lamar was of a different political persuasion than Power (founder of Aransas City), it was apparently an easy matter. Early in 1839 President Lamar signed an order directing the customshouse to be moved to his namesake city. Customs Director Hewes sent a letter to Lamar to "recommend moving it (customshouse) to the city of Lamar, due to its advantages in trade of the Rio Grande . . . . business men at Lamar have offered a lot 100 by 140 feet and promised to erect a one story frame house 16 by 26 feet." [7]

The citizens of Aransas City held a mass meeting and protested; however, President Lamar prevailed and the customshouse was moved to Lamar. The change was temporary, as the people in Aransas City mustered their political muscle in Congress and got the office returned to its original site.[8] It is hard to pinpoint the exact time that the customshouse remained in Lamar, but customs records indicate that the office was moved in June of 1839 and remained there until early 1840.

Business was brisk in the Aransas District in 1839. The April, May, and June report showed fourteen vessels had been in port. In the quarter ending September 30, 1839, thirteen vessels were listed as having been in Aransas Bay. During the same period James Hewes, collector at the time, reported that two shiploads of horses, mules, beef cattle, and hides had been shipped out of the Aransas District bound for New Orleans.[9]

The schooner *Caroline*, which plied up and down the coastal bays, was listed in the customs records as taking on goods at Lamar bound to Matagorda. Thomas Decrow was the boarding officer at Pass Cavallo on February 25, 1840. The sloop *Thomas Jack*, from Galveston, landed merchandise at Lamar destined for John R. Baker with the note: "Landed at Lamar for Live Oak and had no brand marks." All merchandise was identified with the "mark, or brand" of the person, or business, to whom the goods was directed.

This made it easy to sort out goods destined for a specific port and customer.[10]

Like her competitor port, Aransas City, Lamar was seeking to get in on the ground floor with trade to Mexico. This was heightened when the war between the Centralists and the Federalists broke out. But with the end of the Texas Republic in 1845, and the establishment of an uneasy peace with Mexico, trade dwindled at Lamar. A number of the people who had moved to Lamar at the urging of Byrne now followed him back to St. Joseph Island to a settlement on the west end known as Aransas. This later was known as St. Joseph and served as the southern terminal for the shipping and stage business of the two sea captains Peter A. Johnson and Charlie Johnson.[11]

The prospects of making a city out of Lamar were revived in the late 1840s by Col. Pryor Lea. A giant among men who shaped and developed Texas in its formative days, Lea was an educator, a patriot, and a soldier who stood with Andrew Jackson in the Creek campaign in 1813. He turned to law after leaving the army and then represented Knoxville, Tennessee, in Congress. When personal problems beset him, he took his family to Texas in 1846 and housed them in the abandoned church at La Bahía (old Goliad), the only available shelter in that frontier region.

A student of maps, he made a discovery that would change his life and affect an entire region. He foresaw that someday the angle of the Gulf at Aransas Bay would make it ideal as the great western port. His first choice as a terminal for a railroad was Lamar. Despite the fact that he never saw his dream turn into rails, his drive helped develop the coastal region in and around Aransas Bay. His plan called for a railroad connecting Lamar to Goliad and thence to San Antonio and eventually west. The Aransas Road Company was granted a charter from the state on February 14, 1852.[12]

When Lea advanced his railroad plan, Byrne, as well as the other original promoters of Lamar, joined in the project to get a railroad to Lamar. Byrne was successful in getting a number of former residents to return to the projected coastal port. The promoters decided to rename the new terminal city TrePort for the three bays: Aransas, St. Charles, and Copano. The town was replatted, and records show that Captain Byrne sold Lea one-fourth interest in Lookout Peninsula and Goose Island, including the lots not sold at

Lamar, on February 12, 1850. Evidently, the boom fizzled; on March 1, 1853, the land was conveyed from Lea back to Byrne.[13]

Colonel Lea, noted for his fine handwriting, produced a one-page flyer boosting TrePort. Excerpts from it give some insights into the new town:

> The harbor is excellent and vessels drawing nine feet, or more, can run to the wharf at all times. The usual soundings at good tide, over Aransas Bar, being twelve feet. At this place there is an abundance of excellent drinking water and a good supply of firewood. The healthfulness of this region is proverbial and temperature is usually delightful; but, occasional brief cold northers are very unpleasant. The roads are very good in many parts and might become generally admirable by cheap improvements. TrePort has been selected as the natural terminus of some principal roads through western Texas. The TrePort City Company has recently perfected the title to the whole peninsula. In a few weeks the public will have the usual port facilities, with some extra ordinary local comforts and easy access to the interior. Mechanics and laborers are in demand.[14]

While the railroad was never built to Lamar, and the port never fulfilled the dreams of its promoters, Lamar was not abandoned as was Aransas City. In fact, Lamar is the only city that sprang up on Aransas/Copano bays during Texas Republic land speculation days that still exists today. Aransas City vanished by the late 1840s and no trace of it exists today. Copano was gone by the 1880s, and it now takes a sharp eye to find traces of the first port in Texas. St. Mary's bloomed and then withered away until all that exists is an ancient cemetery. Port Preston never really got off the drawing boards, and the remains of its old packery and salt mines have vanished.

Promoters of Lamar did not give up. Since the army was seeking ways to supply their western troops, they sent Capt. Randolph B. Marcy to the Texas coast to find a good port city suitable for their needs. As a result of his survey, Marcy and some of his kin became interested in real estate in and around Lamar.[15]

The most intriguing investors to come to the area were the Colt brothers, Samuel and James, founders of the Colt Patent Fire Arms Company. The Colts, together with Erastus Williams of Connecticut, purchased from Captain Byrne a one-fourth interest in 14,000 acres of land, which included Lookout Peninsula and Goose

Island. Not only did these easterners buy an interest in Byrne's project, they also advanced Byrne money to promote the port of Lamar.[16]

Many stories exist concerning the development of the Colt pistol from a muzzle loader to the later version that "won the west." The best story recalls that Samuel Walker visited a blacksmith shop run by the Colts in Lamar and mentioned to them the great need for a pistol that could be fired and quickly reloaded, especially by a man engaged in rapid pursuit on horseback. The Colts are said to have drawn the plans and hammered out a model in their Lamar shop.[17] It is an accepted fact that the Colts perfected a model known as the Colt Walker revolver that was later made famous by its namesake, Texas Ranger Capt. Samuel H. Walker. His unit operated in the Refugio-Lamar area extensively during the period of Indian raids in the 1840s and 1850s.[18]

Another version of the Colts and their participation in affairs at Lamar is a bit different. It seems that the Patent Arms Manufacturing Company (first company to manufacture Colts) had a bill in 1850 for $12,500 against the State of Texas, incurred during the days of the Republic. Final settlement of the bill is not clear, but it is surmised by some historians that Texas officials ceded to Colt part of the land on which the townsite of Lamar was later built. Having been ceded three-fourths of the Lamar townsite, Colt bought the remaining fourth.[19]

One thing is apparent: Samuel Colt and his brother James knew and did business with a number of people who ended up owning property in Lamar. Among these was John Fuller, a good friend of Mirabeau B. Lamar who had moved to Texas in 1839 as an arms salesman. James Colt was for a time the personal secretary for Lamar, who at that time was a well-known poet in Georgia. Edward Ward Moore, commanding officer of the Texas navy, was also involved in purchasing arms from the Colt Company through Fuller and was interested in land at Lamar. Capt. Samuel H. Walker moved to Texas in 1836 after serving in the Indian wars in Florida. He joined Captain Billingsly's Rangers, was captured by the Mexicans, survived the Comanches, and served in Hays's Rangers. He also is mentioned in real estate deals on Lookout Peninsula. Indeed, the cast of players in Lamar was filled with soldiers of fortune, politicians, and adventurers, mixed with homeseeking pioneers.[20] Anything was possible.

In 1856 Lamar became involved in the famous camel experiment conducted by the army. At that time there was no railroad connecting the east coast with the west coast. Travel over the southern trail was long, hot, and exhausting. Someone had the bright idea of importing camels as beasts of burden for this southern route to the west. The first camels were unloaded at Indianola in May 1856. For several years the experiment was a success, but the camels developed sore feet without their native desert sands. As the Civil War approached, the idea was abandoned, as were the camels, which spread over the countryside and increased in number.[21]

Murdock McRae, son of Archibald McRae, who settled at Lamar in 1836, tells the camel story:

> Some of the camels were sold to circus owners and others were purchased by a Frenchman. He soon turned the animals loose in the desert to shift for themselves. The majority were soon killed off by the Apaches, who developed a fondness for camel meat. The last camels, nine of them, roamed back to Lamar, and were driven off from "Barrel Tree Bend" in Lamar on March 20, 1868. Joe Benson, a faithful old colored man, helped to drive them away. He was fond of relating the tale to us. The camels were sold to a man who put them in a pasture with his mules. The next morning he found some of his mules hung all along the barbed wire fence, while the frightened ones left were scattered all over the surrounding country.[22]

Archibald's wife, Vincey Williams McRae, passed down to her children and grandchildren a number of tales about Lamar from the days when they landed in 1836 until her death in March of 1894 in Lamar:

> Archibald McRae was the second man who settled in the beautiful seaside town of Lamar. They landed at Indianola and came directly to Lamar, where they bought a tract of land from Power and Hewetson and built a home. When they came to Texas the murderous Indians infested the land, cattle ran wild on the prairie and branding was promiscuous. They saw the reign of the six shooter and the Bowie knife. Other settlers soon followed and built homes in the town. Most of the houses were built of concrete [shell-crete] or adobe and are still standing, a mute reminder of the early days.
>
> Lamar was the rendezvous of the Comanche Indians when they roamed the Texas prairies. They were bloodthirsty warriors who loved to plunder and were troublesome neighbors, as many

old settlers could testify. Once the McRaes became so frightened when they saw the Indians coming that they hurriedly boarded their boat, the *Belle,* and crossed over to Live Oak Point where Col. James Power lived.

Lamar was then in its virgin, raw state — a vast flat country, apparently arid and sterile, except for vagrant and stunted weeds, as far as the San Antonio River — no underbrush or mesquite trees in those days.

One of our neighbors, Mrs. Eva Kroeger, had a terrible experience with the Indians. When a child, she and her sister were looking for milch cows about sundown. Their father happened to see Indians coming, so he blew a horn for the girls to come home, but the Indians knew what the signal meant, so they circled around and captured both children. The old squaw could not make Mrs. Kroeger stay on the horse, so they left her on the prairie, thinking she would die, as they scalped her and left her full of arrows. Her brother, John Thomas, found her the next morning. The Indians took the other little girl to the Indian Territory. Later she was rescued and lived to tell the story.[23]

In its heyday Lamar boasted a regular and permanent population. It had two stores, one run by R. Jordan in 1861 and another by R. T. Byrne in 1867. The town had two churches and a post office, of which Capt. Peter Johnson was postmaster for years. There were other adjuncts of old frontier towns, but no saloons.[24]

Sheriff Peter A. Johnson adds a bit to the description of the old port:

> Up to 1886 Lamar was a thriving town and commanded a good shipping business. There were a couple of wharves and large warehouses. There were several store buildings and a hotel or tavern. John R. Talley ran the hotel until the end of the Civil War when it was taken over by Henry Kroeger. One of the stores was operated by the Byrnes and another by the Vineyards. The town stretched from Teal's place at the entrance of St. Charles Bay to Captain Wells' place west of the present Highway 35. There were a number of concrete [shell-crete] houses and buildings.[25]

The Catholic Church, known as "Stella Maris" (Star of the Sea), was built in 1857. The building was made from shell-crete blocks by a Frenchman named Dalbarder. He was assisted by an old Negro slave named Mose Ballou, owned by Seth Ballou who came from East Texas before 1840.[26] The old church was still standing in 1987, having been moved from its original location in

1985 by the Aransas County Historical Commission to a new site close to the Lamar Cemetery.

A Presbyterian church came into existence in Lamar in about 1873, with services held in the home of Murdock McRae. The first preacher was Hugh Wilson of Seguin. It was during his visit to Lamar that a church was decided upon and later built. Prior to the construction of the church, services were held in the McRae home and that of Mrs. L. A. D. Wells. The church was blown down in the storm of 1886. Several years later the lumber was sold to Bert Ballou for $65, loaded onto Hamp Smith's barge, and moved to Rockport, where it was used for another Presbyterian church.[27]

The first school thought to exist in Lamar was the Lamar Academy. Mrs. Sarah Gregory, a widow, arrived at Lamar in the early 1850s and built a large brick house. Her daughter, Jane Gregory, married Patrick O'Connor and shortly thereafter started a school in her mother's elegant home. There was reported to have been a frame house in the yard which housed the school proper, but some teaching took place in the home. Mrs. O'Connor's sister, Mrs. Carrie Byrne (relative of Captain Byrne), taught music on a fine rosewood piano in the home.[28]

Sheriff Peter A. Johnson, son of Peter Johnson, the sea captain, recorded his early memories of Lamar Academy:

> Families living away from Lamar sent their children to board in the town. For several years prior to our removal to Lamar in 1862 Bertha Harris, my half sister, had attended the school. She had many school-mates, among them being the Bass children; Annie Willie, Kate and Charles Byrne; Frances Bower, daughter of John White Bower; James, Lucretia, Lugenio and Wilfred Ballou; Lizzie, Peter and Joseph Fagan; Henry, Isabella, Susan and Tina Finnegan; Margaret Fox, daughter of James Fox; the children of J. Hughes; Mary and Willie Kroeger, children of Henry L. Kroeger; Margaret Lambert, daughter of Mrs. Nicholas Lambert; Mary Murray, daughter of J. Murray; the four children of Capt. Philip D. Newcomb; John Henry O'Connor, son of Mrs. O'Connor; Annie O'Meara, daughter of Edward O'Meara; James and Jennie Patterson, children of James S. Patterson; Augustus M. Peaks, son of Mrs. John R. Tally; Eliza Power, daughter of Tomasita Power, widow of Col. James Power; Angelina and Mary Ryan, daughter of James Ryan; the Lewis and Strikes children; Catherine Sideck; Kate Teal, daughter of William Teal; Florence and Annie Upton, daughters of Edward P. Upton; Liz-

zie Walker; Thomas Wellington, son of Dr. R. W. Wellington; and the J. Wood children.[29]

Peter Johnson and Theodore (Charlie) Johnson were not blood kin. These men were bold sea captains and frontier entrepreneurs who did a great deal to develop Lamar, St. Joseph Island, and the bays of St. Charles, Copano, and Aransas.

Capt. Peter Johnson, a Dane, began sailing the seven seas as a lad and finally owned his own ship, the *Belleport,* a large three-masted, sea-going schooner. He began working out of Mobile, Alabama, and found his calling in aiding colonists during the War for Independence. At its conclusion he moved his operation to Galveston and then to Powderhorn (Indianola). Before long his ship was familiar up and down the coast at Matagorda, Saluria, Aransas City, Lamar, Copano, and Corpus Christi.

Fates of the sea brought Peter and Charlie together. After Charlie Johnson was shipwrecked off Galveston Island, he drifted ashore and found a job on the *Belleport* under Peter. Thus started a friendship that would last a quarter of a century, with Charlie skippering the *Fairy.* Later Charlie married Peter's stepdaughter, Bertha Harris, bringing the two business partners even closer.

As an outgrowth to their booming bay shipping business, the Johnsons organized a transportation system that brought them into contact with thousands of settlers and businessmen up and down the coast. They obtained a contract to carry the U.S. mail from Indianola to Corpus Christi and soon evolved a system to meet the needs of the growing ports. Passengers, mail, and freight were loaded aboard one of the Johnson boats (usually the *Belleport*) at Indianola and taken to Saluria, at the north end of Matagorda Island. From this port mail and passengers were loaded onto Johnson stagecoaches. The route went down the inland side of Matagorda Island to Cedar Bayou (stage stop called Vinson's Slough), where a crossing was made on a Johnson ferry boat. The route continued down the island to a new two-story station house built by Johnson at the town of St. Joseph (formerly Aransas), which was almost directly across the bay from present-day Rockport.

From St. Joseph the passengers, mail, and freight were loaded aboard the *Fairy* which called at Lamar, Aransas City, Copano, and St. Mary's before sailing on to Corpus Christi. Thus, two sea-going vessels, a stagecoach, a ferry, plus sufficient relays of mule teams to keep the stage moving at a fast pace, combined to form a system to meet the needs of the early settlers. This transportation system stayed in place until the Civil War blockade of the Texas coast became effective. The Johnson Line was one of the major factors in binding the coastal ports together. After the war, Capt. Charlie Johnson, with his ship, *Francis,* took over carrying passengers, mail, and freight from Indianola to Corpus Christi, touching at Lamar.

Another sea captain who had a big hand in shaping Lamar was Capt. James B. Wells, who settled on St. Joseph Island in about 1837. Captain Wells was in charge of the Texas navy yards in Galveston for the Republic. Shortly after moving to St. Joseph he entered politics and served as a justice as early as 1845 and in 1848 was appointed master of wrecks. After moving to Lamar he was again elected as a justice and later his name appeared as presiding election officer. He was opposed to secession but remained loyal to Texas. Reconstruction Governor A. J. Hamilton appointed him justice in Lamar at the end of the war.[30]

The Wells home in Lamar is described in family history records as a pretentious home in a large liveoak mott. Part of the mott of trees still stands just west of Highway 35.

Actually, quite a number of seafaring men joined Wells in his move to Lamar. Among them were Captains L. Bludworth, George M. Collinsworth, Peter Johnson, Theodore Johnson, John Low, James Mainlan, Philip C. Paul, George Roberts, William Roberts, Henry Seward, Marion Seward, William Smith, Spears and John R. Baker. Most of these men, with their families, moved to Lamar during the Civil War and remained.[31] Local legends connect part of the seafaring men who settled on St. Joseph Island as being members of pirate Jean Laffite's crews. It is a romantic idea that has failed to produce any "buried treasure."

When the Federal troops made life miserable for settlers on St. Joseph and Mustang islands, many of the island families moved to Lamar, including the Johnsons in 1862, as reported by a family member.

> During the first year of the war the islanders were not molested by the Federals, but the next year the Union fleet became quite active in Texas waters and the islanders began to feel the effects of the war. Landing parties were sent to the islands from the passing Federal fleets. These parties would steal and commit all manner of depredations. Finally the passing war ships began to bom-

bard the houses and settlements, which they could do from a distance of three miles. Life on the islands became unbearable and extremely dangerous.[32]

Johnson managed to hide his ships and ferry and they were not taken over by the Federal troops. After the war Peter Johnson sold the *Belleport,* the *Fairy,* and the ferry boat. In the trade he received the *Francis,* which he immediately sold to Charlie Johnson, who became famous in song and story up and down the coast.

With the coming of the Civil War, life at Lamar changed. A home guard unit was organized in the early part of 1861 under Capt. Edward P. Upton. In the fall, one other company was organized at St. Mary's that had a number of people from Lamar on its rolls.

In the early years of the war the Confederate heavy artillery companies stationed at strategic points on the coast kept the inland bays and Lamar safe from attack. But with the fall of Fort Esperanza, and the compromising of Neal's and Maltby's batteries on Mustang Island, Shell Bank, and at Aransas, Federal ships were free to raid the inland bays.[33]

Lt. Cdr. J. W. Kittredge, on his flagship *Arthur,* brought the war home to Lamar. After working over Corpus Christi in July of 1862, Kittredge sailed into Aransas Bay. There were three ships in Lamar harbor at the time, which Kittredge seized. The *Monte Cristo* had a cargo of powder and supplies, the *Belle Italia* had a load of corn and bacon, and the *Reindeer* had fifty-two bales of cotton. The Federals promptly sent a raiding party ashore, where they found 300 more bales of cotton which they took away on one of their boats. Somehow the *Monte Cristo* was damaged and left by Kittredge to pick up later. In the meantime, Captain Neal sent a crew of four to Lamar that night and burned the ship.[34]

Federal troops staged several raids on Lamar during the next several months as they tightened the blockade. On February 11, 1864, the Federal fleet sailed into Copano Bay. As they passed Lamar, Captain Upton's Home Guards fired on the ships. The Federals returned the fire, but no one was hurt. A landing party came ashore and raided the warehouses and destroyed them and the wharves. A ship in port loaded with cotton was taken by the Federals.[35]

Near the end of the war, Capt. E. P. Upton, of the Lamar Home Guards, was suspected of disloyalty to the Confederacy and was removed from his command and jailed. The native of Maine had rendered service to the Confederacy, but he remained loyal to the Union. Capt. James B. Wells was involved with Upton in the 1864 raid and his Union sympathies also surfaced in a report that Upton sent to his superiors. Wells was an avowed Union man but was not a traitor to Texas.[36]

Toward the end of the war, a Federal force moved into Lamar. These troops remained for several months after the war closed. The encampment of the Union forces was on the Byrne place on St. Charles Bay, below Capt. Charlie Johnson's place.[37]

A post office was maintained at Lamar from its beginning until the early 1900s. Cyrus W. Egery was the first postmaster, followed by James W. Byrne, Mrs. Jane H. O'Connor (during the Civil War), Peter Johnson (1868–1895), and Theodore Johnson. When the Federal government did not immediately resume the post office at Lamar after the war closed, a petition was circulated and the post office was restored.

During the Civil War, salt works were started up and down the coast. At least two were maintained at Lamar and on St. Charles Bay and were run by James W. Byrne and Archibald McRae. The salt works were raided by the Federals a number of times.

Changing conditions brought hard times to Lamar. When Rockport was established, port activities virtually came to a halt. However, unlike Aransas City, Copano, and St. Mary's, the old town of Lamar never quite died. Mrs. Ella McRae Clay wrote these words in 1930:

> Only the names and the memories remain of old Lamar. They stir memories of a romantic past, enshrined now in the hearts of a few remaining who once called it home. But now Lamar has the brightest future before her. The next twenty years will show amazing changes. We are looking forward to having a causeway in the near future, connecting Live Oak Point, scarcely three miles across the bay, with the old town of Lamar.[38]

Mrs. Fred Mires of Taft, a descendant of both Captain Wells and Archibald McRae, recalled in 1987 the first reaction of her aunt, Ella Clay, to the coming of the causeway on Highway 35 to link Lookout Point with Live Oak Point: "It will completely spoil our beautiful peninsula."

The causeway was built, and fifty-odd years have rolled by

since this prophecy. Lamar is still looking ahead and may someday reach the heights that Col. Pryor Lea and Capt. James W. Byrne envisioned.

Port Preston
Dream City

Port Preston was located by Maj. Stuart Perry on the north side of Mission Bay about a mile east of the mouth of the Mission River. It was a classic example of the towns that were visualized along the Texas coast just after the Texas War for Independence.

Perry laid out his town on a grant of land given to Robert Patrick Hearn, one of the Power and Hewetson colonists. Perry, like Henry Smith, proposed to contest Hearn's title. Several lots were sold after the legislature approved its incorporation on January 26, 1839. The promoter sold the venture to John N. Norton, who evidently did nothing to prove the title or develop the town.[1]

Black Point
Copano Bay Landing

Black Point on Copano Bay was a landing in the true sense of the word. Used as an unloading spot for ships dating back to the days of the early Spanish, the old port is located near present-day Bayside. Actually, Bayside is situated on a bluff and it is thought that Black Point was south of the bluff where the beach rolled into the estuary formed by the mouth of the Aransas River. An ancient road led from the Mission Refugio to Black Point and on to Corpus Christi, crossing the Nueces River at the Rock Crossing at Old San Patricio.[1]

The old landing was used by a number of early colonists. Francis Welder and his three sons, Frank, John, and Thomas, and a daughter, Elizabeth, landed there in 1836 after returning from a failed colony in the Valley. He went on to establish one of the longest enduring ranching empires in South Texas. Philip Dimmitt operated out of Black Point in the post-Republic days. Even after moving to his trading post in Corpus Christi, he continued to use Black Point occasionally.[2] In 1842, when Texas was mustering troops to stop the threatened Mexican invasion, Capt. John Wade brought the *Lafitte* into Copano Bay and Black Point, where he tied up long enough for his crew to go ashore and cut wood to fire his ship's boilers.[3]

Smugglers used Black Point as one of their landings in Copano Bay. There was one instance where a trader landed $60,000 worth of merchandise which moved overland through Corpus Christi on the way to Mexico.[4]

Pryor Lea projected his Aransas Road Company turnpike from Goliad to the coast to run across the reef at Black Point,[5] and Joseph F. Smith projected a new port city to be located at Black Point. The plan was switched for a number of reasons and St. Mary's of Aransas was established several miles north.

Smith had a home at Black Point, as did John Welder and later John Wood. The first school in the area was established at Black Point in 1854 and later moved to St. Mary's, as was the first Masonic Lodge in 1860.

As the town of St. Mary's grew and prospered, the settlement of Black Point dwindled away. After St. Mary's was abandoned, Bayside came into its own.[6]

Corpus Christi
Smugglers' Haven

History reveals strange tales. Corpus Christi today is heralded as the Sparkling City by the Sea, Texas Riviera, or the Naples of the Gulf, but back in its beginning it more-than-likely was known as Smugglers' Haven, since it came into being and prospered because of an active group of smugglers.

The bay got its name from Alonso Alvarez de Piñeda, who sailed along the Texas coast and into the area in 1519.[1] Supposedly he was thinking about the Feast of Corpus Christi at the time and thus named the bay after the religious holiday.

Probably the real beginning of the white man's intrusion into the area came with José de Escandón after he was commissioned by the viceroy of New Spain to conquer and colonize the region. Col. Diejo Ortíz de Parilla was in charge of surveying and exploration, making his headquarters at the ranch of Santa Petronila, near Corpus Christi Bay. It remained for Spanish ranchers to become the first settlers in the area. Records of these ranches are not complete; however, from 1757 to 1766 a sprinkling of ranchers braved the hostile environment.[2]

During the mission period in Texas, as well as the period of colonization and the days of the War for Independence, Corpus Christi Bay was largely ignored as a port because of numerous mud banks that hampered passage of ships. This changed after San Jacinto. In 1838 the Federalist revolt was in full swing, as was the French blockade of the Mexican coast. This forced the Mexicans, Federalists and Centralists alike, to seek arms and ammunition north of the border through Texas. Independent Mexican merchants cared little about the "hated Texans." All they wanted was trade merchandise, and they had hard money for payment.[3]

An explosive situation was rapidly forming, but one that made a trader's eyes sparkle with dollar marks. Mexican traders were pushing north seeking trade. Texan traders, who had a flair for adventure and a fast buck, rushed to accommodate the Mexicans. Renegade Mexican bandits, cutthroat *gringos,* as well as Indian opportunists, saw ways to improve their income. Murder, hijacking, and intrigue soon filled the lonesome trails leading from the Rio Grande to Texas trading posts. Recognizing the seriousness of the situation, Congress passed a bill creating a Corps of Regular Cavalry to furnish protection to the frontier.[4] The motive was sincere, but little came in the way of protection on the frontier.

Mexico officially looked on trade with Texas as forbidden, but this did not slow the traffic. President Sam Houston, not wanting to offend the French but at the same time eager to assist the trade, instructed the chief justices in the border counties to protect Texans from hostile acts of the Mexican government or its citizens. Little protection was afforded, but it let Texas traders know that unofficially they were in business.[5]

Into this explosive and dangerous situation the father and founder of Corpus Christi, Henry L. Kinney, made his entrance. He had all of the attributes that were required for success: He was brash, unscrupulous, suave, intelligent, handsome, and, above all, he had a burning desire to make big money fast. He asked no questions, made no promises, and cultivated high-ranking people on both sides of the Rio Grande.

Stories about Kinney are legion. As a youth of eighteen the lure of adventure brought him to Texas and San Patricio, where he became acquainted with Empresarios John McMullen and James McGloin.[6] His restless spirit took him to Illinois and he soon became a prosperous merchant. He fell in love with Daniel Webster's daughter, received the father's blessing, but was spurned by the young maiden. Broken-hearted, he again headed for Texas.[7] Soon he became a friend of Levi Jones, promoter of the city of La Salle (later taken into Indianola) and purchased from him several pieces of property in Nueces County. Later Jones advanced Kinney money and took a mortgage on some of Kinney's property. In the 1870s a number of foreclosures resulted from these unknown mortgages.[8]

Kinney showed up in Aransas City in 1838 and was associated with a group of individuals who were attempting to exploit trade with Mexico. His ability to project himself into a place of leadership is seen in the fact that while at Aransas City he presided over a citizens' meeting on June 15, 1839, to protest the proposed removal of the customshouse from Aransas City to Lamar. While in Aransas City he was involved in several deals, one in particular with Col. James Power, from whom he leased Mustang Island in 1839, which he kept until 1850.[9] In all likelihood Kinney decided to establish his own trading post on Corpus Christi Bay, as opposed to staying in Aransas City, in order to have the whole pie rather than be a participant with a number of other traders. During his brief stay in Aransas City he was associated with men who would shape the history of Texas during the next few years.

Kinney arrived on Corpus Christi Bay in September of 1839 and shortly thereafter took William P. Aubrey as a partner. They simply moved in and took possession of the site.[10] A crude shack was the first company home until they could build a permanent building on the bluff. Historian Dr. W. Armstrong Price, in preparing a historical marker to mark Kinney and Aubrey's Fort and Trading Post, placed the location of the shell-crete building at the site of the present telephone company building. Their pier was between Laguna Street and Cooper's Alley at the mouth of Blucher Creek.

The new trading post has been referred to as Kinney's Rancho, Kinney's Trading Post, Port of Corpus Christi, or Kinney's Rancho at Corpus Christi. It is not clear when the name Corpus Christi was used exclusively, probably not until after Gen. Zachary Taylor's troops arrived, or when Aubrey was named the first postmaster on March 23, 1846.

Kinney's contacts began to pay off. Within a short time a brisk trade was being carried on with the Federalists (camped off and on

Toll Rates

THROUGH

Corpus Christi Ship Channel!

In accordance with an Ordinance passed by the Mayor and Board of Aldermen of the City of Corpus Christi at a called meeting on the 6th day of November, inst., authorizing J. W. Vineyard and assigns to collect Tolls from all Steamers, Sail Vessels and other Water Craft using the Ship Channel between Corpus Christi and Aransas Bays, according to the terms and conditions of the Charter and the Ordinances of said City relating thereto, I will, from and after this date, proceed to collect Tolls from the Captain, Master, Owner or Person controlling any Water Craft, Steamship, Steamboat or Sail Vessel, upon any Goods, Wares and Merchandise of every description, passing through said Channel, at the following rates :

LEAD, (outward), per ton of 2,000	25 cents.
COPPER, " " "	50 "
COTTON AND WOOL, per 100 lbs.	5 "
HIDES, each	1 "
HORSES, MULES, JACKS, JENNIES AND CATTLE, 2 years old and over, each	40 "
Under 2 years	20 "
HOGS, SHEEP AND GOATS, each	5 "
CORD WOOD, per cord	75 "
LUMBER, per 1000 ft. board measure	50 "
SHINGLES AND LATH, per 1000	10 "

All other freights at the rate of one cent per cubic foot.

COMPANY'S OFFICE, OVER N. GUSSETT'S STORE.

JOHN M. MOORE & CO.,

Assignees of J. W. Vineyard.

Per GEO. E. CONKLIN,

Agent and Attorney in Fact for Assignees,

SHIP CHANNEL FOR HIRE — Ships attempting to cross Corpus Christi Bay after the founding of Kinney's Trading Post had shallow water and mud banks to conquer. In the early 1850s the Corpus Christi Navigation Company was chartered to improve channels. Other firms followed until the Morris and Cummins Cut was opened in 1874. In order to pay for work on these channels, a toll was charged. This ad ran in the Corpus Christi newspaper and gave rates charged by the firm of John M. Moore & Co., assignees of J. W. Vineyard.

at Fort Lipantitlan) and private Mexican merchants. Realizing
that he was in a true no-man's-land, Kinney quickly turned his
trading post into an armed camp. His thick-walled, shell-crete
building was complete with portholes, a private army that consisted of as many as sixty men at times, and a twelve-pound cannon.[11] The men who entered Kinney's service were not clean-cut
Texans but men with a past who found living by the gun a good
way to get by on the frontier.

Since he was located in the disputed Nueces Strip (claimed by
Texas but disputed by Mexico), Kinney relished his adopted title of
ex-officio ruler of the territory. President Mirabeau B. Lamar was
in office in 1839 when Kinney started his venture. Without a
doubt, the president depended on Kinney to keep order in the territory and at the same time furnish him information about the activities of the Mexican army. When Sam Houston began his second
term as president in September of 1841, he and Kinney had a close
relationship. In fact, it appears certain that part of the wages of
Kinney's army was paid by the State of Texas. Kinney was equally
at home at the council tables of Gen. Mariano Arista of the Centralist party and commander in chief of the Northern Army of Mexico. He also had just as many friends among the high command of
the Federalist cause. It was with help like this that the newest port
in Texas began to flourish.

Kinney's Trading Post survived many battles with Mexican
bandits, *gringo* renegades or cowboys, and Indians. One classic example came when Capt. Enrique de Villareal showed up at the fort
with 300 soldiers demanding to know why Kinney was squatting on
land granted to him by the State of Tamaulipas on November 16,
1831.[12] There are several versions of how Kinney squeaked by this
confrontation, but the outcome was an agreement whereby Kinney
would pay Villareal for the land. One sidelight was the fact that to
buy the land he had to become a citizen of Mexico — a move that
Kinney said later was the expedient thing to do at the time. Others
branded this act as close to treason.[13]

It is hard to serve three masters and not get caught short by
one. Kinney was implicated at least three times on serious treason
charges, but managed to survive each. One case involved Philip
Dimmitt, a hero of the War for Independence, co-author of the Goliad Declaration of Independence, and respected trader who had
established a rival trading post near Flour Bluff on Corpus Christi

Bay in 1841. Dimmitt and his associates had accused Aubrey and Kinney of having treasonable relations with Mexican authorities on the Rio Grande. After a trip to Matamoros, Kinney was assured that his business would not be molested. Shortly thereafter, Lt. Vicente Sanchez was sent to Corpus Christi with fourteen men to arrest Dimmitt and return him to Mexico to face smuggling charges, which he did. Kinney's establishment was not disturbed, even though Dimmitt's post was sacked and over $6,000 of trade goods stolen. The outcry in Texas was loud, with an accusing finger pointed toward Kinney as conniving with the Mexican army to do away with his competition. Kinney and Aubrey were acquitted after a trial in Victoria. This brought about a bribery charge against Judge Alason Ferguson, who was accused of receiving money from Kinney for favorable testimony.[14]

Trade at the Corpus Christi port continued to increase up to 1842. With the Mexican army making an aggressive move against San Antonio, and war talk in Texas reaching a fever pitch, conditions at Kinney's Ranch were tenuous. After the encounter between Gen. James Davis and Col. Antonio Canales at Lipantitlan in June of 1842, both sides claimed victories. Canales was happy to take his forces back to Matamoros, and Davis was glad to get away with the bulk of his forces. Kinney was back at Corpus Christi by September 1, only to be scared away again when General Woll captured San Antonio on September 11. Kinney just happened to be in Mier at the time Texans were captured in this abortive expedition. He was able to bribe officials to win the release of eight wounded men who made their way home. Woll's intrusion, and the Mier expedition, seemed to put hostilities on hold, as talk turned to annexation of Texas to the United States. By early summer of 1843, Kinney had his port in operation.

Annexation talk brought rumors that the Nueces Strip would be given up for the sake of peace. Lawlessness increased, but so did the power of Kinney — the unquestioned ruler of this no-man's-land. As the rumors of annexation grew, so did Kinney's work in behalf of his city. He was in constant touch with Maj. Andrew Jackson Donelson, U.S. envoy to Texas, pleading his case that the Rio Grande and not the Nueces be declared the new border. He also campaigned successfully to get Gen. Zachary Taylor's army stationed in Corpus Christi.[15]

A new day arrived for the port of Corpus Christi on July 26,

1845, as described in the diary of Major General Hitchcock, USA: "July 26, Arrived last evening within a few miles of the entrance to Aransas Bay [in southern Texas north of the Nueces River] . . . . After breakfast some of us will go ashore in a small boat. General Taylor seems anxious to get the men ashore, on the island. Our lighters are not here." [16] The village of Corpus Christi soon changed from a community of less than 100 to a booming army town. Tents stretched from present Artesian Park, where the army drilled a water well, to North Beach. Within a short time wagons loaded with goods for new businesses arrived and all sorts of new enterprises were ready for the soldiers' dollars. Kinney's cash register was ringing so fast that it was hard to keep up.

Life in Corpus Christi for the next seven and one-half months was completely altered as the number of American troops increased to over 4,000. Troops were landed at Lavaca, Mesquite Landing, and Black Point and marched overland to Corpus Christi. The army set up shops and supply posts to take care of their expanding troops and supplies. Buildings were thrown up for saloons, stores, gambling halls, and residences. Even a theater made its appearance. [17]

As Corpus Christi grew, so did Kinney's reputation and financial well-being. Hitchcock noted in his diary:

> Kinney seems to have a government of his own here and to be alternately the friend and foe of Mexicans, Texans, Americans, and Indians, sometimes defying them and meeting them with force and sometimes bribing and wheedling them. He lives by smuggling goods across the line . . . . Colonel Kinney's position here is an extraordinary one. While an object of suspicion to both Texans and Mexicans, he seems to be regarded as a man of power by both sides. [18]

Later, Hitchcock confirmed what everyone knew when he met with Colonel Kinney and General Taylor and heard a report from Chepeta, Kinney's ace spy, who was just in from the Rio Grande with news about Mexican troops. History was recorded in Corpus Christi on February 16, 1846, when the flag of the Republic of Texas was lowered and the Stars and Stripes floated in its place. Taylor began to get his army ready to leave and on March 11 the main body of troops left. A major milestone in Corpus Christi's history had come to an end. [19]

Corpus Christi became a deserted village almost overnight.

The merchants who had lived on the soldiers' business, the saloons who had kept them in spirits, as well as the ladies of the night, all disappeared. Kinney also followed the army, after being appointed division quartermaster. The title "Colonel" that Kinney carried the rest of his life appears to be purely honorary, since his official rank appeared to be that of a private; however, he continued to council with men in high places. In fact, he acted as the unofficial negotiator between Texas President Anson Jones and Mexican General Arista in the events immediately before the war.[20]

In April of 1846 Nueces County was organized, with Corpus Christi as its county seat. Carved out of San Patricio County, the new county took over all of the area between the Nueces and the Rio Grande. Later the town was established and incorporated. Kinney and William Mann, a merchant, were authorized to hold an election. A citizens' meeting was held in Kinney's home on January 11, 1847, for the purpose of organizing the county government. Shortly afterwards the American forces gained victories at Buena Vista and Monterrey, making it possible to discharge a number of Texans who had joined Taylor's army, or who were members of one of the Texas units attached to the U.S. Army. This brought life back into Corpus Christi and put Kinney back on the job of promoting the city.[21] He began to actively promote Corpus Christi abroad, calling it the Naples of the Gulf.

In September 1848 a weekly newspaper, the *Corpus Christi Star,* made its appearance. About this time Kinney and Aubrey dissolved their partnership. One of the most encouraging bits of news appeared in the *Star* on September 19 when editor Somers Kinney, cousin of H. L. Kinney, announced that a steam dredge had been purchased to deepen the ship channel at the entrance of the bay. From the beginning it had been the dream of citizens of Corpus Christi to dredge a channel across the mud flats of Red Fish Bay to link Corpus Christi Bay with Aransas Bay and gain access to Aransas Pass. Previously all commerce into Corpus Christi was by lighters or extremely shallow-draft boats. This was the beginning of a long struggle that would not culminate until 1926, when the harbor of Corpus Christi was opened to deepwater commerce.[22]

The *Star* heralded new trade opportunities for Corpus Christi with the formation of a wagon company to carry freight between Corpus Christi and the Rio Grande. Promoters of the project were Capt. J. H. Blood, New Orleans; E. Fitzgerald, Corpus Christi; H.

Clay Davis, Rio Grande City; and Benjamin F. Neal, San Antonio. All of these men were destined to play roles in the development of Corpus Christi, with Neal slated to become the first mayor.

The tempo of trade picked up with the discovery of gold in California in 1849. Corpus Christi quickly was touted as the "shortest route to the west." Business boomed as shiploads of gold-seekers sought supplies and transportation going west. Hopes also ran high that Corpus Christi would be named as the army depot for the Southwest, but the anticipation was doused when Indianola received the nod. Increased ship traffic caused William Ohler to build another wharf on the waterfront, with a two-story brick building on shore.[23] Through all of this activity the trade with northern Mexico persisted in varying degrees. Peace had not come to the Nueces Strip. Indians still killed wantonly, Mexican looters made hit-and-run raids on the frontier, and murder was commonplace. Petitions seeking protection on the frontier were slow to be answered, either by the state or federal government.

The overland route to California fell by the wayside. Then, in 1852, Kinney promoted the first State Fair, seeing it as a vehicle to get business moving again and at the same time secretly provide a means for raising money and men for José María Carbajal. Carbajal, a die-hard Federalist, had a dream of creating a separate state in northern Mexico for the Federalists. Kinney saw it as a means for more trade. Kinney spent huge sums of money promoting the project, but few people attended and the affair was considered a flop. The failure started the financial downfall of Kinney, who at the end of the Mexican War was reputed to be the wealthiest man in Texas. One person who did attend the fair was Richard King. A new star for South Texas was rising, since in 1853 King and Capt. "Legs" Lewis jointly purchased the start of the giant King Ranch.[24]

Without a doubt Kinney's influence had made Corpus Christi what it was in the 1850s. With his wealth gone, he immediately began looking for some way to recoup his finances. At that time the Expansionist Movement was getting a big play in the United States, the goal of which was to seize land in Central America and set up small empires of slave states. In 1852 Kinney made a conditional purchase of the Shepherd-Haly grant of the Mosquito Kingdom on the coast of Nicaragua. He ran head-on into a man who was bigger and had more resources than he — Cornelius Vanderbilt. After a brief rule of sixteen days as military governor of San Juan, Kinney was forced out. He returned to Galveston and found out that he had been divorced by his wife. The marriage had been in trouble since Kinney had continued seeing his mistress, Genoveva Perez, by whom he had a daughter that he later adopted. He returned to politics and sought appointments to high foreign diplomatic posts in order to rebuild his image, as well as his fortune. (He would meet his death on February 27, 1862, in Matamoros. Officially, his death was attributed to a stray bullet between two warring factions in the city. Unofficially, it is hinted that he attempted to see Genoveva, who had married, and upon approaching her door in the early morning hours was shot. His place of burial is unknown.) [25]

It became apparent to the citizens of Corpus Christi that if the city was to grow and prosper it would have to secure access to deep water. The stumbling block was mud flats which separated Corpus Christi Bay and Aransas Bay. Even in the best conditions, only shallow-draft vessels could enter Corpus Christi Bay. A charter was granted in 1852 to the Corpus Christi Navigation Company to improve channels for navigation from Saluria to Corpus Christi. Kinney and Benjamin F. Neal were the promoters. Nothing came of the dream. In 1854 the Corpus Christi Ship Channel Company was chartered and a contract was made with the city on May 17. Kinney was again in the forefront and evidently secured the services of a dredge that did some work. Through the years work was started, stopped, and started again many times without meaningful results. On April 15, 1858, D. S. Howard Company entered into a contract with the city, purchased a dredge, and announced big plans before being stopped by secession. A $500,000 bond issue was passed by the city, which was later revoked. The Civil War passed and once again the people of Corpus Christi sought deep water.

In June of 1871 the Corpus Christi Navigation Company was organized, headed by Richard King. This time a contract was made with Augustus T. Morris and James Cummins. A channel known as the Morris & Cummins Cut was actually completed across the mud flats in 1874. It connected with Aransas Pass through the Lydia Ann Channel.[26] J. W. Vineyard of Ingleside figured prominently in channel promotions. At various times all toll collections went to either Vineyard or John M. Moore & Co., assignees of J. W. Vineyard. Vineyard is thought to have been a man of considerable wealth before the Civil War.

The steamship *Gussie* pulled into the new municipal wharf on

Sunday, May 31, 1874. A crowd of 3,000 turned out for the event.[27] While this channel served a purpose, it was not adequate for the ships drawing eight feet of water. The first Aransas Pass-Corpus Christi channel ran through Turtle Cove and across Corpus Christi Bay for twenty-one miles. Built in 1907, it was $8^1/_2$ feet deep by 75 feet wide — increased to 12-by-100 in 1914. By 1920 the channel had shoaled and was not being used extensively. Action was needed immediately.[28]

On June 5, 1920, Congress gave approval to a plan to make a survey of the Aransas and Corpus Christi bay area, with the view of establishing one deepwater harbor in the area. Rockport, Aransas Pass, and Corpus Christi were vying for the designation. The report issued on May 25, 1922, listed the costs for the three concepts as follows: Corpus Christi, cost to U.S., $1,967,000, cost to local interests, $3,084,900; Aransas Pass, cost to U.S. $1,005,000, cost to local interests, $632,000; Rockport, cost to U.S. $1,038,000, cost to local interests, $994,000. The long wait was over — Corpus Christi was designated as the deepwater port for the area. One engineer, H. C. Newcomer, ruled in favor of Aransas Pass, but the Corps of Engineers went with the recommendation of L. M. Adams and ruled in favor of Corpus Christi. Officials of Aransas Pass and Rockport were sure that they would be picked since their proposals were cheaper, but Corpus Christi's homework had paid off. Former mayor Roy Miller had been sent to Washington to lobby for Corpus Christi, with the full backing of the King Ranch. Work started in 1922 and was completed in 1926.[29]

The port of Corpus Christi gradually picked up business as more shallow-draft vessels began calling on a regular basis. Another dock was built at the foot of Peoples Street. As the Civil War approached, it was obvious that the community was divided; however, once war was entered into, most Corpus Christians fought for the Confederacy.

Lt. Cdr. J. W. Kittredge brought the war home to Corpus Christi. After harassing the residents of St. Joseph and Mustang islands, Kittredge entered Corpus Christi Bay on the *Corypheus.* On August 13, 1862, he was joined by the gunboat *Sachem,* the schooner *Reindeer,* and the sloop *Belle Italia,* and demanded to be allowed to inspect public buildings in Corpus Christi. Maj. A. M. Hobby, Confederate commander of forces at Corpus Christi, refused. A forty-eight-hour truce was proclaimed to allow the civilian population to evacuate the city. The battle was joined on August 16. Kittredge withdrew at sunset, with damage to two of his ships.[30]

Kittredge returned the following day and resumed the battle, sending a detachment of thirty men ashore on North Beach to attack by land. The bombardment of the town was heavy, bringing forth several tales worth telling, recorded by Hitchcock in his diary:

> A man confined to bed with rheumatism, in an upper story room, refuses to budge. He prefers death to the pain of being lifted on a stretcher. A round shot strikes the house, passes within a few feet of him. He bounds from bed, clears the steps at a gallop, and leads a party of stragglers up and over the bluff, arrives in camp ahead, never again to experience a twinge of rheumatism.
>
> A warehouse filled with hides is hit by an exploding shell. Hides rain from the sky. A Johnny Rebel, legging it nearby, glances over his shoulder and yells, "My God, they're shooting goat skins at us." [31]

Another of these tales was perpetuated by *Leslie's Weekly*. It was an account of an old German settler who ordered his Negro boy to open dud shells and salvage the gunpowder. Instead of gunpowder, he found to his amazement the unexploded cannon balls were filled with fine bourbon whiskey. The explanation appended to this yarn was that the crew aboard one of the gunboats had stolen a barrel of whiskey from the ship's commissary and, fearful of being caught with the illicit goods in their possession, opened the shells, cleaned them of their explosives, and refilled them with grog. On dull nights the watch, so the tale goes, would tap a cannon ball and mark the passing hours in solitary conviviality. There had been no opportunity in the confusion of battle to set aside the whiskey-laden cannon balls with their esoteric markings, known only to the initiate. When local folks discovered that it was "raining whiskey," there was less dodging of missiles.[32]

Kittredge was captured when he ventured ashore near Flour Bluff into a trap set by Capt. John Ireland. Corpus Christi escaped further direct assault; however, local forces were engaged in skirmishes in the bay and on the islands. When the Federal forces took Fort Aransas and sealed Aransas Pass, Corpus Christi was left to wither on the vine. Shortly after the war ended, Corpus Christi was occupied by two companies of Negro soldiers with white officers. Generally, the citizens of Corpus Christi fared well under the occupation forces. In fact, at least two of the men married local belles.[33]

Still in the throes of Reconstruction, the people of Corpus Christi turned to their port as a means to regain their self-respect and wealth. Like other regions on the coast, Corpus Christi built packeries and shipped out tallow, hides, and bones. Nueces County had at least ten packing houses. Money was scarce, but the demand for all types of goods was great, setting the stage for the revival of traders in the city. Yellow fever hit the community of less than 1,000 in July of 1867 and over 300 died. Economic conditions were slow in improving. However, in 1870, with the Texas legislature ratifying the fourteenth and fifteenth amendments, the way was cleared for President U.S. Grant to accept the Texas Constitution. On April 16, Gen. J. J. Reynolds proclaimed the end of military rule in Texas. Conditions in Corpus Christi improved rapidly.[34]

Corpus Christi in the 1870s was making gains in all phases of her economy. Despite progress in this field, the frontier was still a dangerous place to live, with murders and robberies of isolated ranches commonplace. One of the most flagrant acts of violence occurred in Nuecestown on Good Friday, March 26, 1875. A band of twenty-five to thirty Mexicans, mostly adherents of Gen. Juan Cortina of the Mexican army, appeared on the road leading to Nuecestown and started taking prisoners as people met them, or were overtaken. They proceeded to George Frank's store, where they robbed and terrorized their prisoners. Leaving Frank's store, the bandits went three miles down the river to Thomas Noakes's store. The Mexicans plundered and then burned the trading post. The loot they took included a number of new saddles which Noakes had crafted for sale. A wave of revenge swept South Texas as the result of this wanton raid. For years, anytime a Mexican was caught riding on a new saddle he was accused of having a "Noakes Saddle" and summarily shot. Noakes shot and wounded one Mexican who was later hanged. John Swank was killed in the pursuit.[35]

Railroads brought renewed vigor to Corpus Christi. First, in 1876, Capt. Richard King and Mifflin Kenedy started their narrow-gauge line to Laredo. In 1886 the San Antonio and Aransas Pass Railroad built a line from Gregory across the bay on a trestle to Corpus Christi, arriving in October.[36]

The port city continued to grow with its rail connections; however, the key to expanded growth was still missing — deep water.

When that arrived in 1926, the old port became a new port that reached out to harness the wealth of the region that flowed with gas and oil from below and produced an abundance of cattle and field crops on the surface.

The dreams of Colonel Kinney had been realized at last.

Sharpsburg
River Port

Sharpsburg was located about six miles from the mouth of the Nueces River on a small rise on the north bank in San Patricio County. It was started and developed by S. G. Borden in the early 1870s and at its peak had several stores, a blacksmith shop, grist mill, cotton gin, school, and a post office. Oldtimers remembered boats coming up the Nueces River as early as 1862.

The land surrounding Sharpsburg was suitable for agriculture and cotton was grown in the area, giving rise to the start of the port of Sharpsburg. Borden and a neighbor and business partner, D. C. Rachal, owned a flat-bottomed schooner called the *Nueces Valley*, skippered by Captain Fly. A cotton gin was established in Sharpsburg and the bales were shipped out on the *Nueces Valley*. The Wade Packery was located only a short distance from the port. Hides and wool were two of the products shipped out, along with cotton. Produce, especially watermelons, were rafted down the Nueces from near San Patricio, past Sharpsburg.

Sharpsburg grew as a trading center. Borden operated a ferry at the port, making it the crossroads of traffic out of Corpus Christi and Mexico headed to San Antonio and Goliad.

Borden was evidently in San Patricio County before the Civil War, but returned to his home in East Texas, where he later joined Capt. A. C. Jones's company and engaged in local skirmishes and bushwhacking. In 1867 he returned to the county and settled on a sheep ranch at Sharpsburg. He was influential in county politics and became county judge in 1881.

The first telephone line in San Patricio County ran from Borden's store in Sharpsburg to Corpus Christi in 1900. Borden subdivided Sharpsburg, but after several sales it appears that interest died. A number of farm blocks in the area were sold.

Sharpsburg got its name from a sheep rancher by the name of Sharp who was in the area before Borden. Prior to this time there was a Mexican community called Ramirena in the same general vicinity as Sharpsburg. Hart's Lake was in the area and furnished fresh water to early settlers. The population was listed in 1896–97 at 500. The community gradually faded away when the school closed in 1912 and the children went to school at Odem. Nothing remains now to mark the first port in San Patricio County.[1]

Aransas Pass
Harbor City

The city of Aransas Pass and its deepwater port site, Harbor Island, got started late in the battle to secure a deepwater port in South Texas. Matagorda, Lavaca, Indianola, Saluria, Copano, St. Mary's, and Corpus Christi had been vying for favor from the Corps of Engineers since the days of the Texas Republic. Aransas Pass, as a city, did not get started until 1890, but, due to the Panic of 1893 and failure of the South Jetty to bring deep water over the bar at Aransas Pass, the big push did not come until 1909, when Burton and Danforth arrived on the scene.

While the city of Aransas Pass did not get started until 1890, promoters who were seeking to establish a port on Harbor Island and the mainland were stirring by 1858.[1] The United States Corps of Engineers expressed an interest in the pass as early as 1853. After an extensive investigation the Central Transit Company, backed by the Great Baring Brothers of London, selected the present site of Aransas Pass over all other points in the area to build a port city to carry commerce between Europe and the Orient. They quickly arranged for the purchase of land. Construction on a terminal railroad and harbor improvements were in progress when the Civil War intervened. The building of the Union Pacific Railroad from coast to coast also put a damper on the project.

Pryor Lea was a planner and dreamer who traveled to Texas in 1846 and settled in Goliad. Lea's dream, for which he received a charter, was to build a railroad from Lamar on the coast to San Antonio, going through Refugio and Goliad. Lea's charter was later amended to a turnpike. Some grading and bridges were apparently constructed on this project. However, Lea is thought to have merged his idea for the Aransas Road Company with the Great Baring Brothers project.[2]

After the Civil War, Lea and several other railroad and deep-

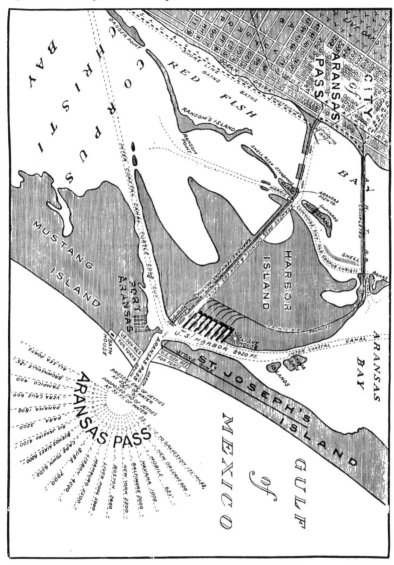

ARANSAS PASS residents, with great dreams of creating the first deepwater port of the gulf, were not modest in the literature they sent worldwide to advertise the new city. This map ran as a full-page ad in the Aransas Pass Progress *and was mailed across the United States. Deep water was brought to Harbor Island in 1912. The oceangoing liner* Brinkburn *arrived in port on September 7, 1912, to set off a week-long celebration.*

water promoters were back working on their projects. The focus for deepening Aransas Pass between St. Joseph Island and Mustang Island was in Rockport during this period. The cattle packery business was centered in the Rockport-Fulton area and the local interests, as well as the Morgan Shipping Line, sought help in getting deep water over the bar and a channel brought into Rockport.[3]

The Texas-Mexican Railroad (originally Corpus Christi, San Diego, and Rio Grande) was chartered in 1875 and shortly was taken over by the Mexican National Railways. At that time a branch was projected to the city of Aransas Pass. Again, deep water over the pass was the ultimate goal in order to be able to divert seaborne trade over the railroad to Mexico.[4]

The first attempt to get the pass deepened came from the citizens of Rockport in 1868 when they raised $10,000 for a 600-foot dike on St. Joseph Island.[5] No confirmation of this can be obtained from local sources.

Congress passed a resolution in 1879 authorizing the deepening of Aransas Pass. This came after a survey by the Corps of Engineers which recommended two parallel jetties and protection for the eroding head of Mustang Island. Maj. Samuel M. Mansfield worked on this project from May of 1880 until 1885. Known locally as the Old Government Jetty, or the Mansfield Jetty, the work consisted of repeated layers of rock and brush. The project was a failure, as the jetties settled and no significant deepening of the water at the pass occurred. Maj. Oswald H. Ernst recommended that two parallel stone jetties be built and that the continued erosion on Mustang Island be accomplished by laying an eighteen-inch-thick riprap cover. Mustang Island was repaired, but a shortage of funds prevented the new rock jetties from being built.[6]

One of the biggest boosters of deep water during this period was Col. George Fulton. His correspondence to government officials and influential politicians shows his keen interest. Newspapers of the time carried many of Fulton's ideas for deep water.

The next chapter in the saga of deep water was written by private enterprise. In March of 1890 a charter was granted to the Aransas Pass Harbor Company for the purpose of "constructing, owning, and operating deep water channels from the waters of the Gulf of Mexico and across Aransas Pass." [7] At the same time the Aransas Harbor City and Improvement Company was formed, with a list of nine directors and investors from all over the United

States. Political clout was seen in the form of Russell B. Harrison, son of President William Henry Harrison. T. B. Wheeler, former lieutenant governor of Texas, was the key organizer in charge of the operation and worked tirelessly to bring their dream into being. The list of stockholders included men of money and influence.[8]

With the two organizations in place, the promoters launched a nationwide publicity campaign. What followed was one of the most remarkable stampedes for land and lots in the history of the settlement of South Texas. Notwithstanding the numerous disappointments, the failures of the past, and the disasters that had overtaken all previous efforts to develop the harbor, the people had perfect faith. There never was a question in the mind of the public but that the success of the harbor enterprise would open a great port to the world. The Bay View Hotel (originally called Hoyt Hotel) was built and opened for business in 1893. It was a three-story showpiece designed and built to impress visitors who flocked to town to buy lots. Of course, not everyone got to stay in the fancy hotel. Early pictures show a tent city under the oak trees.[9]

One of the projects in the master plan was to build a railroad from the city of Aransas Pass to Harbor Island. Construction got started and continued to the Morris and Cummins Cut. Rock for the planned jetty was shipped in on the San Antonio and Aransas Pass Railroad, transferred to the terminal railroad, and delivered to the end of the line at the Cut, where it was loaded onto barges headed for the jetty at the pass.[10]

The developers had hoped that SA&AP would eventually take over the terminal railroad and thus serve the new deepwater port at Harbor Island. However, the Panic of 1893 caused SA&AP to suffer business reverses and, as a result, the line was taken over by Southern Pacific Railroad. Since SP had financial ties with the port of Galveston, they were not eager to lend a hand to the new port. With Wheeler's urging, the state legislature conferred upon Aransas Harbor Company the right to acquire certain land immediately around the harbor, thus giving the company an additional selling tool. Almost immediately they secured a commitment from Alexander Brown and Sons of Baltimore to furnish the money necessary to construct the project (a considerable amount of the money was provided by local interests). The company adopted the single, curved jetty concept and went to work immediately. Two engineers, Lewis M. Haupt and H. C. Ripley, did the work. When finally completed, water over the bar had been deepened slightly but only immediately adjacent to the jetty. The project was a miserable failure.

With everything gone sour, lot sales turned to zero and people left the city in large numbers. Aransas Pass Harbor Company had expended $401,554 on the dream. In a final effort the company contracted with C. P. Goodyear to provide a twenty-foot channel in any way he could. He used 23,350 pounds of dynamite to blast a channel and some 13,000 pounds to blow out 500 feet of the old Mansfield Jetty.[11] He failed to deepen the channel. Not completely discouraged, the company turned to the government and petitioned them to take over their work and finish the project. Deliberations lasted for years.

In 1899 the Corps of Engineers was authorized to tackle the project. They removed the old Mansfield Jetty and the north jetty was completed according to Haupt's plans. Finally, the engineers recognized that a lone jetty would not do the job. In 1907 authorization for the south jetty and extension of the north jetty was approved. As the water deepened across the pass the engineers turned their attention to a channel and basin for Harbor Island. Work on this project continued for several years. On September 7, 1912, the oceangoing liner *Brinkburn* arrived at Harbor Island and took on a load of over 10,000 bales of cotton. A weeklong celebration was held in Aransas Pass and Harbor Island to commemorate the coming of deep water to South Texas.[12]

When the land boom of the early 1900s fizzled out, the Aransas Harbor City and Improvement Company was unable to meet its commitments and as a result two sheriff sales were held on April 24, 1906, at which time the land purchased from T. P. Mc-Campbell was bought back by his widow, Mary E. McCampbell. By this time the prospects for deep water were almost assured, as the Corps of Engineers was busy on the project. Wheeler, who had weathered the storm of financial reverses, had been working behind the scenes to get the city of Aransas Pass launched. By the time the water crossing the bar had reached twenty feet, Wheeler and his associates had everything ready. E. O. Burton and A. H. Danforth, well-known San Antonio real estate developers, had become interested in Aransas Pass and they negotiated a deal with Mary McCampbell for 12,000 acres of land, including the old townsite of Aransas Pass.[13]

Burton and Danforth believed in doing things in a big way. First, they made arrangements with W. H. Vernor to start a newspaper in Aransas Pass. By the time they were ready to put on their big land sale, the *Aransas Pass Progress* had been in print for several months. Vernor, while an independent editor, was fully cooperative with Burton and Danforth and filled the pages of the *Progress* with true stories of the wonders of Aransas Pass. Press runs of over 5,000 enabled the promoters to send the news of their big land sale to selected audiences. The land sale plan was a simple one, carefully crafted to avoid being a lottery in the eyes of the postal department. Editor Vernor, in his book *A Rugged American,* gives the details:

> There were 6,000 tickets. They sold for $100 each to people who lived mostly in the states of Texas, Oklahoma, Kansas, and Nebraska. While the tickets were sold at $100, it did not take all cash to buy one. $10 cash and $10 monthly, without interest, was considered sufficient and that's the way most of the tickets were sold. Each ticket, called a certificate by the promoters, represented a town lot in the City of Aransas Pass, of which there were 6,000. Each holder of a certificate would get at least one town lot, and would also have a chance at a first, second, or third prize.
>
> The first prize was a 3-story, 72 room hotel [Bay View]. The second prizes consisted of 10 modern cottages, which had been built by the promoters especially for the occasion of the drawing or "distribution," as they called it. The third prizes consisted of farming tracts, ranging in size from five to forty acres each, directly surrounding the townsite of Aransas Pass. The key to the whole scheme was that all certificate buyers had agreed to bid $100, no more, no less, and no one else would bid. Purchasers were told: You can bid more than $100 and you will find that all other buyers have agreed that they will bid no more than $100, and there will be in the place of distribution, nooses hanging down from the ceiling in the front and in the rear of the building, and on the noose will be wording as follows: "This is for the man who overbids!" [14]

Special trains arranged by the promoters began arriving in Aransas Pass the day before the sale. By the time Col. A. D. Powers opened the sale, the crowd overflowed the two large tents put up for the occasion. The only hitch in the day was the fact that the postal inspectors managed to buy a certificate from a land prospector on the third day of the sale and forced the price of some of the lots to go as high as $300. As a result, the total of the sale exceeded

$600,000 by $203,600. Postal inspectors claimed that the break-through which they made in Aransas Pass doomed similar sales all over the United States.

Everything was on schedule to carry out the master plan. Aransas Pass Channel and Dock Company was chartered June 22, 1909.[15] A contract was let to Bowers Southern Dredging Company to dig a channel from the deep water at Harbor Island to Aransas Pass, 100 feet wide and 8½ feet deep, thus giving the city a channel to deep water.

While the dredging was being done by the Corps of Engineers at Harbor Island, all of the dredged material was pumped onto the island itself, thus raising the level by eight feet. The material out of the channel to Aransas Pass was thrown to one side, making a roadbed for Harbor Island Terminal Railroad, which was eventually completed in 1912. Eight bridges were necessary to complete the roadbed for the new railroad, which now reached the deep water at Harbor Island on one end and connected with Southern Pacific Railroad in Aransas Pass on the other end.

With all of the pieces put together, Aransas Pass began to expand in all directions. New businesses began to locate in the city, including a $50,000 cotton compress. An electric plant was built by C. J. Stanzel. Oceangoing vessels were calling regularly at the new port at Harbor Island and on September 7, 1912, a weeklong celebration featured the ocean liner *Brinkburn* as the centerpiece. Records show that in the two weeks ending on September 13, 1912, 47,093 bales of cotton were shipped. The compress, which was first located in Aransas Pass, moved out to Harbor Island, and in 1913 over 100,000 bales went through the compress and were shipped.[16]

Growth brought about many changes in the city. On April 7, 1910, a commission form of government was adopted, with W. H. Vernor named as mayor by three votes over T. B. Wheeler. J. D. Powers, Jr., and W. F. Stegal were named commissioners.

The new twin ports had just about gotten over their growing pains when the hurricane of 1916 hit the coast. The *Progress* ran this headline the next week: "Hurricane and tidal wave sweep coast. One dead here, hit at 1 a.m. on August 18." Damage in the city was heavy, and the terminal railroad was hit hard. It took several weeks to repair all of the trestles and roadbed, and in about two months business was back to normal.

Aransas Pass was just getting back to normal after the end of

World War I when the hurricane of 1919 hit on September 14. Damage to the entire coast and Aransas Pass was extensive. As a result, voters of the city unanimously approved a bond issue and special tax levy to build a seawall to protect the city. The terminal railroad was completely washed away and received a $300,000 loan from railway revolving fund to rebuild. Shipping out of Harbor Island and along the terminal railroad returned to normal.[17]

The issue of deep water had been a constant bone of contention among the ports in Aransas and Corpus Christi bays. The competition between Harbor Island-Aransas Pass and Corpus Christi had been especially keen after deep water was brought into Harbor Island in 1912, and it began to heat up again. On June 5, 1920, Congress decided to pick one harbor to be designated as the deepwater port. A preliminary survey of the coast in the vicinity of Aransas Pass, Port Aransas, Corpus Christi, and Rockport was ordered, with one to be picked as the site for a "safe and adequate harbor." [18]

Two officers from the Corps of Engineers, Maj. L. M. Adams and Col. H. C. Newcomer, submitted conflicting reports. Adams urged the selection of Corpus Christi and Newcomer picked Aransas Pass as the best. Cost figures showed that it was cheaper by far to dig a channel to Aransas Pass. The controversy waxed hot and heavy for a short time. Corpus Christi got endorsements from Houston, Beaumont, New Orleans, and others in their battle. Corpus Christi had the upper political edge in that they were able to send Roy Miller to Washington to lobby their cause. Also, Robert J. Kleberg, with the backing of the King Ranch, headed the Deep Water Harbor Association for South and West Texas.[19] Aransas Pass and Rockport worked hard, but the Corps ruled in favor of Corpus Christi. On May 25, 1922, Congress passed an appropriation to begin work on a 25-by-200-foot channel through Turtle Cove and across Corpus Christi Bay. On September 14, 1926, Corpus Christi officially opened its harbor to commerce.[20]

In an effort to bring deep water to Aransas Pass, leaders in the city sought to gain support for a deep channel from Harbor Island to Aransas Pass. On June 9, 1922, the secretary of war approved a permit for Aransas Pass to construct a channel 25 feet deep and 120 feet wide from Port Aransas to Aransas Pass, to allow for oceangoing vessels drawing up to 22 feet of water. The formation of a navigation district to carry out this program was put on the county ballot for September 28, and a spirited campaign was carried on throughout the county. The vote tally was 1,192 to 800 against the proposal. The *Aransas Pass Progress* on September 29 declared that "Corpus Christi and Taft Ranch interests" could be blamed for the defeat. Harbor Island continued as an oil terminal, but for all practical purposes no further cargo shipments were made in and out of Harbor Island.[21]

Disappointment over the loss of the deepwater port slowed the growth of Aransas Pass for a short time. Eventually the channel, which had been dredged in 1909–10 by the Aransas Pass Channel and Dock Company from Harbor Island to Aransas Pass, was widened and deepened and taken over by the Corps of Engineers.

Shrimping and fishing, with their associated industries, have made Aransas Pass into one of the foremost small harbors on the Texas coast. A shrimp cannery started at Aransas Pass in 1925, and gradually the fleet of shrimp boats operating out of the harbor increased to the point that the harbor had to be expanded. The largest expansion of Conn Brown Harbor came about in several stages after WWII. Today the largest shrimp fleet on the coast operates out of the harbor, with allied services, packing, and shipping businesses filling up the waterfront.

Aransas Pass was born with a dream of being a great port city. While the dream got sidetracked, a drive around Conn Brown Harbor shows that it is still a city that lives from the sea.

Rockport
Village Port

Port cities are born out of need. Rockport was no exception.

At the close of the Civil War, cattlemen in the area needed a place to ship cattle by sea. Two warehouses and the largest wharf at the bay's leading port, St. Mary's, had been damaged by the Federals, and a port nearer to Aransas Pass was needed.[1] James M. Doughty and Richard H. Wood, area ranchers who were also investors in St. Mary's, picked out the site for Rockport and built the first cattle pens on the location in 1866. They were joined in the venture by Capt. Dan Doughty and Jeremiah and Robert Driscoll. In 1867 J. M. and T. H. Mathis, cousins, moved to Live Oak Peninsula to live, seeing the possibilities in Rockport as a shipping point. They associated themselves with James M. Doughty in the cattle business. Joseph F. Smith and Col. John H. Wood built facilities in 1868.[2]

Doughty and Wood had cattle pens on the coast. After the Mathis cousins joined the firm, they constructed ramps from the pens to the wharf so that cattle could be loaded directly from the holding pens onto ships. Arrangements were made with the Morgan Shipping Line to bring one of their cattle boats into the new port on a regular basis. This partnership lasted a short time, but the Mathis cousins continued in the business and acted as agents for the Morgan Line.[3]

In 1871 a partnership was formed, composed of Youngs and Tom Coleman (one-third), John M. and Thomas Henry Mathis (one-third), and George Ware Fulton (one-third), known as the Coleman, Mathis, Fulton Cattle Company. They built what was known as the "Big Wharf" on Rocky Point. The wharf extended about 1,100 feet into the bay and was thirty-five to forty feet wide. Along one side was built a six-foot-high chute to drive cattle from the pens to the ship. The dock proper was wide enough for two wagons to move abreast to haul freight to and from the two large warehouses at the base of the wharf. There was a 400-foot "T" head where the ships docked.

In 1879 the Mathis cousins dropped out of the company but continued to live in Rockport and invest in the city. The Coleman-Fulton Pasture Company continued to headquarter in Rockport until the early 1900s. The company sold the wharf to John Wood and Samuel Allyn in about 1900; it was torn down and moved to St. Joseph Island and the lumber used for cattle pens.

Youngs Coleman had come to Texas from Lancaster, Pennsylvania, shortly after the War for Independence and settled near Liberty, moving soon to Jackson County. He went to the Coastal Bend with his son Tom in about 1854 and built a plantation manor on the banks of the Chiltipin Creek in what is now San Patricio County. Youngs and Tom both served in the Confederate army. After the war Youngs, an adamant southerner, refused to swear allegiance to the Union and moved to Mexico, where he bought an island estate. He died in Mexico. Tom returned after the war to run the family business. He later served as county commissioner and county judge in San Patricio County.

Thomas Henry Mathis grew up in Tennessee where he became an educator. In 1859 he joined a cousin in Texas, J. M.

Mathis, who was engaged in a trading venture with Mexican firms. When the Civil War put an end to the business, T. H. joined the Confederate army. After the war the two cousins were drawn to Aransas Bay, where they exploited the packery business which was booming in the area. Shortly, they chartered their own steamboat, the *Prince Albert,* and began regular cattle shipments to New Orleans. After the loss of the *Prince Albert* they formed an alliance with the Morgan Lines.

Col. George Fulton was born in Philadelphia and as a young man became an impassionate supporter of the cause for independence in Texas. He organized a company of young men and started down the Wabash River on a barge, heading for New Orleans and Texas. By the time he reached Texas the Battle of San Jacinto had been fought; nevertheless, he joined the army and was commissioned a second lieutenant. Serving but a short time, he was commissioned by John P. Borden, first commissioner of the Texas land office, to convey from San Antonio to Houston all of the ancient land archives. In this period he also formed a friendship with ex-Governor Henry Smith, who was destined to become his father-in-law. Shortly after his marriage to Harriet Smith in 1840, Fulton and his wife moved to the north, not returning to Texas until 1867. Since Colonel Fulton was the executor of Smith's rather large estate, including land in the Coastal Bend, the family moved to Aransas Bay. Fulton was quick to join other businessmen in the packery business.[4]

The city of Rockport actually was started and built by ranchers and businessmen who were seeking a means of marketing their immense herds of Longhorn cattle. The long trail drives, before and after the Civil War, were time-consuming, expensive, and dangerous.[5] The ranchers were quick to embrace a method that would help them get rid of their cattle at a profit. In 1866 it was estimated that 260,000 head of cattle went up the trail from Texas to northern markets. In 1867 only 37,000 went north.[6] This was an indication that something was changing, and the change was the advent of the packeries, or hide and tallow factories. The time was right, and the place was Rockport. The 1871 *Texas Almanac* emphasized this point:

> Rockport and Fulton are but two or three years old; but the former is now doing most of the trade of this and several other counties, and promises to become one of the most important marts of West Texas. There are some excellent schools in these towns and

several Catholic churches and congregations of the Methodists and Baptists.[7]

Times were so good in Fulton that a dividend of $200 per share was declared in 1873 and another of $67.50 in 1874 by the Coleman, Mathis, Fulton Cattle Company.[8]

Rockport and Fulton rode to real prosperity in the period between 1865 (when W. S. Hall built the first packery on the coast three miles from Rockport) and the mid-1870s (when cattle became too valuable to slaughter for just the hides and tallow). Hall moved to Texas from Maine and prospered in the cattle business before the Civil War. After the war, with no market for his cattle, he decided to slaughter the herd for the hide and tallow. In one year alone he slaughtered over 11,000 head of cattle and over 40,000 during the time that his business was active. His success brought Fulton, the Woods, Mathises, Colemans, and others to Rockport to get into the booming packery business.

During the heyday of the packeries, as many as a dozen large concerns were doing business in the Rockport-Fulton area, with perhaps five or six smaller outfits. In addition to the packeries operated by Hall, Mathis and Fulton, there were the American Beef Packery, West and Weiser Company, Boston Packing Company, Butler and Company, John W. Baylor Company, and Cushman and Company. Cushman was the largest of the group, slaughtering 5,000 head annually. He also pickled or salted beef to ship in barrels to European markets by way of New Orleans and the east. The Meade and Nash Packery at Fulton was not only killing cattle but also slaughtering turtles for their shells. Some turtles were also shipped live to be used as meat on their arrival.[9]

A large packery employing forty men could process 200 to 250 head of cattle in a day. Since the bulk of the meat was discarded after rendering the fat, the dump grounds near town turned into a mountain of meat which could be smelled for miles. Mrs. George Fulton, Jr., whose home was near the Fulton Packery, says that the meat at their packery was burned, making a terrible odor.[10] Oral tradition tells of ducks and geese gorging themselves on the rotting flesh to the point that their meat was not fit to eat. It is also reported that a Yankee came to Rockport in later years and bought the mountain of waste, called "hash," turned it into fertilizer, and sold it for a handsome profit.

During the peak of the "packery boom," at least one Morgan

ship was in port each day and as many as six ships might be tied up at the Fulton and Rockport docks to take on products from the packeries or live cattle headed for New Orleans and Havana. Payment for products in these days was made in hard money, usually silver. Mrs. Fulton tells of bags of silver sitting around on the floor of the office of the Coleman, Mathis, Fulton Cattle Company until measured out by her father. Such a bulk of silver was usually measured rather than counted. Andrew Sorenson remembered rolling fourteen barrels of silver from the dock to the office. Silver could be left on the docks overnight without fear.[11]

In June of 1873 most of the freight consigned for Corpus Christi was offloaded at Rockport and sent by lighters to Corpus Christi.

Starting in about 1875, the packery business in Rockport began to decline. Packing houses began to move closer to centers of population in order to utilize the entire carcass. Blood was sold for fertilizer, the tongues and lean beef were cooked and canned, while the rougher beef was dried, salted, or canned. Bones were ground up and boiled to get the fatty content for neat's-foot oil, with the remainder going into bone meal. The thing that finally killed the packeries was improvement of the price of live cattle to the point that it made sense for a rancher to go to the live market rather than the packery with his cattle. Within a short time most of the big packeries were closed, and the ones left bought only the culls.

The packeries had brought Rockport from a lovely, deserted beach to a booming city which once held about 2,000 people at its peak. The once prosperous port slowed to a walk, businesses closed, and people moved away. Buildings could not be sold for what the nails to build them had cost.

Rockport boomed largely because of the shallow-draft, sidewheeler steamers operated by the Morgan Line. These ships ran with ease in the shallow (seven to eight feet) water of Aransas Bay. The steamer *Aransas* was built especially for the Rockport trade by the Morgan Line. Others which carried coastwise trade in and out of Rockport were the *Alabama, Mary, St. Mary, Gussie, Morgan, Hudson, Hewes, Harris, Hutchinson, Clinton,* and *Harlen.* These steamers were built for shallow water but at the same time took on big loads. For instance, the *Harris* carried 133 beeves and 241 calves on a trip from Rockport to New Orleans in January of 1877. The ship also carried passengers and other freight.

While the packery business was gone, the coastwise business remained, as goods were moved into Rockport to be lightered to other ports in the area. Wool from South and West Texas was being shipped out of Rockport. Freight destined for Mexico arrived in Rockport and was lightered to Corpus Christi to be loaded on ox carts for the long haul.[12]

A United States customs collector, Victor Bracht, had his office in Rockport in 1881. Records show that a considerable amount of tonnage was passing through the port; however, it was a different type than that of ten years earlier. For instance, in 1881 imports were listed as: lumber, 15,110,467 feet; shingles, 1,722,000; merchandise, 23,000 tons; iron rails, 10,683 tons; coal, 611 tons; animals, 418 head. Exports included dry hides, 38,708; wool, 2,400 tons; cotton, 65 tons; bones, 45 tons; miscellaneous, 575 tons; green hides, 1,202; horns, 1,760; tallow, 28 barrels; animals, 1,466 head. The bulk of the lumber came out of Florida.[13]

The townsites of Rockport and Fulton grew together; however, the bulk of the growth was in Rockport. James M. Doughty and the Mathis cousins had platted the southern half of the town and named it Rockport. A ledge of shellrock that projected into the bay gave the town its name.[14] Previous to the naming of the townsite, the name of Rocky Point had been used. Later the name Rockport was changed to Aransas Pass and then changed back to Rockport. The surveying was done by William Benson. The northern portion of the townsite was developed by John H. Wood and Joseph F. Smith, who had surveyed and platted the townsite of Fulton. Most of the land on which Rockport is located was included in the land purchased by Empresarios James Power and James Hewetson and later patented by Joseph Smith. Smith entered into a land contract with T. T. Williamson to locate and survey land for him including the Rockport tract.[15]

The surveyors had hardly finished their work before people began lining up to purchase lots. The first wave of buyers were ranchers and other landholders in the area who wanted to get in on the ground floor of the new real estate development. Workers for the packeries, ship captains, and businessmen provided a ready market for the lots. The main business area of Rockport flourished in the Doughty and Mathis survey, as businesses of all types began moving to the new city on Aransas Bay.

Texas's military government recognized the new city and its

CAROLINE was one of the coastal vessels which delivered freight up and down the coast from Matagorda Bay to Corpus Christi Bay. It had a shallow draft, allowing its skipper to successfully approach all of the ports and landings. Some of these coastal vessels had a center board which could be raised, allowing them to run up on the sandy beaches. At El Copano shippers drove wagons loaded with freight out into the water to meet the coastal vessels.

leading industry in 1869 by assigning an inspector, William Maynard, to Rockport as inspector of animals and hides. This move was made by the state government to help curtail the selling of hides from stolen cattle.

The population had increased enough by 1869 that Capt. Charles F. Bailey and G. A. Beeman established the *Transcript,* which operated for a number of years under Bailey's editorship. They had founded the St. Mary's *Vaquero* in 1868 but became discouraged with its progress, although Beeman continued in St. Mary's for some time.

On August 13, 1870, the state legislature approved a bill incorporating the City of Rockport and setting its boundaries. The governor appointed John M. Mathis as the first mayor, with Edward Moffett, S. D. Robb, Charles L. Dean, Richard H. Wood, Victor Bracht, and W. R. Archer as the aldermen, and George Dye, secretary.[16]

Growth was steady on all fronts. Victor Bracht was named the first postmaster in 1868. At this time mail came to Rockport from Saluria and was carried on horseback down the length of Matagorda Island and across Cedar Bayou to St. Joseph Island, to Aransas Wharf (later Aransas), and by boat to Rockport. In the fall of 1871 the first telegraph line was constructed through Refugio County. Rockport citizens raised $6,000 to bring the line to their city, with customers receiving a one-half rebate on messages sent over the wire. In 1878 the CMF Cattle Company put in the first telephone from Rockport to their ranch on the Rincon and to Tom Coleman's home on the Chiltipin.[17]

The commissioners court in Refugio County in March of 1871 issued a permit to J. M. Doughty and the Mathis cousins to operate a steam ferry between Live Oak Point and Lamar. A ferry existed at this point until the 1930s, when the Hug-the-Coast Highway was completed. By that time the population of Rockport was larger than that of the rest of the county. After a prolonged battle of petitions between Rockport, St. Mary's, and Copano, the state legislature on March 15, 1871, provided for the removal of the county seat from Refugio to Rockport. In July 1871 the court signed a contract with S. C. Skidmore to furnish a building for the courthouse in Rockport for $20 per month. The courthouse was moved, but it brought about bitter feelings. As a result, a compromise was reached and the legislature on September 18, 1871, created a separate county of Aransas, with Rockport as the county seat. The last meeting of the commissioners court for Refugio County was held in Rockport on September 25, after which the old records were moved back to Refugio County and Aransas County was started.

A new Moorish-style courthouse was built in Rockport in 1889 and served until the mid-1960s, when it was torn down to make way for a modern building.[18] The first officers in Aransas County were J. Williamson Moses, chief justice (county judge); Berry Merchant, commissioner, Precinct 2; S. E. Upton, commissioner, Precinct 3; Arthur Lott, commissioner, Precinct 4; P. E. Jordan, commissioner, Precinct 5.[19]

Minutes of the Aransas County Commissioners Court reflected the growth of Rockport as a county seat and the center of trade for the area. A road was approved from Rockport to Ingleside, running along the coast. Another road ran from Lamar to Heard's Crossing on Copano Creek and was thirty-five feet wide. Still another road ran from Lamar to Salt Creek settlement.[20]

In 1871 the Rockport, Fulton, Laredo and Mexican Pacific Railroad was chartered by the state. This railroad was planned as a trade route between the United States and Mexico. George W. Fulton was the president; James M. Doughty, vice-president; John M. Mathis, treasurer; and J. H. Hynes, secretary. A lot of time and money went into promoting the project that finally folded without breaking ground.[21] A fitting closing for this packery era can be pictured from descriptions by an early writer, H. S. Kneedler:

> . . . . Rockport was the wealthiest town of its size in the South, and the name was known to all Texans of that day — before the railroads came — as one of the largest beef-canning centers in the Union, in fact, the Chicago of the South as regards this industry. Now it is one of the\most beautiful and restful summer resorts to be imagined.[22]

Frontier ports usually had several faces. Rockport was no exception, boasting numerous saloons and gambling houses to take care of the restless, growing population. One of the most famous gambling houses was the "Finish," owned by Oliver P. Reed and Maj. Andrew J. Hogan. The establishment became renowned all over South Texas. J. C. Herring in the *Rockport Pilot* described the action:

> Near the Big Wharf, on the spot where the First National Bank stands today, was a big gambling house and saloon, the *Finish*. It is

supposed it was so called because it often "finished" up a cattle-man's herd. It is told that one time the Methodist Church needed $500, so old Uncle Myers, who was the minister, went down to the *Finish* and told the boys what he wanted. They "dug down" and gave him the five hundred. He thanked them and invited them all out to church, so they shut up and went to hear him preach. Nothing smaller than silver dollars was ever used . . .[23]

Rockport was "on hold" for the next eight to ten years. The population dwindled and very few ships called. During this period, leaders in the community worked tirelessly to secure a deepwater channel to their port city. They also worked to get deep water over the bar at Aransas Pass. (This struggle will be dealt with in detail in the chapter on the ports of Harbor City, Aransas Pass, and Corpus Christi.)

A new phase in Rockport's life started with the coming of the San Antonio and Aransas Pass Railroad in 1888. The population was about 600 when the railroad arrived and in ten years grew to 2,500. In 1888 the Rockport Chamber of Commerce published a booklet entitled "Beautiful Rockport, the Unrivaled Gulf Port of Texas, the coming City of 200,000 people." Perhaps the writer was a bit too enthusiastic, but Rockport's location on Aransas Bay did become the focal point of tourists rather than merchants.

Several resort hotels were built where the packeries once stood. Col. John H. Traylor arrived in Rockport during this time and became one of the leaders in making Rockport a tourist resort. He also became Rockport's mayor in 1908. Traylor built the Aransas Hotel, which later became famous as the Del Mar, drawing guests like Governor James Stephen Hogg. The dining room could accommodate 100 couples for dancing. Orchestras played twice daily in the dining room, where the menu included turtle steaks, as well as choice cakes from the hotel's own bakery.[24]

The late 1880s and early 1890s were truly boom days, with tourists arriving daily by train and the local gentry building fine homes in the city. Real estate auctions were being held. Literature distributed by salesmen not only featured the luxury resorts, but pointed out that the "coming deep water" would make Rockport a great seaport. One glowing letter pointed out that Rockport had the finest harbor, a new $50,000 hotel, a street railway running from Rockport to Fulton, electric lights, and fine schools.[25]

When deep water failed to materialize and a series of fires gutted the business section, the glitter faded from the boom and Rockport settled down as a lovely coastal town. Vessels with deeper draft sought ports that could accommodate them. The storm of 1919 wiped out many of the old landmarks and inflicted deep economic wounds on the cattle industry. In 1988 Rockport is undergoing still another boom, as people from all over the country have discovered once again the beautiful seaport on Aransas Bay.

Standing as a stalwart witness to most of the turbulent events that have swirled around Rockport and Fulton is the Fulton mansion. When Col. George Ware Fulton came to Fulton in 1867 with his family, he built a modest one-story home that existed until about 1910. As he grew in power and wealth, he erected a three-story mansion fitting of a man of his position. Started in 1871, its completion came four years later at a cost near $100,000. Hurricanes, hard times, vandals, and neglect ravaged it over the years, but today it stands proud as a state historical site fully restored to its original glory.

Portland
Storm Victim

Portland was never destined to be a port city. However, in the early 1900s the Coleman-Fulton Pasture Company began extensive cotton raising in San Patricio County and needed a means to get the cotton to market.

On May 1, 1910, John G. Willacy organized the Portland Development Company and struck a deal with C-FP Co. to sell lots in the Portland townsite, originally platted in 1891. The pasture company also heavily invested in utilities and roads in the new development. Part of the program authorized by the C-FP Co. board of directors in June of 1910 was the construction of a wharf in Portland from which the company could ship their own cotton.

On October 13, 1911, the *Corpus Christi Caller* carried a story on the awarding of a contract to D. M. Picton to build a $40,000 wharf at Portland. The wharf was 1,500 feet long, reaching into the bay far enough for shallow-draft vessels to approach. Records show that they started shipping their cotton from the wharf in 1913 and continued until the wharf was heavily damaged by the hurricane of 1916 on August 18. The wharf was cut back to half its length and continued to serve the cotton trade until it was completely demolished by the hurricane of 1919. It was never rebuilt.

There are no records of others using the wharf for shipping of anything other than cotton. The company used it as a port of entry to bring lumber and other supplies, and it is presumed that other merchants took advantage of the wharf during its short life.[1]

San Antonio Bay / Espiritu Bay

(Hynes, Mesquite, Guadalupe, Mission bays)

The San Antonio Bay area was visited by early explorers and mapmakers, as were Aransas and Matagorda bays; however, due to the fact that no major pass led into this bay system it seems to not have been so widely used as the others.

Pass Cavallo led into Matagorda Bay. By astute navigation, ships could bear to the left, after clearing the old town of Saluria on the tip of Matagorda Island, and head into Espiritu Bay and then into San Antonio Bay. Entering at Aransas Pass, ships had to go the distance of Aransas Bay, seek the passage into Mesquite Bay, and then enter San Antonio Bay. Of course, Cedar Bayou cut between Matagorda Island and St. Joseph Island. Few ships were able to find this channel, or successfully slip through its narrow passage even when the tide was running high. Pirate Jean Lafitte seems to have been the only sailor who mastered the use of Cedar Bayou.

Perhaps the trials necessary to get into the great San Antonio Bay contributed to the fact that few landings were developed along its shores in the days of the Spanish or the Texas revolutionary periods. With the advent of modern times, channels have been cut

102

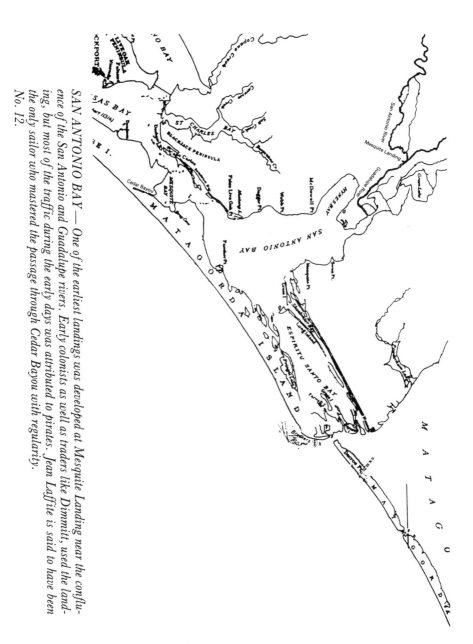

SAN ANTONIO BAY — *One of the earliest landings was developed at Mesquite Landing near the confluence of the San Antonio and Guadalupe rivers. Early colonists as well as traders like Dimmitt, used the landing, but most of the traffic during the early days was attributed to pirates. Jean Laffite is said to have been the only sailor who mastered the passage through Cedar Bayou with regularity.
No. 12.*

through shallow areas so that barge traffic and small boats use many harbors along its shores.

Did the legendary Jean Lafitte really use Cedar Bayou? Did he and his men seek refuge in the many secluded inlets of this vast bay system? And later, did the crew meet at False Live Oak Point to disband and divide their loot?

No historian has ever claimed real proof of the presence of Lafitte in the Cedar Bayou area. However, legends usually have a shred of truth at their root. So, briefly enjoy the story related by "Grandma" Frank, who claimed that her husband was one of Lafitte's men. She was living at False Live Oak Point when she related the story passed down by Will Bickford to historian Hobart Huson.

> After Lafitte was ousted from Galveston Island by the United States Navy in 1821, he decided that the day of the pirate was over, and he would disband his organization. All of the booty and loot accumulated over a long period of years was loaded into several vessels, which sailed down the coast. Whether or not any further piratical operations were indulged in, it appears that prior to the time he arrived in Refugio County waters, Lafitte had aroused the opposition not only of the American navy, but the British as well. The combined naval units chased Lafitte down the coast, and were pressing him hard, when he arrived off Paso Cavallo.
>
> At the time the pirate reached this historic point he was beset by no less than five British frigates, besides such United States vessels as were in the pursuit, and the position of Lafitte was desperate. To add to his troubles a dreadful storm was raging at the pass, which made it almost suicidal to attempt to go over the bar. Lafitte however, was hard pressed, and ordered his ships to run the bar, which sent shivers down the spines of his hardened seamen. Some of these pirates afterwards said when they saw a bad storm brewing that it reminded them of the night Lafitte made them cross the Matagorda bar, and that all of them had been scared to death that night.
>
> The pirates, by great good fortune, crossed the bar safely, but the British frigates, which attempted to follow, had hard luck. Two of them were lost and others went aground. Lafitte's ships scattered through the inlets and hid in the mouths of the rivers. The vessel, on which Lafitte was, sought refuge in Garcitas Creek, a place formerly known as Center Board Reef (but now known as Chicken Reef). The name Center Board Reef originated

due to the fact that a dowel pin on Lafitte's vessel became loose, and the center board slipped and stuck in the mud.

When it was deemed safe to do so, the pirate ships emerged from their hiding places and assembled in Espiritu Santo Bay, off False Live Oak Point. There for three days and three nights the pirates labored to unload their accumulated booty. There was held an executive meeting of the freebooters. Lafitte told them that they were through, that the days of profitable piracy were over, that he intended to go to Campechi and live a retired life, and that his men were released from any further obligations to him. He advised his men to settle in Texas, as that land belonged to no one, but that those who cared to accompany him in his retreat were welcome to do so. He further stated that the accumulated profits of their long association would be now equitably divided among them. Most of the men were married men and practically all agreed that it was time to disband and settle down to peaceful lives. Most of the men stated they would take the chief's advice and settle in Texas. Some few stated they would remain with the chief to the last. All were to see that the ships were brought into the port of Lafitte's selection, whereupon the combination would be disbanded and the members could go to wherever they chose.

Having reached this understanding, the booty was divided to the entire satisfaction of all. Lafitte, being the captain and underwriter, received a share far in excess of the share of any one individual. He decided to cache most of it at False Live Oak Point, and it was so large that it took three nights to bury it. Madam Frank, who fraternized with the men, watched the bearers go into the woods with the chests and boxes. During the progress Lafitte came to her house and took refreshments. Once he exclaimed, "There is enough treasure in those woods to ransom a nation!" When the last trip was made into the woods, Mrs. Frank noted that the bearers did not return. Lafitte desired to be the sole repository of his secret and dead men tell no tales.

After all this business had been accomplished, the pirates took to their boats and headed toward the sea. Lafitte had been informed that the British and American vessels were blockading the passes at Cavallo and Aransas, thereby bottling him up in the inlets. He decided to get to the gulf through Cedar Bayou, and in order to lighten the draught, as that channel was shallow, he had all excess cannons and baggage thrown overboard into Espiritu Santo Bay. All of the pirate vessels got through Cedar Bayou but the last, which got stuck and was wrecked. Mrs. Frank heard a cannonading in the direction of Cedar Bayou which lasted for

FALSE LIVE OAK POINT — *Legends tell that pirate Jean Laffite sailed into San Antonio Bay and set up camp at False Live Oak Point after being ejected from Galveston Island. Treasure-seekers have failed through the years to turn up the treasure he supposedly buried there, but they still look.*

three days and three nights, then ceased. She was always confident that Lafitte beat the British and American fleet, as she never saw him again.[1]

Was this Culebra Island, reputed to be Lafitte's base? No one knows. Perhaps Jean Lafitte's "forgotten port" was Culebra Island, supposedly composed of St. Joseph and Matagorda islands.

Mesquite Landing
Place of Mosquitoes

Ortíz Parrilla was delegated by the Spanish government in 1766 to lead an expedition into southern Texas to explore the area and furnish detailed information about the rivers and bays. This was a result of the "English scare" caused by rumors of Anglo intrusions into Texas. Parrilla headed north from the Rio Grande, crossed the Nueces River near Mathis, followed it to its mouth, and then explored Padre and Mustang islands. He moved on to La Bahía (at Goliad) and then moved down the San Antonio River to its confluence with the Guadalupe.

As a result of this expedition, Captain Piscina of La Bahía recommended to the governor that a fort be established halfway between the Guadalupe and Nueces rivers (Aranzazu on Live Oak Point) and a little fort at Mesquite Landing just below where the San Antonio runs into the Guadalupe. Its Spanish name was El Muelle Viejo, or "the old wharf." Above the landing is a swampy area called Bayou de los Mosquitos. This is also the site of the ranch of Refugio mission called El Rancho de los Mosquitos, and the place to which the mission was moved from Calhoun County.[1]

Capt. Joaquin Orobio y Basterra, commandant of the Presidio of La Bahía, left Goliad on January 29, 1747, and explored the San Antonio River to the Guadalupe. He noted Mesquite Landing as a possible landing site. With this and Parrilla's exploration it is considered likely that Mesquite Landing, called the place of the mosquitoes by the Spaniards, came into being in this era.[2]

Early historians like Hobart Huson mention ancient military works, or a fort, erected to protect the landing. Several references of supplies going to La Bahía seem to indicate that Mesquite Landing was the landing spot. Some historians believe that a wharf of some type was built during this early period.

Probably the first Anglo to use the port was Dr. James Long

when he mounted his expedition in 1821. He entered Paso Cavallo with a schooner and two brigs, then left the schooner with twenty to thirty men and proceeded into Espiritu Santo Bay and Mesquite Landing with roughly fifty-three men. His objective was to take Goliad and help oust the Royalists from Texas and to aid the cause of Mexican independence. Long took Goliad but was overwhelmed the next day by Col. Ygnacio Perez. Upon learning that Long had boats at Mesquite Landing, Perez sent a detachment of men and seized them.[3]

During the settlement of South Texas by empresarios, at least one shipload of the McGloin and McMullen settlers got confused and landed at Mesquite Landing rather than Copano. They made their way to Refugio, where others were camped. The Toole family landed on St. Joseph Island in 1829 and then went to Mesquite Landing, stopping at Nicholas Fagan's home for several days.[4] Several other settlers, with garbled directions, turned into Espiritu Bay rather than continue on to Copano Bay, and, as a result, embarked on their new life from Mesquite Landing.

During this colonial period the Guadalupe and San Antonio rivers were considered navigable by seagoing vessels. The boats went up the San Antonio as far as the Carlos Ranch — a distance of perhaps thirty miles from Mesquite Landing.[5]

The road running from Indianola to Chihuahua, which was traveled by the silver wagons, crossed at Mesquite Landing on a ferry that operated until as late as 1890. Peletiah Bickford was the last operator. When the first telegraph line came into South Texas in the 1870s, it ran through Mesquite Landing to St. Mary's.[6]

Peter and John Hynes established ranching in the area, but it was Col. Newton C. Gullett who founded the Tivoli Ranch in 1876 and started development in the area. In 1902 Jesse McDowell and Preston R. Austin formed the Refugio Black Land & Irrigation Improvement Company. Austin established the town of Tivoli, which was several miles from the ancient Mesquite Landing.[7]

Until the railroad came to Tivoli in 1912, most of the freight and some passengers came by the Guadalupe River to the old Boat Landing, probably established by Gullett a short distance from Mesquite Landing. The Refugio Black Land & Irrigation Improvement Company maintained a good wharf and warehouse at the Boat Landing and homes for its employees. Cattle were shipped by barge for a while but later were abandoned.[8]

Matagorda Bay/
San Bernardo Bay

(Manhattan Bay, Live Oak Bay, Tres Palacios Bay,
Turtle Bay, Carancahua Bay, Keller Bay,
Lavaca Bay, Garcitas Cove, Powderhorn Lake)

San Bernardo Bay was one of the focal points for early explorers to the Texas coast. Spanish and French schooners and three-masted men-of-war explored the many bays and inlets as they sparred for control of a territory so vast that they could not comprehend its scope. The clear, blue water and sandy beaches seemed to beckon these early explorers and, in many cases, lulled them into a false sense of security as the treacherous reefs, currents, and sand bars claimed many a ship. Each sought to lay a claim to the vast territory.

The Spanish had long laid claim to the territory to their north, but it was not until René Robert Cavelier, Sieur de La Salle, founded Fort St. Louis on Matagorda Bay that the Spanish got moving. Actually, La Salle crossed the bar at Paso Cavallo and came ashore on February 15, 1685. One of his ships was wrecked entering the pass on February 21, giving it the dubious honor of being probably the first of many ships to fall victim to the shifting channels, squally winds, and lack of adequate charts. After initially

109

EDNA

and information
cote charts

Dry Creek

NAVIDAD RIVER

Texana

LAVACA

RIVER

Garcitas Creek

Sixmile Creek

Placedo Cr

Dimmitt's
Landing

LAVACA

Wenoke

Noble Pt

Linnville

Lavaca

Cox's Point

Cox Bay

Rhodes Pt

Keller Bay

BAY

Sand Pt

Chocolate B

Cerancahua Cr

E. Carancahua Creek

Lavy Cr.

Blessing

TRES P

Turtle Creek

Reed Creek

Now Cr.

Palacios

Turtle Bay

Well Pt

TRES PALACIOS BAY

Oliver Pt

Palacios

CARANCAHUA BAY

Lake

Indianola

M   A   T   A   G

Powderhorn Lake

DeCrow's Landing

Port O'Connor

Calhoun
Saluria

Decros Pt

M   A

Mustang

Swan Pt

HYNES BAY

Dowell Pt

SAN ANTONIO

Webb Pt

Mesquein Pt

ESPIRITU SANTO BAY

Shoalwater Bay

Long Island

Shoalwater Pass

Grass I

Dewberry I.

Snail I.

Turtle I.

Vanderveer

Pringle Lake

Beaver I.

S   L   A   N   D

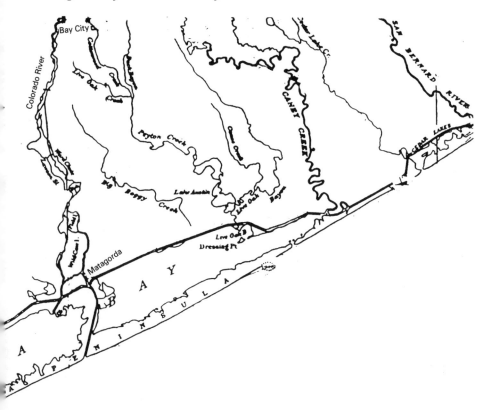

MATAGORDA BAY — *Early history was made along the shores of this bay system. The old Port of Matagorda thrived in the early days, despite its many drawbacks. The bay's greatest recognition as a shipping point came when Indianola reached its peak in the pre-Civil War days. Fort Esperanza and Fort Washington were designed to guard the approaches of Paso Caballo. Fort Caney had its moment in history during the Civil War. Tres Palacios Bay and the Tres Palacios River brought goods to the open water, with a lot of shipping being done from Palacios Point.*

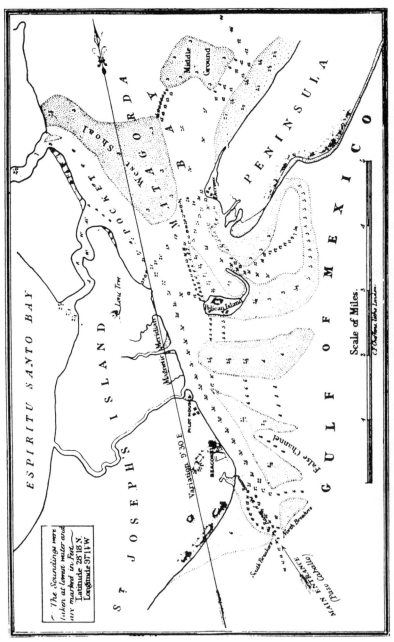

MATAGORDA BAY was charted in 1839 by W. D. Wallach, civil engineer, with notes telling that Paso Caballo was always safe for vessels, drawing from eight to nine feet of water. (First published in Kennedy's Texas in 1841)

establishing a settlement on the beach where he came ashore, La Salle moved inland and built a permanent fort out of logs about five miles inland on the west bank of Garcitas Creek.[1]

Despite the fact that La Salle was murdered by his own men, and the Indians eventually wiped out the settlement, the Spanish were alarmed at an intrusion into what they considered their private domain. Alonso de León was sent from Monclova in 1689 to seek the French settlement. He arrived at Fort St. Louis on April 22, 1689, and found only a few bodies in the ruins of the fort. Later he found a few French survivors being held by the Indians; these he rescued and returned to civilization. In 1690 de León was sent into the area again, this time with instructions to establish a fort and mission near the site of Fort St. Louis. The trip was made but the mission never materialized.[2]

Although the Spanish hated the appearance of the French, they moved slowly with any counter measures. It was not until the 1730s that the string of nine missions from deep East Texas to South Texas was completed. The movement to establish missions moved close to Matagorda Bay in 1721 when the Marquis de San Miguel de Aguayo established the presidio Nuestra Señora de Loreto (La Bahía) Presidio on the supposed site of La Salle's Fort St. Louis. It stayed at this location only a few years until it was moved northwest to the Guadalupe River near Victoria in Mission Valley.

Actually, the Spanish sent their first explorer into the Texas area in 1519, when Alonso Álvarez de Piñeda was given the assignment to explore and map the entire coastline from Florida to Vera Cruz. Without a second thought as to the magnitude of the job, he sailed with a four-ship convoy with all sorts of illusions of great wealth for himself and prestige for the crown. His maps were creditable, and even today offer insights into how these early Spanish explorers viewed the New World.

Without a doubt, Piñeda explored the Matagorda Bay area. One bay system that he labeled as "Matabrigo" is thought by scholars to have been the Matagorda Bay system. The explorer named the vast territory that he surveyed as "Amichel," a name which lasted in official reports for a number of years.[3]

The maps prepared by Piñeda are said to have been in the possession of Panfilo de Narvaez when he mounted his expedition in 1527. Cabeza de Vaca was a member of the expedition. Narvaez landed his fleet on the west coast of Florida and set out with a body of men to explore the interior. He instructed the fleet to continue on down the coast until they found a suitable harbor where he would join them after exploring the interior.

The landing party ran into all sorts of trouble and, with the fleet gone, they were stranded in a dangerous land. Narvaez eventually drowned while aboard a raft which the crews had fashioned to travel down the coast. Cabeza de Vaca was aboard another raft and was eventually washed ashore on an island. Historians have never quite agreed on the island, but most think it was Galveston Island.

Cabeza de Vaca's diary furnishes historians with what the Gulf Coast and its inhabitants, the Karankawa Indians, were like. Only five of the 242 men who started out on the expedition survived, including Cabeza de Vaca.[4]

The French explorer Jean Béranger explored the bays up and down the Texas coast in 1720. He was sent to explore the Bay of Saint Bernard with a view to finding a suitable place for a settlement. In his first voyage he missed the entrance to Matagorda Bay and came across the bar at Aransas Pass. A second voyage was commanded by Bernard de la Harpe. One of his original maps is labeled: "S. Bernard." [5]

Despite all of this interest on the part of the Spanish and French, little was done to bring settlers into the area. The mission period sought to bring Christianity to the Indians, but the coastal bays were left largely to the Karankawas and their dugout canoes.

From 1782 through 1810 there was an increased interest in the Matagorda Bay area. Traffic had increased to the point that ships regularly called at either the Port of San Bernado or at Matagorda. In fact, ships in and out of the harbor had reached a point that Indians lay in wait on the coast watching for ships in trouble. Sailors unfortunate enough to run aground in these waters were immediately set upon by the Karankawas, with chilling effects.[6]

In November of 1782 Joseph Santoja, interim commander of the presidio of La Bahía del Espíritu Santo (Goliad), wrote to Señor Don Domingo Cavello, viceroy of Coahuila, urging the construction of a fort on Matagorda Bay to protect the ships from the Indians. His plea for help was urgent:

> These occurrences [pillaging of ships] take place almost every year. For though the letter is present to guard the coast, and to succor ship wrecked sailors who come upon it, when any news is acquired, or any cannon shot heard, no matter how soon [aid] is called for, it

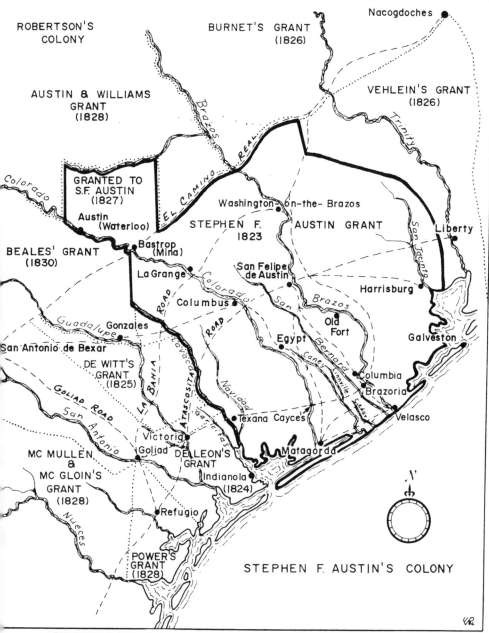

AUSTIN'S COLONY — Stephen F. Austin brought the first colonists to Texas, set-tling at San Felipe in 1823. By 1829 the port of Matagorda had been established at the mouth of the Colorado River. (Map courtesy of Matagorda County Historical Commission)

is impossible to help. For the said heathen Indians, and some Christians traveling among them as fugitives, have come to terms with each other on the bays and islands, so that whenever they see the misfortunes of any luckless [persons] who arrive there, they take possession of all they are carrying, even if they do not take their lives. I am of the thought that to remedy such grave occurrences, and so that the miserable men coming to these shores shipwrecked may not perish at the hand of those tyrannous murderers savagery, it would be appropriate [to build] a fort on one of the islands that extend along the harbor of Matagorda.[7]

Asked later whether the harbor of Matagorda was better than that of San Bernardo, Joseph Santoja replied: "It [Matagorda] was, though no more ships could be anchored there than [the number] aforementioned [20]." [8] The Port of San Bernardo is thought to be a coastal region rather than a definite location.[9] The Port of Matagorda (sometimes referred to as the harbor of La Bahía) is presumed to be in the general locality as the present city of Matagorda. The fact that the Port of Matagorda was one of the supply points of the presidio of La Bahía was made in the same letter by Joseph Santoja:

Matagorda lay due north, that from where ships could be anchored it must have been a quarter of a league, and that from the beach where one disembarks to the presidio of La Bahia del Espiritu Santo it seemed to him that it must be twelve leagues by land. This proximity caused the schooner's captain, Don Luis Landrin, to come in the said port of Matagorda with the intention of being supplied with provisions from the aforementioned presidio of La Bahia.[10]

Again it was pointed out in the letter that "a new settlement was planned at the mouth of the Colorado River on the Northern Sea [Gulf of Mexico]." But like the plans to build a fort, these 1785 plans also failed to materialize.

In an 1804 report of the Royal Presidio of Bahía del Espiritu sent to the governor of the province, a number of changes were evidenced in the First Division (which covered the area served by La Bahía). The population was noted at 945, of which 240 were "Indian casts." The seaports were listed as Matagorda, Bergantin, and Aranzazu. Bergantin was located on St. Charles Bay and Aranzazu on Live Oak Point in Aransas Bay. A note on Matagorda listed the port as "having a good depth, inferred from the record for the year

1690, when the viceroy, Conde de Galve, sent two expeditions to Texas, one by land and one by sea to explore Bahía del Espiritu Santo. The second one, while waiting for the first expedition, anchored in the port several days and the pilots made soundings. Its depth in feet [is] not recorded." [11]

In 1805 Don Miguel Serrano was ordered to take a party of twenty men and, making use of canoes belonging to Indians who inhabited the coast, make a thorough inspection of the Port of Matagorda.[12] It was noted later that the expedition had difficulty because the "place has been made terrible by the Indian Fresada Pinto, who, until his recent death, instigated the depredations committed by his tribe." In November of 1805 Fr. José Man. Gaitan wrote this letter: "We arrived at what was once thoughtlessly called the port of Matagorda. It was sounded by my workman, who has been a sailor many years. He assured me that it was the port and that it was in good condition." [13]

The possible growth of the area can be seen by a letter addressed to Governor Antonio Cordero from Bahía del Espiritu Santo on March 17, 1806: "As a result of the publication of the royal order of September 29 of last year, which has opened the port of San Bernardo to trade free from all duty, a merchant inquired if this free trade includes merchandise from Louisiana or other ports in the United States." [14]

Unfortunately, the Spanish never carried through on many good intentions in regard to this area. There were several good reasons for this, the chief being that internal political strife was taking most of the nation's resources and attention.

Matagorda
Started as Austina

Traditions run deep in Matagorda. Probably no other pre-Republic frontier settlement has more nostalgic roots that dig as deep into the traditions of the Old South — stately plantations, a culture that boasted opera houses alongside barrel houses, and a wealth that contrasted sharply with the average frontier town.

Matagorda was a cut above the average, proud of its culture, schools, trade and, yes, its wealth.

Austina was planned as the first settlement in Austin's Colony, but after some initial discouragements, the empresario elected to move his headquarters to San Felipe, which he deemed to be closer to the center of his feudal-size grant of land.[1]

Moses Austin probably began having thoughts of securing a land grant as early as 1813; by December of 1820 he was in San Antonio seeking permission to bring 300 families to Texas. At that time Texas was in the Eastern Interior Provinces of New Spain, which included Texas, Nuevo Leon, Coahuila, and Santander or Tamaulipas. Joaquín de Arredondo was the supreme civil and military officer. In San Antonio, Antonio Martínez was the Spanish governor of Texas (also the last) and it was to him that Austin addressed his request. Rebuffed by Martínez, Austin met Baron de Bastrop, an acquaintance from several years back, as he left the meeting. Bastrop used his influence with Martínez and the governor approved Austin's request to settle 300 families and forwarded it to the supreme officer, Arredondo.[2]

Moses Austin died in June of 1821, but not before turning over his dream to his son, Stephen F. Austin, who had been a partner to his father's planning from the beginning. Martínez recognized Stephen as the heir to his father's plan and cooperated with the son in working out details for the new colony in August of 1821 in San Antonio. Leaving San Antonio, Austin and his party traveled over the territory on the lower San Antonio, Guadalupe, Colorado, and Brazos rivers.[3]

Austin returned immediately to New Orleans and started making plans to implement the settlement of the colony. He purchased the *Lively*, a small vessel of about thirty tons burden, for $600. The money came from a loan made by Joseph Hawkins.[4] The ship sailed toward the end of November with sixteen to seventeen families, together with a supply of farming tools, seeds for planting, and other provisions. The plan was for the ship to proceed to the mouth of the Colorado, make soundings, and discharge its passengers and cargo. Austin left New Orleans and was joined by ten men at Natchitoches. They proceeded to the mouth of the Colorado River, arriving in January. Despite the fact that they did not have a large amount of supplies, they waited for the *Lively* a number of days, existing on catfish and wild onions. They finally returned to a settlement on the Brazos.

According to an article written by Lester G. Bugbee, the *Lively* left New Orleans November 20, 1821. On December 3 it was supposed to have sailed past the mouth of the Brazos and on December

23 returned there and discharged passengers and cargo. It then sailed south to make soundings and was expected to return; however, it showed up in New Orleans and took on another cargo of passengers and provisions. This time it was wrecked off the shore of Galveston Island with a total loss of cargo. One of the passengers was Thomas M. Duke, who later became a customs official.[5]

The group of settlers left on the Brazos sought to find other settlers and then finally tried to raise crops. Adverse conditions in 1822 turned their efforts into disaster. Eventually, most drifted back to the United States.[6]

In March of 1822 two ships arrived with colonists. The *Only Son* was first, landing near the mouth of the Colorado River. Included in this group were William Kincheloe, Horatio Chriesman, Mr. Abram, M. Clare, Mr. Bray, George Helm, Charles Wilson, Mr. Morgan, and G. Hayes. Some brought their families. Several days later another vessel arrived and unloaded the following: Samuel M. Williams and Jonathan C. Peyton and family. The supplies from the two ships were left in charge of four men while the remainder of the party proceeded to the settlements in the interior to get transportation. When they returned for their supplies, the four guards were dead and the supplies stolen, presumably by the Karankawa Indians. James Cummins had been stationed at the mouth of the river to act as a guide for the party. Jesse Burnham, an Indian fighter hired by Austin, together with Cummins, organized a group of men who tracked the Indians down and practically annihilated the entire party.

For a while the Indians did not bother the settlers. Soon, however, stealing, killing, and other depredations caused Cummins on August 25, 1824, to ask Austin for twenty-five men to quell the Indians. The Indians, upon hearing of the war party, retired to La Bahía and sought shelter in the mission. Cummins extracted an agreement that the Indians would stay west of the Lavaca River. In 1826 they broke the agreement, raiding the homes of the Cavanah and Flowers families, murdering Mrs. Cavanah and several of her children. They also murdered Mrs. Flowers and left her young daughter, presumed dead, with an arrow in her back. She survived and spread the alarm. The settlers gathered sixty men and caught them at Little Boggy Creek and exterminated the entire group. After this a fort was built at the mouth of the Colorado and the battleground has since been called Battle Island. The same group of men meted out similar justice to another small band of Indians at what was later called Dressing Point, because of the dressing given the Indians.[7]

Trouble in getting final approval from the Mexican government caused Austin to have to leave his colony in March of 1822 to go to Monterrey to straighten out the problems. He went to Mexico City in April. Austin learned in the coming months about the meaning of *mañana*. Procrastination lasted over a year while Austin suffered financial and mental hardships. Before Austin left for Mexico he had appointed Josiah H. Bell as the person responsible for government while he was gone. During this time *alcaldes* had been elected in the two centers of population, settlements on the Brazos (now Washington County) and those on the Colorado (present town of Columbus). Probably as many as 217 titles were issued during this period by Baron de Bastrop.[8]

When Austin returned to his colony he found three pressing needs: the issuing of land titles, restoring the settler's confidence in the permanency of the colony, and bringing the Indian problem under control. He made a contract immediately with Seth Ingram to begin the survey work. In May of 1823 Governor Trespalacios ordered the recruiting of fourteen men for protection to be stationed near the mouth of the Colorado. This brought no results and Austin employed ten men, at his expense, to serve as rangers, with Lt. Moses Morrison in charge. One of the acute problems was the piracy of belongings of incoming settlers. Ships would discharge passengers on the coast, along with their possessions. Since the new arrivals had no means of transportation for their goods to their new homes, it was necessary for someone to go to one of the areas of settlement and borrow carts or wagons. Many times the goods were stolen and the guards killed.[9]

By the fall of 1824 the colony was firmly established and a semblance of local government was in place. Crops were abundant, cabins were replacing makeshift shelters, and the Indians were less troublesome. Austin submitted an application for permits to settle another 300 families.[10]

When Austin secured his initial grant there were restrictions against the establishment of towns on the coast. In 1826 the restrictions were lifted, at Austin's request. He saw the need of having a port city to serve his growing colony.[11]

San Felipe de Austin was the capital of Austin's Colony. Since the surveying of grants was probably the most important activity carried on in the city, it follows that several surveyors made their home in the capital. Among them were Seth and Ira Ingram, Elias R. Wightman, William Selkirk, and Horatio Chriesman. Austin was keenly aware of the need of a seaport to receive the incoming flood of settlers and their goods, as well as a port to handle exports. Elias R. Wightman put the idea in perspective when he proposed the establishment of the town of Matagorda to fill this need.[12] Wightman, along with Hosea H. League, James C. Ludlow, and Richard Matson, were granted permission by Austin to found the City of Matagorda.[13]

The young surveyor lived a life of adventure and enterprise. A successful merchant before the War of 1812, Wightman found himself insolvent after the war was over. He taught school for a year (his future wife was a pupil) before heeding the call of adventure in Texas. He joined Stephen Austin as a surveyor in 1825 and is credited with correcting the maps of the day through his careful work. When commissioned to found the seaport of Matagorda, he returned to his native New York state to recruit colonists for the city. The girl he had taught, Mary Sherwood, was now six years older and a young maiden. He married her and they founded their home in Matagorda. A number of friends and relatives joined the young couple on their journey to Texas. They started by wagon train to the Allegheny River, where they boarded two large flatboats built especially for immigrants. Through many hardships, they finally reached the Mississippi and the Port of New Orleans. On the day after Christmas, 1828, the colonists boarded the *Little Zoe*, skippered by Captain Alden, for the trip to Matagorda, arriving January 27, 1829.[14]

The colonists aboard the *Little Zoe* had heard chilling stories about the savage Karankawa Indians (spelled Carancahua in Austin's Colony). Ed Kilman, in his book *Cannibal Coast*, introduces the natives of the Colorado River Valley in this way:

> The warm seashore season of 1822 was over, and this band of Kronks was seeking winter camping and hunting grounds in the woods upstream. They hugged the reedy bank in their dugout canoes, keeping a sharp eye out for white poachers on their hunting preserves.
> They pulled into "Skull Creek" and pitched camp. The squaws began boiling or roasting half spoiled buffalo meat or ven-

ison and brewing yaupon tea. The men slipped out to reconnoiter
the country for any white settlers who might be abroad from
Buckner's Camp up the Colorado, or from Jennings' camp across
the prairie below.[15]

Peaceful, perhaps; but these Indians were on a collision course
with the white man who wanted the land that the Indian thought
the Great Spirit had given him.

Sorting out the true story of the fall of the Karankawa Indians
in and around Matagorda would fill a huge volume, and even after
years of verification the events, places, and people would still be in
question. The Karankawa Indians were a part of history, but unfortunately neither victor nor vanquished had the time, or inclina-
tion, to really chronicle the events of the day.

The accounts of the voyage of the *Little Zoe* by Mrs. Wightman
and by another passenger, Thomas J. Pilgrim, a Baptist missionary,
give some chilling insights into their voyage that lasted one month.

> The supplies and fresh water ran short, causing real illnesses to
> go along with the colonists being seasick most of the time. Water
> was rationed at one-half pint per day. Hurricane-like winds battered
> the little ship as it neared its destination, sweeping them out to sea.
> To make bad matters worse, the ship sprung a leak and the crew
> eased their pain by hitting the grog a bit heavy.

> Most of the winds were exactly ahead of our desired course,
> and after a long calm (in which we rolled most unpleasantly), we
> were greeted by a norther. Many times when our port was in
> sight we would fall to the leeward, and it would be impossible to
> beat up to it before another norther would strike us.[16]

> * * *

> Just as they were about to enter Pass Cavallo, another strong
> wind blew them to the south. When it subsided they found them-
> selves at Aransas Pass, where they anchored. The women went
> ashore to wash and twelve men went to hunt for fresh meat. Soon
> two canoes of Indians were seen making straight for the schooner.
> The captain fired a musket, which had been left on board, but the
> Indians paid little attention to it. Then the men, who had been
> hunting, came back and as soon as the Indians saw their guns
> they paddled away as fast as they could. The Indians came back
> and a few were allowed to come to the ship. They manifested no
> hostility. Their canoes were stored with fish, all neatly dressed,
> which they bartered to us.[17]

The little ship finally arrived at Matagorda on January 27,

1829, and the people were gratified to find a newly constructed fort manned by four men, just as Austin had promised. The military men were James Cook, Daniel Decrow, Andrew Jackson, and a Kentucky youth named Helm. Mary Wightman organized a school and Sunday school immediately, a job that she continued for many years while her husband was absent on surveying trips. Josiah Wilbarger also taught school in Matagorda.[18]

Others who were living at the new townsite included Jesse Burnham, an Indian fighter stationed at the mouth of the Colorado since 1822. He lived in a small log cabin. James Cummins, also an Indian fighter and guide, lived with his widowed daughter, Maria Ross. Her husband had been killed by the Karankawas. Mrs. Parker, the grandmother of Mrs. Wilbarger, lived at the Cummins house.[19] No doubt these folks were all on hand when the slightly bedraggled men and women filed off of the *Little Zoe*. Everyone who had been living in the fort moved out to make room for the immigrants.

The list of colonists aboard the *Little Zoe* included Elias R. Wightman and his wife, Mary Sherwood Wightman; Benjamin Wightman and his wife, Esther Wightman (mother and father of Elias Wightman); and the Wightmans' three daughters: Margaret Wightman (single); Jerusha Wightman Yeamans and husband, Asa Yeamans, and their children, Joseph, Horace, Esther, Elias Robert; Esther Wightman Griffith and her husband, Noah Griffith, and their children. Other passengers were Maria Demmiss Pierce, T. J. Pilgrim, Henry Griffith, F. W. Grasmeyer, R. R. Royall, Philip Dimmitt, H. Wooldridge, Gail Borden, Jr., John P. Borden, and Paschal Borden. Each family coming to Texas during the colonization days was granted a league (4,428 acres).

In the writings of T. J. Pilgrim and Mary Wightman Helm, it was pointed out that the colonists were unloaded near the mouth of the river (two miles from the townsite) with their chattels. Then the little vessel was manhandled over onto its side, thus raising the keel, and maneuvered through the shallow inlet across Dog Island into the river. This was truly a Matagorda-style portage.[20]

The site for the new City of Matagorda had been selected by Wightman, assisted by a group commissioned by Austin. On August 2, 1826, this group submitted a petition to Austin to proceed with the development of a seaport for the colony. In 1827 Wightman laid out the town and early in 1828 Austin dispatched Wightman and David G. Burnet to the United States to secure people for the new town.[21] At about the same time the empresario received a grant for an additional 300 families. In describing the site, Wightman wrote:

> We, the said petitioners, having viewed Matagorda Bay as the most important and safe harbor on the coast. . . . that there may be a town erected on the east side of the Rio Colorado some two or three miles from the mouth on the margin of the bay. We have discovered one of the most beautiful situations for the building of a large, commodious, and commercial town that our imagination could conceive. A large amphitheatre, a semi-circular bluff of about six or eight feet above high water mark of the very permeable dry soil and ascending back to an extensive and beautiful prairie. . . . We are confident that a mere trifle will open a canal from the Colorado through this low land to the bay and a bayou already flows up to meet it.[22]

When Wightman submitted his petition he mentioned that the bayou "meanders in a northerly direction for about two city blocks, thus cutting off the southwestern ends of Matagorda and Fisher Streets and terminating at an intersection with Lewis Street." [23]

Generally all of the land lying between the Colorado River and Caney Creek, extending northward from the bay, was called Big Prairie in those early days. It was in this area that most of the early settlers received their land grants. Matagorda was to grow not only as a seaport, but as the home of farmers who settled in the area but preferred to have their families live in the city as opposed to on the plantation. Some of the plantations in the area became leading cotton and sugarcane producing areas, especially before the Civil War.

The settlers immediately began work on making their economic lives secure. Within a few months the log fort had been dismantled and the logs and lumber used in other buildings. Individual log cabins began to appear. A constitution for the city had been drafted in 1827 that set out in detail how the new city would operate under the guidance of the owners, or proprietors, who were Elias Wightman, Stephen F. Austin, H. H. League, and Ira Ingram. For administrative purposes, League was named president; Ira Ingram, secretary; Seth Ingram, treasurer; and Wightman, surveyor. In the 1827 constitution the ownership was listed as: one-fourth each to James B. Austin, Thomas R. Duke, William Selkirk, and Elias R. Wightman.

By 1831 the community had progressed to the point that a lot auction was held, with residential lots going for $30. As an inducement to specialized tradesmen, some lots were given to people with a needed skill in the community. The streets were all laid out, with the courthouse square (now the public schools) in the center.[24]

The community's priorities were evident in that the first school was opened in the winter of 1829, with Josiah P. Wilbarger as the teacher and Mary Wightman as assistant. After several years, Wilbarger moved to Austin.

Mary Wightman married Meredith Helm after her husband died in 1841 and continued teaching for many years. She is credited with organizing the first Sunday school in 1829. Thomas J. Pilgrim, who came to Matagorda on the *Little Zoe,* established a Sunday school in San Felipe, also in 1829. Sumner Bacon, a Presbyterian, was the first to hold church services in 1829. Despite not being an ordained minister, he distributed Bibles and taught Sunday school during the early 1830s. It must be remembered that the colonists all professed allegiance to the Catholic church, as one of the requirements of securing a grant of land in Texas. Very few Catholic priests were in the area and, as a result, Protestants practiced their religions in private.[25]

Despite the fact that some of the oldest churches in the state were established in Matagorda a few years later, there does not seem to have been an organized group during the early pre-revolution years. Several letters written by Ira Ingram to a friend in the East deal with the subject. The friend had written to inquire how it was "possible to live under a state religion." Ingram replied:

> On the subject of the freedom of religion and religious worship, there has never been any restraint to any settler either by the government or officers. Strife and animosities too often are the offsprings of a well-meant zeal for the cause of a true religion, and invariably the hand-maid of intolerant fanaticism. We hear no ravings and see no rompings or indecorous and indecent exhibitions under the cloak of a religious assemblage. . . .[26]

Later Ingram pointed out that Austin required that all of his colonists have a character reference before their acceptance, and this brought a sober, hard-working, God-fearing type of people into the frontier. When Ira Ingram died in 1837 he left an estate estimated to be worth $75,000 to the schoolchildren of Matagorda.[27]

The early 1830s was a time of growth for Matagorda. It became known as the gateway port into Texas. Immigrants began to arrive in a steady stream by sea and overland by covered wagons.

COURTHOUSE OF 1849 — The two-story wooden structure was destroyed by the hurricane of 1854, then was rebuilt and served until 1894, when the county seat was moved to Bay City. Seth Ingram gave the land for the building and John Rugeley paid for the materials. In 1876 D. E. E. Braman received permission for his son to hold school in the building. (Photo courtesy of Matagorda County Historical Commission)

In the next few years literally thousands of new arrivals would walk down Matagorda's main street. As with the original settlers, the people who came as settlers were usually men and women of good moral character and the homes and institutions that they fostered reflected this tone. Early writings show that most of these pioneers built one- or two-room cabins with a lean-to on one side. Two-room structures were usually built with an open passageway between the rooms, but roofed. This later became known as a dog run, a mark of homes of the time. Since there were no large stands of timber in the area, the log cabins gave way to rough plank homes just as soon as it was possible to get lumber ships in from Florida. Most of the floors were made of dirt or split logs, with the split side smoothed somewhat.[28]

Matagorda had been destined as the port city for the colony and, as such, people arrived in large numbers. However, not all viewed Matagorda through rose-colored glasses. S. Rhoads Fisher arrived with his family in the early days and later his daughter wrote these impressions:

> Although situated on Matagorda Bay, and at the mouth of the Colorado River, neither circumstance was of any advantage. The navigation of the bay was obstructed by Dog Island bar, six or eight miles below the town, so the passengers and goods had to be sent ashore in small boats called "lighters," and the navigation of the river was obstructed by a large raft in the river, a short distance above the town.

The tales told by the daughter, Mrs. Annie P. Harris, are many, but the most touching deals with their arrival.

> Mr. Fisher had planned months ahead to make the move to Texas and had sent plans and money to build a home for his family. On arrival he did not find a home waiting. After finding the agent, entrusted with the job of building the house, the man answered: "I had other uses for your money, sir. My brother was in difficulty, and I required your money to clear him." It is not known if Harris had to resort to *frontier justice* to get his house built.[29]

Matagorda began to fulfill its destiny as being the port of Texas in the early 1830s — after all, it was the closest port city to New Orleans and also the closest port to the growing number of colonists. Things looked bright for the economic growth of the city when a Mexican customshouse was established in 1831. The population of the city was growing, several stores were built, and two salt factories were in existence.[30]

As Matagorda grew, so did discontent among the new Texas colonists. Accustomed to American-style democracy, they chafed under Mexican laws that restricted their freedom. There was always a group of Texans who wanted complete freedom from Mexico, but by far the larger part of the colonists were happy with their Mexican landlords; they just wanted a share in their own self-government. Stephen Austin was one of the latter.

Finally, the Mexican government sought to turn back the tide of American colonization with the law of April 6, 1830. Basically, this law sought three things: (1) military occupation of Texas; (2) counter-colonization by Mexicans and Europeans, particularly by Swiss and German immigrants; and (3) the development of an economic bond between Texas and the rest of Mexico by establishing coastwise trade.[31] Even as Austin sought for clarifications to the law concerning immigrants from the United States, other Texans were taking things into their own hands, leading to uprisings against the Mexicans.

The Convention of 1832 was the first manisfestation of this inner struggle. The delegates met in San Felipe on October 1 and elected Stephen F. Austin president. Action at the convention was aimed at redress of standing complaints made by the colonists against the Mexicans. A total of fifty-eight delegates from sixteen districts responded to the call. Ira Ingram and Silas Dinsmore were representatives from Matagorda. Austin wrote extensively concerning the work of the convention, only now the emphasis was shifted to a separate state organization for Texas. The Second Convention met April 1–13, 1833. Its purpose was to form a constitution for the State of Texas, with the approval of the general government. Sam Houston, a delegate from Nacogdoches, chaired the meeting.

In the spring of 1833 Austin made a trip to Mexico City to try and work out problems between Texas and Mexico. He ended up in prison. Austin returned in September of 1835 and Texas united behind his bid for a consultation at Washington-on-the-Brazos. The Committee of Safety from Matagorda was composed of Hamilton S. Cook, Ira Ingram, Seth Ingram, R. R. Royall, and W. J. Russel. When the consultation was held on November 3, 1835, the following from Matagorda were listed as delegates: R. R. Royall, Ira R. Lewis, Charles Wilson, and John D. Newell.

With General Cos known to be en route to Texas, the consultation was faced with problems that they had no experience to fall back upon. When the convention met on March 1, 1836, Matagorda delegates were listed as Ira Ingram, Bailey Hardeman, S. Rhoads Fisher, and James Collinsworth. Probably they turned to Austin and his words: "No more doubts, no submission. I hope to see Texas forever free from Mexican domination of any kind." [32] Oral tradition places their meeting in a blacksmith shop owned by Noah T. Byars.

General Cos landed with his army at the port of El Copano in September of 1835 and, after unloading supplies, headed for Goliad, arriving on October 1. He quickly garrisoned the old fort of La Bahía and left for Bexar on October 5, leaving behind a small force. When Cos landed at Copano, Col. James Power had opportunity to send word to other communities that Cos's army was on the move. No doubt people in Matagorda were aware of the troop movement since John Linn, a trader out of Victoria, was in Copano to monitor Cos's movements. [33]

When word reached Matagorda, George Collinsworth took charge of organizing an expedition. Before he even arrived in Goliad, he was joined by men from Refugio and San Patricio, and others, including Col. Benjamin Milam. Milam had been captured in Mexico, escaped from Monterrey, and had reached the San Antonio River about a mile below Goliad on the night of October 9 when a party of Collinsworth's expedition came by. The exhausted Milam heard English conversation and called out: "Who are you?"

"American volunteers bound for Goliad, who are you?"

"I am Ben Milam, escaped from prison in Monterrey, trying to reach my countrymen in Texas," cried Milam. He was killed later in the successful assault on San Antonio, in which he had encouraged men to enter into the battle with these famous words: "Who will go with old Ben Milam to San Antonio?" Before the battle, the men of the Matagorda and Bay Prairie Company signed a pledge of protection for the town of Goliad. [34]

Accounts of the actual storming of La Bahía vary; however, that night the citizen expedition organized by Collinsworth overwhelmed the twenty-four defenders. Ira Ingram, who was company adjunct, wrote later that a group composed of the *alcalde* of Victoria, Juan Antonio Padilla, Philip Dimmitt, Dr. Erwin, and Colonel Milam called on the fort's commander, Lt. Col. Francisco Sandoval, and demanded surrender. Upon being refused, the Texans laid siege and received an almost immediate surrender. Only one man, a Mexican, was killed.

Texas at this point had not declared independence from Mexico. On December 20, 1835, the Goliad Declaration of Independence was proclaimed after being drafted by two Matagorda men — Philip Dimmitt and Ira Ingram — who were part of Collinsworth's company. It was signed by the Matagorda men of the fort and ninety-two residents of Goliad. They hoisted the flag of independence, now known as the Goliad Flag, which displayed a severed right arm holding a bloody sword.

Afterwards Collinsworth's men were joined with those of Ben F. Smith, John Alley, Ira Westover, and Benavides to form a regiment, with Smith in command. Smith's command did not last. Remnants of the Matagorda squad, for the most part, settled in with Philip Dimmitt and followed this illustrious Texan through the war. Dimmitt came to Texas in 1822 bearing a letter of introduction from Stephen F. Austin. He married Luisa Laso, daughter of Carlos Laso, one of de León's colonists, and as a result had access to high Mexican officials. He had a mercantile business in Bexar, established Dimmitt's Landing on Lavaca Bay, and operated a line of carts from the port to Bexar. His squad stayed in command at Goliad until dismissed by the acting governor, James W. Robinson, on January 18, 1836. The next day his men again named him as their commander.[35]

During the early part of the war an increasing amount of supplies were being funneled into Matagorda. More and more of the men joined in the battle. Captain Collinsworth's company was broken up after the assault on Goliad. As a result, some left the service; others were with Dimmitt and not with Col. James Fannin when his men were slaughtered. Two of the men killed at Goliad were the Yeamans brothers, Elias and Erastus. Another cavalry group, commanded by Col. Albert C. Horton of Matagorda, was spared the fate of Fannin's men when his squad was sent ahead on a mission and thus missed the final battle on the Coleto and the subsequent surrender. Some of the members of Horton's squad were Daniel Martindale, William Haddon, Charles Smith, Francisco Garcia, Ransom O. Graves, Napoleon B. Williams, Lewis Powell, Hughes Witt, George Pain, Thomas Dasher, John J. Hand, Duffield, Spencer, and Cash. Captain Caldwell also commanded a Matagorda squad.[36]

Matagorda's stock took a nose-dive when Gen. Sam Houston started his famous retreat toward San Jacinto. People who were left in the countryside, and in towns behind Houston's line of retreat, joined in the pell-mell evacuation known as the Runaway Scrape. Texan resistance had been wiped out at San Patricio, Agua Dulce, Refugio, Goliad, and the Alamo. Everyone evacuated the best way possible. Those who could, got aboard a boat; those who had a wagon or cart, rode; others walked. Roads became clogged with broken-down wagons, abandoned family heirlooms, and people too sick or weak to travel any further. It was a headlong flight for the sanctuary of the United States border. The blood-chilling tales of the fate of the defenders of the Alamo and the slaughter of Colonel Fannin's men gave credence to any tale told about Santa Anna. The number of people fleeing the Matagorda area can be ascertained by Gen. Juan N. Almonte's economic report on Texas, issued in 1835, which gave Matagorda a population of 1,400, with another 250 in the surrounding area.[37]

A tale involving Capt. Thomas Stewart's company of volunteers and drafted men from Matagorda fits into this nitch in history. The newly formed company was ordered by Gen. Sam Houston to Cox's Point to oversee supplies that were consigned to this port. By the time they arrived, the war had gone against the Texans and Houston ordered the company to retreat and take their families with them. The company then returned to Matagorda to assist in the evacuation of the town. Most Matagorda families left by boat to Beaumont and Sabine and some even farther. Stewart's company proceeded to Velasco, with some of them serving there and at San Jacinto.

When General Urrea arrived in Matagorda he found the city deserted. He left a Prussian colonel by the name of J. J. Holzinger in charge of a company of eight soldiers to guard the empty town and six Texas prisoners. This is the same Holzinger who had saved the life of Herman Eherenberg, a fellow German, from the firing squad at Goliad. After the war, Eherenberg informed on Holzinger and his actions as head of the occupation unit. Eherenberg later wrote that Holzinger broke into the vacant homes and helped himself to anything he wanted, storing the goods in a warehouse.

When the Battle of San Jacinto brought the downfall of Santa

Anna, General Urrea immediately left the area and ordered Holzinger to do likewise. He found an old vessel, loaded it with his stolen goods and the Texas prisoners, still under the guard of the Mexican soldiers, and sailed south. Eherenberg and two of the prisoners finally escaped and sounded the alarm. Holzinger was returned to Matagorda, with the stolen goods, to be reclaimed by the returning colonists. Holzinger later was set free after exposing Urrea in a letter to John Wharton.

Members of Stewart's company were Capt. Thomas Stewart, J. Q. Hoit, William Frewm, Benjamin Joins, Daniel Yeamans, Hamilton Cook, George Elliott, John Plunket, William Russel, Joseph Yeamans, William Rolin, Samuel Brigham, John Devoit, J. Burnet, and John Krowlin.[38]

One other wartime story bears telling since the cast was made up of men from Matagorda. In the fall of 1835 the Mexicans had two gunboats, the *Bravo* and the *Montezuma,* patrolling the Texas coast. They gave chase to the American schooner *Hanna Elizabeth,* running her aground. Stories vary about the incident, but essentially a group of men from Matagorda boarded the grounded ship and took possession of the prize. Another American schooner, the *William Robbins* (under Captain Hurd), was brought onto the scene to assist in moving the prize ship to Matagorda. S. Rhoads Fisher commanded the marines. The case ended up being heard by Charles Wilson, first judge of Matagorda Municipality. Evidently, acquiring title, by right or might, to the prize schooner could be equated to winning a giant lottery today.[39]

With the ending of the war, the economic pace in Matagorda began to accelerate. The fact that oceangoing ships had to lighten their loads to get through the shallow water channels at Dog Island Pass did not seem to stop the rapid growth of the shipping industry. Dog Island, sometimes called Dog Reef, was a moon-shaped reef that stretched across the bay with two entrances — Dog Channel, close to the mainland, and Tiger Channel, on the island side. Devil's Elbow was an area between the two river channels, where a gigantic whirlpool existed. It was also an excellent place to fish.

The channel around Dog Island was not the only thing that impeded water transportation for Matagorda. The Colorado River offered an excellent waterway to move freight in and out of the uplands. But there was one big hangup — the logjam in the river known simply as the "raft." Throughout the years, efforts have been made to clear the raft in order to allow ships to sail up the river. The raft was an insurmountable obstacle. Flat-bottomed keel boats were able to navigate the river, but their load capacities were limited. At different times steamers managed to slip past the raft (which was usually just about twelve miles above Matagorda), but in periods when the river was low this was impossible.

Starting as early as 1839, public meetings aimed at removing the raft were held up and down the river. The Colorado Navigation Company was organized in 1842 and in 1846 the *Kate Ward*, a steamboat built above the raft, arrived in Austin. Through the years many ideas were explored; for instance, a channel around the raft. But all dreams perished for lack of adequate funds. In 1851 W. T. Ward cleared a twenty-mile channel up from the mouth of the river and was at the brink of success when funds ran out. The United States Corps of Engineers purchased the *Kate Ward* in 1853 and sought to dig a series of by-pass channels around the raft. By 1854 boats were using the new channel, and for the next eight years ships moved freely up and down the river. The Civil War, the coming of railroads, and the reforming of the raft snuffed out the gains of decades.

Flood control districts were formed to take care of flooding caused by the new rafts. Finally, in 1934, a channel was cut from the mouth of the Colorado River across Matagorda Island and into the Gulf of Mexico. Reclamation districts joined with the Corps of Engineers, and in 1938 the Rivers and Harbors Act authorized the construction of a barge channel from the mouth of the river to Bay City, making it a port city.

So Elias Wightman's dream had come true — but too late for his city of Matagorda.[40]

Civil and criminal procedures had been handled through the local governments set up by the Austin Colony. Oliver Jones was *alquazil* (sheriff) in 1829–30 and in 1834 represented Austin's Colony in the legislature of Coahuila and Texas. He was also in the annexation convention of 1845. Matagorda had its *alcalde,* the first of which was Ira Ingram, who served from 1834 to 1836. Matagorda County was organized, together with twenty-three others, on March 17, 1836. Uneasy times with Mexico and Indians were still ahead, but Matagorda was unfurling full sail.[41]

The growth of Matagorda as a shipping point probably can best be told through the history of the family of William Selkirk,

taken in part from the notes written by Wyatt O. Selkirk of Blessing
in 1937. William was one of the "Old Three Hundred" and was
one of Austin's trusted associates, as well as the leading surveyor.
His son, James Henry Selkirk, arrived in 1836 just after San Jacinto
and settled in Matagorda, marrying Lucille Hall of England. Sen-
sing the urgency of the lack of commercial shipping facilities, Selkirk and his cousin James Selkirk built the first dock in the old port.
It was a large pier extending out into the bay.

> This pier joined onto the southeast end of Market Street and
> extended from the bluff out into the bay for a quarter of a mile or
> more, with a "T" head on the outer end. The pier was built to
> support wagons loaded with cotton and from it many thousands
> of bales of cotton were shipped.
>
> Large warehouses for storage were constructed on the bay
> shore at the end of Market Street, and from stories handed down
> from older people, cotton had been seen stacked from the bay-
> shore end of Market Street north to the courthouse on Wightman
> Street, or where the present school house stands.
>
> During the summer months the "T" head became a favorite
> gathering place for the younger set on moonlit evenings. The pier
> also afforded a fine fishing place. Shrimp were caught in abun-
> dance from the pier with casting nets.[42]

Henry Selkirk became active in the business, social, and political life of the community. He was city clerk and treasurer, county
clerk, surveyor, treasurer, and held other minor posts. He was also
a Mason and establisher of the American Art Society in Matagorda. He died in 1862, the victim of yellow fever, and is buried in
Matagorda.

In 1837 J. W. J. Niles moved to Matagorda and opened the
Matagorda *Bulletin*. Niles was not only wrapped up in Matagorda
affairs but was also involved in state politics. Even at this early date
the contract to do state printing was quite a financial prize. Niles
absented himself from Matagorda frequently to work on the possi-
bility of getting the juicy printing contract from Moore and Cruger
of Houston. To this end he opened the *National Banner* in Houston
to better campaign for Mirabeau B. Lamar for president.[43] A great
deal of the history of Matagorda is held in these old pages printed
on a Washington hand press. Fortunately for researchers today, the
newsprint that was used in those days was of a high quality with a

linen basis and as a result has not discolored as badly as more modern papers printed on wood pulp paper.

In one of the first issues on August 9, 1837, the editor introduced George M. Collinsworth as the new collector of revenue at the customshouse. A typical ad from a merchant ran like this: "Clapton and Mostly of Matagorda are receiving by the schooner *Oscar* a well selected assortment of fancy and staple dry goods, hardware, queensware, cutlery, saddlery, clothing, hats, shoes, etc."

An issue dated September 6, 1837, gave another indicator of the economic conditions: "Lawyers in Matagorda are Chas. DeMorse, John Childress, Edw. Holmes, Spencer Jack, and Wm. DeLap." Only one doctor, Dr. A. M. Levy, was listed in the professional column. A medical advice column gave these homespun remedies: "A new cure for hydrophobia — copious blood letting, 48 ozs. at short intervals. Cure for croup — Mix 2 ozs. of squills, 40 grams epecacuana, 1 gram tarter emetr and give every ten minutes from onset of disease until free of vomiting."

Mail schedules were good: "Mail from the east will arrive on Tuesday at 1 P.M. and will depart Wednesday at 9 A.M. under the watchful eye of Postmaster S. B. Brigham."

The newspaper carried a list of the ships in and out of the port for the week. During the week ending February 6, 1838, there were ten schooners from New Orleans and one from Mobile, Alabama.

In the paper of January 31, 1838, the election of Harvey Kendricks as mayor was proclaimed, with the aldermen being Edward L. Holmes, W. J. Maynard, A. Wadsworth, G. M. Collinsworth, Charles Howard, Thomas Stuart, Rupes McLellan, and R. H. Wynne.

A constitution drafted in 1827 was the basis of early county government, and on August 1, 1829, the proprietors met and elected officers. H. H. League was named president; Ira Ingram, secretary; Seth Ingram, treasurer; and Elias R. Wightman, surveyor. Ira Ingram took over as president in January of 1831 and served until his death in 1837. The town was incorporated in 1830. Matagorda County was organized in 1836, and Matagorda was declared the county seat in 1837. A chamber of commerce was in operation in 1840, as evidenced by items in the local newspaper.

The first countywide election was held in 1837, with Isaac Vandorn the new sheriff and H. L. Cook the chief justice. Silas Dinsmore was the first chief justice, having been appointed by Sam

Houston on December 20, 1836. Where the county government operated is not known, but it stands to reason that the county government probably met in the same hall as the city government.

The date generally given to the construction of the first county courthouse is 1846, but this is not backed by evidence other than oral tradition. From best information, the 1849 courthouse was a two-story wooden building located on courthouse square (now used by public schools). It was destroyed in the storm of 1854. In 1855 the commissioners court authorized the rebuilding of the courthouse by the same plans. Seth Ingram gave the block of land for the courthouse. The hurricane of 1875 also did extensive damage to the building, but it was repaired.[44]

The Civil War brought Federal troops to the peninsula and Union ships frequented the bay, but no landings were made at Matagorda. Blockade runners worked out of Caney Creek and Matagorda, evidently with a degree of success. Early writings reflect the fact that the sugarcane plantations in the vicinity of Hawkinsville reached their peak of prosperity as prices hit all-time highs. Naturally, the labor-intense industries, such as cotton and sugarcane, suffered in the post-Civil War days. Matagorda declined; however, export figures in the early 1870s show that cotton was making a comeback. Another success was a shipyard in Matagorda which specialized in repairs and construction of shallow-draft vessels.[45]

Increased interest in land sales in the northern part of Bay Prairie sparked a movement to seek the removal of the county seat from Matagorda to a more centrally located spot. On September 18, 1894, an election was held, with the newly established Bay City receiving 778 votes to 141 for Matagorda. A new courthouse was built in Bay City in 1896.[46]

The importance of shipping to the new state was evidenced with the organization of a customs system on June 12, 1837. The District of Matagorda covered that part of the coastline commencing at the mouth of the San Antonio River and following the coast eastward to the mouth of Cedar Lake.[47]

Records of the customs service during Republic years, carefully preserved in the State Archives, trace rather faithfully the trends in shipping and the type of goods moving in and out by these pioneers. Politics played a big hand in the appointment of customs officials.

George Morse Collinsworth, the same man who organized

COLORADO HOUSE— One of the finest hotels in Texas, built in 1852 by John Ives, featured mahogany, walnut, and cherry furniture. It had fourteen guest rooms upstairs, each with its private dressing room; downstairs were two great rooms which could be joined by opening folding doors. Owned by Galen Hodges, the hotel was the center of the plantation social circle, but its guests included men and women from all walks of life. Andrew Jackson registered on May 3, 1857. (Photo courtesy of Matagorda County Historical Commission)

planters who ran the Mexicans out of Goliad,[48] was named the first collector of customs for the Matagorda District, with the office projected for the City of Matagorda. This action was taken May 23, 1837, and by the next month his name is to be found on port entries. Rent receipts during this period show that $25 per month was paid to a Jack Spencer for an office for the collector. A warehouse/office was built in June of 1840. Two other employees in the office were Thomas H. Brown and a Mr. Balfour. Hugh O. Watts was a deputy collector assigned to the Lavaca Bay area.

All goods up until January 23, 1839, moved through the Matagorda office before going to its final destination. On this date the separate District of Lavaca was created, with Hugh O. Watts as the collector. Linnville was named as a port of entry, but, when the collector was murdered by Indians, the job went to William H. Watts and the office moved two miles. The District of Calhoun was created January 21, 1841, by abolishing the districts of Matagorda and Lavaca, with several deputy customs collectors at the ports of Dimmitt's Landing, Texana, Lavaca River, Linnville, and Matagorda. Port Calhoun and Port Cavallo were ports of entry. Port Cavallo on the pass was named the temporary port of entry. Collinsworth was confirmed as collector for the Calhoun District on January 22, 1841. Deputy collectors were authorized for Matagorda and Linnville. Thomas M. Duke replaced Collinsworth as collector for Calhoun on March 15, 1841. With the office at Port Calhoun, Richard West was appointed deputy collector at Linnville and Galen Hodges at Matagorda. Duke was replaced by Alexander Somervell on December 14, 1842.[49]

The fact that Texas was still a troubled land could be seen from the bill of lading registered by the schooner *Aurdra* on January 10, 1836: "Richard D. Lanxay received 94 kegs powder, $611; 60 canisters powder, $25; expenses to keep powder until ready to take, $3. Total, $639. [Signed by Geo. Collinsworth]." [50]

Merchandise arrived in a number of instances C.O.D., with the warehouseman called upon to collect the bills before releasing the merchandise. On July 28, 1837, the schooner *Oscar* arrived with $2,220.78 in merchandise for Thomas W. Mather (clothing store), who paid a $515 duty on dresses, frocks, prints, plaids, shirting, sheeting, handkerchiefs, ruffle shirts, white cotton hose, shoes, brogans, muslin, sewing silk, slips, pistols, gingham, and coats. The bill was $2,678.12, and the seller deducted twenty percent for prompt payment, or $457.34, plus $515.60 for duty.[51]

On July 12, 1837, Clopton and Mosby (Matagorda merchants) received eighty-seven packages from New Orleans on the schooner *Oscar*, all marked "B.M.C. and Co." The invoice was $7,053.12 and covered thirty pages. The duty collected amounted to $1,699.28. On November 12 the *Oscar* was back with a list of goods covering fourteen pages for the same company. Each package consigned was labeled by the sender with the "mark" of the customer, which usually consisted of initials, or in some instances cattle brands. This way any dock laborer could sort through cargo for certain marks that were due to be offloaded at Matagorda. In most instances the ports up and down the bays were served by captains who made their living plying their trade up and down the bay rather than hauling in goods from New Orleans or New York. In 1838 the following owners were licensed to operate lighters, schooners, and sloops up and down the coast: Elijah Decrow, *Tom Payne;* Howard Decrow, *Polly Hopkins;* Harvey Frisbee, *Yankee Traveler;* John Williams, *Oscar;* Thomas Bridges, *Enterprise;* Samuel Cummins, *Geo. M. Collinsworth;* Jas. Farwell, *Eliza;* J. W. Byrne, *Cora;* Wm. Alhert, *Black Lake;* Jacob Mussind, *Infant;* and A. E. White, *Louisa.*[52]

On July 13, 1837, one of the first of hundreds of slave ships tied up at Matagorda docks. The log kept by the customs office showed the schooner's name, arrival date, the owner, and the age, height and sex of the slave. For instance: "Sloop *Dream,* 7-13-1837, owner Creacy, F, 35, 5 ft." Records in the courthouse show that the bulk of the slaves in Matagorda District were owned by the people who lived in Matagorda and had plantations on Bay Prairie near Caney Creek.[53]

The start of a great industry was noted in 1841, when the editor of the *Colorado Gazette and Advertiser,* published in Matagorda, noted that the time was drawing near when large quantities of beef (live) would be packed and shipped from Matagorda. He especially mentioned the large herds of cattle, left over from the mission days, that still roamed the Bay Prairie and the Caney area. Matagorda's lack of deep water cut her out of this lucrative trade that eventually ended up at Indianola.

On November 9, 1839, editor W. D. Wallach reported that

yellow fever was running rampant in Houston and Galveston. The next week it was in Matagorda. Hundreds died.

William Chester ran a typical ad in the paper that week: "Just received a large assortment of groceries and provisions which we will sell for lowest retail prices for cash or in exchange for cotton, hides, skins, or pecans. Included are claret, madeira, Maloga, port, sherry or champagne wines, gin, whiskey, brandy, cordials, crackers, soda bisquits, coffee, sugar, salt, rice, chocolate, nails, candles, starch, etc." The bulk of all merchants ran similar ads — always with the spirits listed first. This gave rise to the name "barrel houses," or stores where spirits could be purchased along with a bit to eat. Most liquor was shipped in barrels.

On November 16, 1839, chamber of commerce officers were elected: James Lann, president; Edward Sanders, vice-president; James Belknap, secretary; W. W. Stewart, treasurer. Committee of arbitration members were J. W. Morse, G. R. Jaques, A. Wadsworth, and G. W. Ward.

On June 4, 1842, it was noted in the newspaper that the patent office was closed until further notice. And another issue reflected the times: "$100 reward runaway from Talbat Plantation on Caney, a Negro man named Dosson, age 30, black complexion, stout, thick and well set, carried with him a double barrel shotgun and small sorrel pony."

The importance of Matagorda as a point for cotton export was seen in the June 2, 1851, issue of the *Colorado Tribune:* "Schooner *D. C. Foster* cleared port for New York with cargo of 176 bales of cotton, 163 bbls. of molasses and 20 bbls. of sugar." Some of the largest sugarcane crops in the state of Texas were being grown in the Caney Creek area at the time. In the early 1850s James B. Hawkins built and operated one of the largest sugar mills in the state at Hawkinsville on his 30,000-acre Caney Creek plantation (about fifteen miles up the creek from Matagorda Bay). This business reached its peak during the Civil War, with sugar and molasses bringing premium prices. The sugar, cotton, and molasses were floated down Caney Creek to Matagorda Bay and thence south to the Port of Matagorda.[54]

The fight for this rich trade was fierce, as seen by an ad in the same issue of the *Tribune.* The ad announced a new port on Decrow's Point with "Repaired and refitted warehouse and strong wharfs. No wharfage in any case for vessels or for goods landed, unless such goods shall remain on wharf over 24 hours."

The ship clearings from Matagorda for one week, as reported in the *Tribune*, underline the mushrooming cotton and sugar business:

> Lighter *Caroline* with 21 bbls. of sugar;
> Schooner *Matthew Bird,* 249 bales of cotton;
> Schooner *Joseph Henry,* 195 bales cotton, 11 hhds. sugar, 206 bbls. molasses;
> Schooner *Freeman,* 171 bales of cotton, 111 hhds. sugar, 206 bbls. molasses;
> Schooner *Buena Vista,* 165 bales cotton, 37 hhds. sugar, 92 bbls. molasses.

The raising of cotton has been the cornerstone of the wealth and growth of Matagorda and the immediate area. The first cotton gin was thought to have been built by Col. Robert Williams, who arrived with nine slaves in 1825, planted cotton, and built a cotton gin in 1827 at Caney. A gin is reported to have been built in Matagorda in 1825. For the next few years, gins sprang up throughout the rich plantation area. Since the gins of this period could not gin more than about 200 bales in a season, it was imperative for each large plantation owner to have his own gin.

Gins were composed of two separate buildings. The ginhouse was a two-story frame building which housed the gin stand on the second floor and power machinery on the first. It also contained two storage rooms, one for seed cotton and one for the ginned cotton. The second building housed the press, a strongly braced box where the ginned cotton was placed to be made into bales. A huge hand-chiseled wooden screw, with a foot at the bottom, did the compressing. Mules usually furnished the power for compression by means of wings attached to the screw. A complete gin could be built for about $800. About ten hands were required to run the operation.

Developed almost at the same time was the sugarcane industry, which was probably centered in Hawkinsville, since this was the plantation headquarters of Col. James B. Hawkins. Other farmers on the cutting edge of this change were Abram Sheppard and John Rugeley and his son, Edward Rugeley. The raw sugar was imported for years through the Port of Matagorda in barrels until the plantation mills refined their sugar a little more and began selling it to local customers. With the coming of the Civil

War and the Union blockade, Colonel Hawkins is said to have made a fortune by selling sugar to the Confederacy, after increasing the capacity of his mill to the largest in the state. During this period he had as high as 2,400 acres devoted to sugarcane. After slaves were freed, Hawkins contracted for convict labor to keep his mill running.[55]

Not only were these men leaders in the farming community, they were political and civic leaders as well. Edward Rugeley was a member of the Constitutional Convention of 1875 and then was elected county judge. He was instrumental in the movement of the courthouse from Matagorda to Bay City. Col. Robert Williams helped organize Company D in Matagorda and was a staunch Episcopalian, owning a pew in the Matagorda church when it was rebuilt in 1860.[56]

If the Old South ever existed in Texas, then its best example was in Matagorda and the fertile Colorado River, Caney Creek, and Brazos River bottom lands. In many family histories of these early settlers the stories reveal that rich families of the Old South had picked up and moved from the "worn-out land" on the eastern seaboard to the fresh, virgin soil of the Texas Gulf Coast. In many instances these families brought pieces of their old life with them. A stained-glass door, a cherished piano, fine china, and silver helped them pick up the old plantation life without ever missing a beat. There are instances of a family bringing all of their furniture, as well as personal possessions like horses and pets.

A letter written by Ira Ingram to his uncle, Roswell Ingram, in Michigan, dated January 9, 1835, told something of the "pot of gold" that awaited cotton farmers. He boasted (but backed the brag with figures):

> The prosperity of our country the past year, while it rewards the cultivator abundantly, challenges a comparison with any country whatever. . . . many have sold cotton at 14$\frac{1}{2}$ cents per lb. At this price the labor of a hand may fairly estimate at $400 (per acre, per year). One of my friends who works about ten hands, sold his crop for $4,500. . . . Land that sold for $1 per acre, has lately been sold for $3 or $4 per acre. Slaves sold from $500 to as high as $1,500. Once a planter had 20, 50 or 100 slaves paid for, all he had to worry about were boll worms and getting the money to the bank.[57]

Success stories of this nature were leaving Texas like a riptide, and the results could be seen daily with the increasing tide of immigrants. This especially became true after San Jacinto, and finally with the end of the Mexican War.

From the landing of the first settlers at Matagorda, a special emphasis was placed on education and the cultural adjuncts of life. School, churches, theater, and social graces were at the core of Matagorda pioneer life. Actually, Matagorda was the center of social life in the area. A live theater was established as early as 1838, and by 1840 the Matagorda Thespians were in full bloom. The Colorado House was Matagorda's finest hotel, boasting fourteen private guest rooms. Gen. Andrew Jackson registered at the hotel on Sunday, May 3, 1857.

So, as the planters from the East arrived with their stained-glass doors and fine china, they quickly elected to live in the city of Matagorda and let the plantation work be carried on somewhere out on Bay Prairie. A gentleman farmer had only to ride out occasionally to check on the progress of work if he had good overseers.[58]

Real estate records and early stories reveal that these plantation people usually built large two-story houses with a wide front veranda. Each house faced the bay, since the cool, prevailing breeze made the city especially attractive. Most houses also had a back veranda extending along the ell of the house that probably contained the kitchen and dining room. Since every plantation had a host of skilled workers, most city homes had an assortment of outhouses that included a second kitchen, cooler room, smoke house, privy, and anything else that was needed. Most lumber came directly from saw mills in Florida.

When Wightman laid out Matagorda, he left plenty of room for homes of this type along the broad streets. Early in the growth of the city the abundance of oyster shell was put to good use in paving most of the streets in town.

Many of these plantation-type homes were presided over by the beautiful ladies of the house, affectionately known as Matagorda belles. Most of the homes had broad halls that reached to the back of the house with a stair that ascended to the second floor. There was usually a parlor, or library, off the hall, and Mama's Room. Young ladies usually had bedrooms upstairs, while the young males in the household were apt to have a bedroom apart in the rear of the house. Often the second floor was enhanced with dormer windows.

No doubt gracious living in the fashion of the Old South was

CHRIST EPISCOPAL CHURCH was established in 1839. Caleb Ives arrived December 12, 1838, and held communion on Christmas Day for eight men and women in the school house. Ives not only ministered to the church but also opened a school on January 24, 1839. The sketches of the Episcopal church, courthouse, and the Colorado House were made by a German artist, Helmuth Holtz, from memory after he had visited the frontier port in the early 1850s. Galen Hodges used the lithograph on his letterhead, despite the fact that the artist had misspelled the hotel's name [Colonado]. (Photo courtesy of Matagorda County Historical Commission)

carried on in the ante-bellum days in Matagorda. Truly, it had its day in glory.[59]

Matagorda's early settlers were deeply religious. This is evidenced by the fact that Mary Wightman organized a Sunday school shortly after arriving in the winter of 1837. Organized church services started soon after San Jacinto and the end of Catholicism as a state religion.

In 1838 a group of the Protestants, who had been meeting regularly, petitioned for aid in establishing an Episcopal church in Matagorda. Reverend Caleb S. Ives of the diocese of New York was selected and sent to Matagorda, arriving on December 12, and on Christmas Day holy communion was administered to eight men and women. The Matagorda Parish of Christ's Church was organized February 27, 1839 — the first and only Protestant Episcopal church in the Republic of Texas. Services were held in the Masonic Hall until the first church was opened Easter Sunday of 1841. This, the first Christ Church in Texas, was destroyed in the hurricane of 1854. It was quickly rebuilt under the direction of Rector Stephen R. Wright. Through the years, the work of Christ Church has been recognized worldwide.

Methodists got started about the same time as Christ Church. Jesse Hord was appointed as itinerant preacher in January 1839. His circuit included Matagorda. Reverend Isaack Strickland's circuit included Fayette County all the way to Matagorda; later, Robert Hill was assigned to the circuit. Reverend Homer Thrall began his career as a Matagorda circuit rider in 1840. The name of John Wesley DeVilbiss appears on a circuit that extended from Fayette County to Matagorda.

A public report lists churches in Matagorda in 1851 as being Episcopal, Methodist, and Baptist Sunday School. Baptists in Matagorda date back to T. J. Pilgrim, who came with Wightman's first group of settlers. Despite the fact that he settled in San Felipe, he was active in Baptist church work at Matagorda. Throughout the city's long history, constant mention is found about its representation in the Southern Baptist Convention.[60]

Education was on the minds of Wightman and his followers when they came ashore in 1829 to found Matagorda. Within a few weeks school was being held in the fort and soon had its own log cabin, with Josiah Pugh Wilbarger as the teacher, assisted by Mrs. Elias R. Wightman. Not much is known about schooling for the next several years. However, when General Almonte issued his report on Texas in 1835 he failed to list a school in Matagorda. In the issue of the Matagorda *Bulletin* for May of 1838, there is a notice signed by Henry M. Shaw stating that the Matagorda Academy would open for business. Tuition for reading, writing, and spelling was set at $15, with higher branches of English at $20. In 1839 Reverend C. S. Ives and his wife took over the schools, which remained for at least ten years.

As more and more people moved to Matagorda, there seemed to be a constantly changing menu of private schools. However, writers of the time point out that the rich planters sent most of their children back to their original homes in the East for their education, leaving public schools for the less affluent. However, ads for the colleges, schools, or academies promised impressive course offerings and instructors. Lafayette Academy during the late 1840s and 1850s seems to have been one of the leading institutions. Room and board was usually offered by the academy, or by nearby residents, in the range of $10 per month.

The Young Ladies School at Matagorda, with Mrs. Catherine Wright as the principal, ran an ad in the March 6, 1858, *Chronicle of the Times*. The school ran twenty-six weeks for a fee of $40 for the academic year. Advanced classes were $60; modern languages and piano and vocal classes were $50. Room and board, including washing, was $15 per month.

Public schools started making their appearances after the Education Act of 1854 set aside state land for school purposes. Matagorda County was divided into six school districts. The commissioners court minutes for May of 1854 list the boundaries and name S. W. Fisher, D. E. E. Braman, and J. H. Selkirk as the trustees from the Matagorda District. In the same year William Russu, assessor and collector of taxes in Matagorda County, noted that there were 290 free white children between the ages of six and sixteen. The State paid at the rate of $179.80 per student in 1854.

Early commissioners court records and newspapers of the day indicate that wealthy planters continued to send their children to private schools. In all probability education in Matagorda was a cut above the average even before the advent of the law of 1854, which started the foundation of public education.

Most public schools in Matagorda County appear to have been in the city of Matagorda. Court minutes of February 1861 reveal voting held in a schoolhouse at Palacios. A move was noted in the court proceedings in 1864 to realign the education districts in the county.

After the Civil War, public schools largely took over from private academies and seminaries. However, any type of growth in these days was slow due to lack of resources of all types.[61]

True to their Southern slant on life, men of Matagorda lined up to volunteer for service when the Civil War broke out. The young and the old, as well as farmers, ranchers, boatmen, and gentlemen, all answered the call. Courthouse records at Bay City tell that Dr. E. A. Peareson was authorized to form a company. Capt. John Rugeley, John W. McCamley, and Robert H. Williams were given the job of raising money to support this company.

One of Matagorda's active units, the Matagorda Coast Guards, reported for duty at a post in Arkansas and fell into vicious fighting within a short time. They were forced to surrender, but later part of the men got back into the battle. Most were killed before the end of the war.

Word came to Capt. Rugeley on December 31, 1863, that a force of Yanks planned on attacking Matagorda. All of the reservists volunteered to meet the enemy. Finally, a group of about forty-five embarked at night in Henry Cookenboo's sailboat, the *George Burkhart,* to meet the enemy. In the meantime a stiff blue norther had blown up, dropping the temperature below freezing. When the little boat was within about 200 yards of shore it capsized, spewing the men into the ice-flecked water. A total of twenty-two died and are buried in one large common grave in the Matagorda Cemetery. The names of the heroes are

> James Matthews, J. H. Jones, D. A. McKinley, A. D. Hines (bugler), George M. Bowie, J. M. Connor, J. N. Howell, N. M. Kennerly, A. J. May, J. B. Seaborn, B. H. Walton, Thomas E. McKinley, Tom Wadsworth, T. C. Secrest, J. G. Secrest, Henry Gibson, A. C. Johnson, James Rugeley, E. Duggan, E. Lake, Julius Shaw.[62]

Federals fired several cannonballs into Matagorda, but no troops came ashore in the county seat during the war. Federal troops who came ashore at Paso Cavallo pretty well controlled the entire bay. At one time a Union army marched down the peninsula and threatened the Confederate earthen fort at Caney. The only casualty was a defender who climbed on top of the earthen works to get a better look at the Yankee gunboats. A cannonball took his head. The site of the old fort is now at least one hundred yards seaward. Hurricanes, erosion, and relentless tides have taken their toll.[63]

Perhaps Matagorda has always been just a step away from being a great city. Visioned by its founders as the "Great Western Port City," Matagorda at times did reach pinnacles of near greatness, but never were its fathers able to harness outside political muscle with their rose-tinted dreams.

In the first decade of Matagorda's existence, a channel was cut across Dog Island and work was started to remove the raft from the Colorado. Without a doubt, if these two obstacles had been taken care of, dreams conjured up by Wightman and his followers would have turned Matagorda into a City of Gold.

But it was not to be. Looking at history through the small end of the telescope, the problems faced by Matagorda were too many: the ever-silting shallow channels of Dog Island; yellow fever in 1862; Mexican Army occupation following the Runaway Scrape; Civil War in the midst of an economic upswing; removal of the county seat (1894); and ravaging hurricanes (1854, 1875, 1886).

Even the coming of the railroad had little economic impact on the port city. The Cane Belt came to Matagorda in December of 1901, but by that time shipping patterns had already been established. Probably more tales can still be picked up today about the "Saturday Special" than any other feature of the rail line.

The Cane Belt Railroad Company, now the Gulf, Colorado and Santa Fe, was chartered March 4, 1898. It ran service into Matagorda six days per week, earning such endearing names as "Try Daily" or "Religious Line" (no trains on Sunday). The most popular run was on Saturday, when young folks from all up and down the line would pack the trains to enjoy the Saturday night dances in the old pavilion. Most of the guests would be booked into the Matagorda Hotel on the Bay, a huge hotel that served the vacation trade for a number of years.

Trains no longer run to Matagorda; however, the tracks are still in place. Who knows? Maybe, just maybe . . .

Linnville
Trader's Port City

Linnville was sacked and burned by the Comanche Indians on August 8, 1840. That fleeting moment earned this early Texas port a place on history's list of infamous deeds. But, actually, the old port city was a thriving center of commerce before and after the Indians put on their big show.

The Texas coast was developed by a hardy breed of men — traders who were out not only to make a dollar, but also driven by the spirit of adventure. This brought John Linn to Corpus Christi Bay in August of 1829 with a load of tobacco. He disposed of that cargo and immediately put together another shipload of trading merchandise, which met with official Mexican resistance on the Rio Grande River. The merchandise finally ended up in Matagorda Bay. Linn found the atmosphere for trading ripe in Victoria and soon had established himself as a respected businessman in that community. The spot where his ship unloaded in Matagorda Bay became Linn's port of entry for trading ships. Other traders also began using the facilities. All of this took place in 1830; by 1831, it is thought that Linn had warehouses and a wharf in operation at Linnville. The site of the port was roughly three to four miles north of the present city of Port Lavaca.

Linn never made his home in Linnville, as he soon became the last *alcalde* and then the first mayor of Victoria. However, as he grew as a trader and politician, so did Linnville grow as a trading port. Linn was also a man of action in the Texas Republic. He represented Victoria in the Consultation of 1835, fought in the Battle of Gonzales, and was quartermaster for the Texas army. He worked with Gen. Sam Houston at, and after, the Battle of San Jacinto. As a trader, he was ordered to provide retreating Mexican soldiers with supplies. When the Republic was formed, he served as a representative in the second and third congresses.

Shortly after Linn got Linnville in operation, and received his second shipload of merchandise, he made a deal with General Terán to supply his Mexican army troops with supplies. Terán had been commissioned to establish a fort on the Lavaca River and at that time had about 200 men, according to Linn. After the Battle of Velasco on June 26, 1832, and after the death of General Terán, who committed suicide by falling on his sword, the Mexican army began making plans to close the Lavaca fort. Captain Artiaga, base commander, prevailed on Linn to furnish the troops enough supplies to leave the area and take a check drawn on the Matamoras customshouse for payment. The master of Linnville never received payment for the goods, but he confided in friends that it was worth the loss to get rid of the Mexican troops.

Business was good enough at the young port that Linn purchased a copper-bottomed schooner called *The Opposition*. Capt. John Pierce delivered the first load of merchandise and set out for

Boat Bill No 6

Packages of goods unladen from
Brig Cruso & put on board
Lighter Tom Payne Nov 10th
1843. All sent to Public Store.

[W] 4 Bags Coffee (Damaged)
" 20 Bags Salt
" 9 Bales Domestic
" 15 Kegs Nails
" 5 Boxes Merchandize
" 5 Bbls Ditto
" 2 Half Bbls Mackerel
" 55 Bars or Pieces Iron
" 2 Bundles Shapes
" 12 Tea Kettles
" 36 Bake Pans
" 14 Covers
" 12 Spiders
" 22 Bake Pan Covers
" 42 Kettles

M 5 Bales Bagging
" 4 Coils Manilla Rope
" 25 Do Kentucky Ditto

S.W. 1 Bale Mer or Twine

J.A. 1 Box Merchandize
" 2 Trunks Baggage Examined

Augustus Storrs Inspector.

[W] It may be a mistake but
I make twelve pieces of
hollow ware more than
stated on this bill or on the
manifest. A. Storrs Inspector.

07-14

BRANDS OR MARKS were used in the early days to identify all merchandise. This manifest list was from the brig Cruso, *put aboard the lighter* Tom Payne *and sent to public storage at Matagorda on November 10, 1843. The merchandise was destined for Linnville and Cox's Point. Brands made it easy for dock hands to separate cargo. Albert Storms, the inspector, made a note of what he considered an error in the merchandise count.* (From the Texas State Archives)

New Orleans for another load. When the ship was six or seven days out of Paso Cavallo, a strong wind hit the vessel that was under full sail. It capsized before the sails could be lowered. The loss of the schooner was a blow to Linn's business, but he got new supplies and continued to serve the area.[1]

The fortunes of Linnville in the years immediately preceding the Texas War for Independence seemed to go up and down with the state of John Linn's political standing at the time. Linn had many friends, made while trading with Mexico and while serving as *alcalde* and mayor of Victoria. Therefore, when the shifting winds of Mexican politics favored Linn, business was good at Linnville. Linn was also a loyal Texan, as evidenced by his being an advisor to General Houston on trade affairs before and after San Jacinto. These tides all affected the growing port.

During the war, provisions and men destined for the Texas army came through Linnville. In a letter written by a soldier, James Johnstone, dated Linn's Landing, the tone was upbeat:

> Our army is well furnished with provisions. There are one hundred and fifty tons on hand in this place. There is, however, a great want of wagons and horses to convey the provisions to the army. . . . Tell all who intend to come, to come quickly. Gen. Houston has not yet arrived. He and Col. Harrison are expected daily.[2]

As the fortunes of war turned against the Texans, and Gen. José Urrea began his sweep up the coast as Santa Anna pursued Houston and the Texas army, the Texas coast was evacuated. Capt. J. J. Holzinger, Urrea's hatchet man, was sent to the coast to plunder Cox's Point, but upon arrival found that the Texas navy had gotten there first and destroyed the warehouses and stores. For some reason Holzinger made no move to destroy Linnville. This could have been the basis for the charge of treason leveled at Linn by Ira Ingram. S. R. Fisher, justice of the peace in Matagorda, after hearing the charges, sent Linn to General Houston in charge of a nominal guard. Upon arrival, just before the Battle of San Jacinto, Houston scoffed at the charges of disloyalty to Texas and immediately put Linn to work.[3]

After Texas became a republic, the growth of Linnville can be traced through the customs records in Matagorda Bay. In 1837, when the Matagorda District was created, Linnville was one of the shipping points noted in the records. A letter from George Collinsworth, head of the customs district, to Hugh O. Watts, deputy collector at Lavaca, marked Linnville as a growing port. As early as June of 1838 a move was underfoot to establish a Lavaca customs district because of the inconvenience of shipping goods to Matagorda prior to shipping them to Linnville and Texana. The separate district became a reality on January 23, 1839, and Watts was named the collector, with the right to name the new port of entry. He selected Linnville as the port of entry and in the following months the ships destined for Linnville increased dramatically.

In addition to Linn's warehouse, there was at least one other major warehouse at the port operated by William H. Watts and Hugh O. Watts. These brothers also operated a warehouse a short distance from Linnville. Notes in early writings about this period indicate that several stores were started in the community in the mid to late 1830s. W. G. Ewing was one of the merchants. His sister was Mrs. H. O. Watts. No mention of a church or school is found in early records; however, Z. N. Morrell, who is credited with establishing the first Baptist church in Texas, preached in Linnville and Lavaca.[4]

Growth of Linnville can be measured by the number of boats that called at the port during the next several months. The days of growth and tranquility were doomed to be limited.

On August 8, 1840, a war party of Comanche Indians, thought to number as many as a thousand, appeared just after sunrise at Linnville. The settlers had worked out a plan to follow in case of an Indian attack and immediately put it into action. The plan called for everyone to run to the shore and take small boats out to a lighter that was anchored nearby. Just as it appeared that everyone would be safe, Mrs. Watts remembered a cherished keepsake that she was determined to retrieve. Her husband accompanied her back to their home, but by that time the Indians were everywhere. Watts was killed and Mrs. Watts was taken prisoner. John Linn gives a good description of the scene.

> While the Indians were cutting up fantastic antics before high heaven, in Linnville, the refugees on the schooner were the spectators, and witnessed with whatever feelings they could command the wanton destruction of their property. Judge John Hayes, however, became so exasperated that he vowed he would have one shot at the "red Devils" any way. So, grabbing a gun, the judge jumped overboard — the water was not over three or four feet deep — and waded to the shore, where, gun in hand, he stood upon the beach anxiously waiting for a Comanche to come within range. But the Indians imagined the judge was a "big

medicine," and so steered clear of the awful fate in for him who should invite the judge's fire. Finally the earnest petitions of his friends on the boat availed and the judge returned to them. Now, upon examining the old "fusee" which threatened so lately to consummate such slaughter, it was discovered that *the piece was not loaded!*

In my warehouse were several cases of hats and umbrellas belonging to Mr. James Robinson, a merchant of San Antonio. These the Indians made free with, and went dashing about the blazing village, amid their screeching squaws and "little Injuns," like demons in a drunken saturnalia, with Robinson's hats on their heads and Robinson's umbrellas bobbing about on every side like tipsy young balloons.[5]

The Indians were punished in the Battle of Plum Creek. Mrs. Watts was rescued after being shot in the breast by an arrow. Her steel corset kept the arrow from killing her. Mrs. Crosby, who was captured near Victoria, did not have a corset to protect her and was killed a few minutes before her husband and rescue arrived.

Oral tradition tells the tale that Linnville was burned to the ground and never recovered. Old records prove these hand-me-down tales to be not quite accurate.

On August 21, 1840, William H. Watts, who was the deputy collector and brother of Hugh O. Watts, was appointed collector of the Lavaca District. The office was moved two miles below the site of Linnville, where the Watts brothers owned a two-story warehouse. Richard West replaced William Watts on February 24, 1841.

On April 16, 1841, Thomas M. Duke, collector of the Calhoun Customs District, of which Linnville was a port of call, received a letter from George Earlee, Elijah Bennett, and Oren Prescott — all citizens of Linnville. They offered to build a customshouse at any point on Matagorda or Lavaca bays for $2,500 in par money in New Orleans or $15,000 in Texas treasury notes.

In July and September of 1841, three material bills were paid for a customshouse in Linnville. The first was for $222.50, for part of a lumber order; the second was for $2,080; and the final was for $193.44. A. John Burton was listed as the builder. No exact location of the building was given; however, a sketch in the State Archives is clearly labeled as the Linnville customshouse. In 1845 a receipt was issued for twelve chairs for the Linnville customshouse.

Without a doubt the customshouse at Linnville was built. Whether or not it was rebuilt at the old location, or at the location of the Watts brothers' two-story warehouse, is unknown. It is possible that it was built at a spot close to old Linnville, but not the old location, since records indicate a silting problem at old Linnville.

From the time the District of Lavaca was formed on January 23, 1839, until the Lavaca and Matagorda districts were combined into the Calhoun District, a lot of overlapping occurred. In June of 1841 some merchandise destined to Linnville was still coming through Matagorda; however, most of the goods headed for Linnville were being cleared through Port Cavallo, the port of entry for Calhoun District.

Records show that customshouses were built in Matagorda, Lavaca, Linnville, and Port Cavallo during 1841. Arrivals at the Port of Linnville were listed primarily through Port Cavallo in the April to December reports of 1841. Shippers out of Linnville during this period included James Ross, ComGame, August Stories, C. L. Owen, William G. Ewing, Cornelius Lane, Thomas J. Walton, Ferguson & Smith, John M. Smith, and Richard West. Hayes Linn was a deputy collector at Linnville during this period.

Exports out of Linnville included cotton, beef hides, deer hides, wool, and pecans. Some of the prices placed on the exports were as follows: 349 bags of pecans, $783; dried hides, $25; 26 bales of cotton, $1,040. Customs records are not present for most of the years 1842 and 1843. However, records of shipments into and out of Linnville are recorded in 1844 and 1845.[6]

Just when did the port of Linnville go out of business? A good guess would be that by the mid-1840s Lavaca was growing and Indianola was booming. With competition like that, Linnville probably withered on the vine. Merchants moved to other locations and homeowners went where schools and churches were available.

The Comanche Indians put the spotlight of the state and nation on Linnville, but in the end it was competition from other ports, not the Indians, which wrote its epitaph.

Cox's Point / Dimmitt's Landing

Philip Dimmitt came to Texas in 1822 from Kentucky. In 1828 he married Maria Luisa Laso and became a naturalized citizen. In 1829 he petitioned for a league of land as head of a family, and an additional one-fourth league because of his Mexican wife. He received title to the land on the east side of Lavaca Bay. Since he was a trader, he established a landing near the mouth of the Lavaca

River and built a warehouse at the site. His warehouse was used to receive supplies destined for the Texas army.

On February 15, 1836, there was a public storekeeper at Dimmitt's Landing. The port was still in use in 1838, as evidenced by an entry in Texas customs records showing where O. Balfour was paid $210 for three months of service as a clerk in the customshouse at the Port of Dimmitt. Goods destined for Dimmitt's Landing were cleared in the beginning through the customshouse at Matagorda. When the Lavaca District was formed, the port of entry was Linnville. Later the Calhoun District was formed to cover all of Matagorda Bay.

Dimmitt's Landing was identified in 1840 and 1842 by early writers like George Bonnell. William Kennedy in 1841 listed Dimmitt's Landing as one of the new towns on Lavaca Bay.

Sometime around 1840, Dimmitt opened a trading post on Nueces Bay and evidently devoted most of his energies toward this new project. He also landed merchandise at Black Point on Copano Bay during the same period. Dimmitt's Landing seems to have faded as the city of Lavaca began to grow. The death of Dimmitt in Mexico in the summer of 1841 no doubt hastened the end of the port.[1]

Cox's Point was located east of the mouth of Lavaca River on a small neck of water still known as Cox's Bay. Like Dimmitt's Landing, this port also came into existence shortly before the days of the Texas Republic. Thomas Cox, a hero of the Battle of San Jacinto, is listed as a resident of Cox's Point, and oral tradition credits him with having founded the port. Sometime in 1834 or 1835, a wharf and warehouse were constructed there.

In December of 1835 Gen. Sam Houston sent out a general notice advising all volunteers to land at Copano, Cox's Point, or Matagorda. As the fortunes of war changed, Houston began to issue orders for supplies to be diverted to Dimmitt's Landing or Cox's Point. In March of 1836 Houston ordered Col. James Fannin to proceed to these two ports to secure the landing of supplies and men. Fannin never carried out this order.

Supplies did start coming into Matagorda Bay. On February 14, 1836, the *Caroline* discharged cargo at Cox's Point and Dimmitt's Landing; however, very little of the provisions found their way to Colonel Fannin. Numerous mentions are made in both the *Southwest Historical Quarterly* and in *Jenkins' Papers* about supplies for the Texas army being stockpiled at Dimmitt's Landing and Cox's

Point. A letter from John S. Rutland to Capt. John W. Moore outlined the difficulties of securing wagons in the area for transporting
the goods into the interior. He even indicated that the supplies
should be moved up the Lavaca River to Santa Anna (name
changed later to Texana).[2]

Unlike other port cities that just faded away, Cox's Point holds
the dubious honor of having been blasted off of Lavaca Bay by the
Texas navy. Oral tradition tells the story that the navy had orders
to destroy the port's facilities just before the Runaway Scrape, in
order that the Mexicans could not use them.

Alcoa Aluminum now occupies the site of Cox's Point.

Lavaca
(Port Lavaca)

The early roots of Lavaca (Port Lavaca was called Lavaca
until the 1840s) were planted around 1815, when traders and the
Mexican government used landings in the area to unload supplies
destined for the interior.[1]

As early as 1832, citizens from the Lavaca settlements took part
in a meeting held in the home of William Menefee on the Navidad
River as part of a discussion of the rights guaranteed to the colonists
by the Mexican Republic. The communique was signed by the citizens of Lavaca and Navidad settlements.[2] Evidently, settlers had
worked their way down the Lavaca River in the early 1830s to establish homesteads along the river and reached Lavaca Bay.

The area in the vicinity of the Lavaca River was in an un-
claimed area. Empresario de León claimed the coastal lands on
Lavaca Bay to a point one league above the crossing of the Atas-
cosito Road, sometimes called the old La Bahía Road, then in a
straight line to a point on the Guadalupe River. However, there
were thirty-one settlers in the Lavaca area when Commissioner
José Antonio Navarro arrived in 1831 to issue land titles. Empresario DeWitt commissioned James Kerr to survey the area on January 6, 1826. On July 26 DeWitt arrived at the mouth of the Lavaca with several families and established the Lavaca Station (now
Leonardo Mauso's ranch, twenty-one miles up the Lavaca River).[3]

This evidently marked the establishment of a settlement up
the Lavaca River that was later used by the Mexican government
as a post when they beefed up their forces in Texas in 1831. General

TEXAS NAVY — *Small in number, the ships of the Texas navy played an important part in the struggle with Mexico, during and after the Battle of San Jacinto. Among the ships were the* Independence, *skippered by Commodore Hawkins; the* Brutus, *under the command of W. W. Hurd (merchant captain); the* Liberty, *under Capt. W. S. Brown; and the* Invincible, *an ex-slaver, guided by Capt. Jeremiah Brown. The Texas navy kept supplies from reaching Gen. Antonio López de Santa Anna and sent captured ships and their supplies to bolster Gen. Sam Houston. After San Jacinto, the little navy staved off an invasion of Texas by sea. Samuel Rhoads Fisher was appointed by Houston to the cabinet post of secretary of the navy, headquartered at the port of Matagorda.*

Mier y Terán was in charge of increasing the troops at Bexar, La Bahía, and Nacogdoches. Garrisons were established on the Brazos, at the head of Galveston Bay, on the Neches and the Lavaca. These establishments surrounded the settlements and guarded all approaches to them. Their object was to prevent violation of the law through the entrance of unauthorized immigration from the United States and to control smuggling through Texas ports to the interior states of Mexico.[4] By this time, there were approximately 1,000 Mexican troops in the Department of Texas.[5]

Was there a connection between the landing on the bay called Lavaca and the landing twenty-one miles up the Lavaca River, also called Lavaca? It appears that the same people were involved in the use of both landings. Once the Mexican troops were pulled out, the reference to the landing up the river does not appear again in early records; however, early traders like John Linn make numerous mentions of Lavaca as a landing.

In his book *Fifty Years in Texas*, Linn describes his early business:

> On my second trip to Texas [the first was to Corpus Christi Bay] I had purchased a fine schooner called the *Opposition*. She was coppered [bottom] and put up in the best possible manner. I landed my cargo in Lavaca Bay and carted the effects to Victoria. Shortly afterwards I sent the vessel back to New Orleans for other goods that I had contracted for, and she returned in good time.[6]

In 1831 Linn established his own port known as Linnville just a few miles up the bay from Lavaca. He listed 140 lots for taxation in 1840; however, the plat in existence now shows only about ten lots abutting the bay.

Just exactly when the first port facilities were built at Lavaca remains lost in the past. But as the people of Texas geared up for the coming War for Independence, it appears that a community had begun to jell at Lavaca amid the swirl of military operations. On January 27, 1835, the Mexican military chief ordered a detachment of troops to Matagorda and Lavaca to prevent smuggling which was going on in great volume.[7] As the fortunes of war waffled back and forth, Col. James Fannin in February of 1836 decided to withdraw to Goliad and look to Lavaca, instead of Copano, as his port. Fannin concluded that Aransas Pass was unsafe.[8] It was during this period that the ports of Cox's Point and Lavaca were confused several times. On February 14, 1836, in an official Texas army dispatch, it was noted that the "cargo of the schooner *Caroline* was landed at Cox's Point (now Port Lavaca) and another cargo which followed was discharged at Cox's Point and Dimmitt's Landing. None has reached Col. Fannin in larger quantities than an overnight supply." [9] On March 17, 1836, Gen. Sam Houston ordered Colonel Fannin to take a position at Lavaca to protect supplies at Cox's Point and Dimmitt's Landing.[10]

Very little information is available about activities in Lavaca Bay during the 1835–36 period. One bit of information comes from an early traveler, Gideon Lincecum, in 1835. He wrote:

> The pass into Matagorda Bay has 7 feet of water. The La Vacca bay, which is the western arm of Matagorda Bay, has a pass of 8 to 10 feet. The greater portion of the vessels make their landing at Cox's Point up the Labvacca of late, as being more safe than any of the other landing places. . . . There are many more new towns rising at different points in Texas, all of a very late date. One, 15 miles north of Coxes Point on the Nevidad, is called Santa Anna in honor of the Mexican general. The name of the port was changed to Texana.[11]

Another bit comes from the memories of George Washington Trahern, who moved to Texas when he was fourteen, settling first at Texana and then moving to Lavaca. He described life in Lavaca:

> At that time, you know, Texas was in war with Mexico and we were all minute men. Every man kept his gun and horse — man and boy — that could carry a gun did. We had to fight Mexicans and Indians; any minute [we] might be called out, and would all rendezvous at a certain place and start out and fight Indians or Mexicans or whatever it was.[12]

No doubt any settlers who made Lavaca their home as early as 1835 joined other Texans in the area when they fled their homes after the fall of the Alamo on March 6, 1836. After the Alamo fell, General Santa Anna started his march toward East Texas in pursuit of Gen. Sam Houston and the Texan army. During the great Runaway Scrape, families abandoned everything that they owned to flee ahead of the advancing Mexican army. After the defeat of Santa Anna at San Jacinto on April 21, 1836, and the retreat of General Urrea down the coast shortly thereafter, people slowly started returning to their homes. It is thought that during the next few years a number of homes were built at Lavaca and at least one wharf was built out into the bay to make loading and unloading ships easier.

With the destruction of Linnville on August 8, 1840, it appears that John Linn and other traders chose not to rebuild their city and instead moved their trading operations to Lavaca. There is also evidence that some of the traders who operated at Linnville also had interests in Lavaca, making it a logical transfer.

In this same time frame the State of Texas recognized the need to establish a control of shipping in and out of the ports along the coast. An act was passed on June 12, 1837, setting up a system of customs districts. The Matagorda District was created, commencing at the mouth of the San Antonio River and following the coast eastward to the mouth of Cedar Lake.[13] George Collinsworth was appointed the head of the district, with his office at Matagorda.[14] A deputy collector in the region of Lavaca Bay was authorized, and Hugh O. Watts was appointed. He was assisted in his work by inspectors, or boarding officers, who would be sent by the collector to discharge the goods at the port of landing. Alexander McDonald and Philip Dimmitt were two of these officers. D. G. Williamson was a boarding officer who was stationed at Paso de Cavallo.[15]

Due to Matagorda's location at the extreme end of Matagorda Bay, an attempt was made in 1838 to establish Lavaca as a separate port of entry; however, the bill did not pass the Texas Senate.[16] On January 23, 1839, the separate districts of Lavaca and Matagorda were created by Congress. Lavaca took in the coastal region surrounding Lavaca Bay. Hugh O. Watts was confirmed as the collector of the new district of Lavaca, and he selected Linnville as the port of entry for his district.[17] The office remained there until Linnville was sacked by the Comanches on August 8, 1840, and Watts was killed.

William H. Watts, brother of Hugh O., was confirmed for the job by the Senate on December 24, 1840. The office moved two miles down the bay, perhaps to Lavaca, where the Watts brothers owned a warehouse. However, on July 24, September 6, and September 24, 1841, bills in the amount of $222.50, $2,080.00, and $193.44 were approved for a customshouse at Linnville, with A. J. Burton as the builder.[18] Since the bills were paid it is assumed that the new customs building was built; no records indicate whether the new customshouse was at Lavaca or at a point just below Linnville.

On January 21, 1841, the districts of Matagorda and Lavaca were abolished and a new district called Calhoun, with the same boundaries as the original Matagorda District, was formed. Port

Cavallo on the pass was named port of entry, with customshouses to be retained at Matagorda and Linnville.[19]

Mist has a way of settling on Lavaca Bay that completely blocks out landmarks that are only a few yards distant. Such a mist lies over the closing of the port of Linnville and the start of business at Lavaca. Records in the State Archives show that the office at Linnville was operating until at least December of 1841, with the schooners *Henry* (three times), *Maria,* and *Callas* arriving.

It is not clear where the District of Lavaca customshouse was at this point. During the same period, records show baggage entries at Port Lavaca. People entering Port Lavaca with their baggage included Franz Riemer, G. W. Garnett, Aug. Herrlich, Jas. Vanhopper, Hiram Fisher, Geo. Wilson, R. H. Hines, Wm. Patterson, Joseph A. Clark, Chancy Johnson, John Tibble, Thomas McConnell, Samuel Hace, Margory McCraft, T. K. Clark, Erastus Clark, James C. Henry, Abram Baker, David W. Muligan, G. Stephen Ryan, William Ryan, Wm. Duryen, E. L. Peck, S. A. Dennis, Benjamin I. Hannis, J. M. Baker, E. B. Nichol, Bryan Callagham, I. B. Tuck, and I. M. McClean.[20]

An earlier passenger list in 1838 for the schooner *Sarah Hughes* showed eight passengers coming ashore on Christmas Day. The *Champion* checked in at Lavaca on December 28, 1839, landing seventeen passengers, including the Spears family and H. O. Watts. The Ashby family landed, bringing their farming equipment. In 1839 the brig *Sam Houston* and the schooners *Amazon, Henry, Maria* and *Martha* brought the following new residents: Boyles, McDonald, Gallagher, Walker, Lane, Dale, Hall, Blair, Klatche, Hughes, Guilbeau, Monod, Radaz, Brown, Noble, Stern, Beck, and James. It is difficult sometimes to determine, from the existing customs records, whether the ships were destined to the Lavaca District, which included Linnville, or to the Port of Lavaca.[21]

Tucked away in the customs records at the State Archives is a rough drawing of a warehouse in Port Lavaca. The drawing, signed by William G. Ewing, a customs office clerk during the early 1840s, shows a building 25 by 60 feet with a pier extending 300 yards into the bay. Unfortunately, there is no date on the sketch. Was the building built? Was the old Port of Lavaca being called Port Lavaca in 1840? From all evidence it appears that Port Lavaca, or at least the Port of Lavaca, was the name used for the new community and that by the mid-1840s it was being officially called Port Lavaca.

By 1844 all customs records were made out to Port Lavaca and a thriving business was apparently being carried on in the young port city. A note in the customs records on November 22, 1844, showed the presence of a public storage at Port Lavaca. Goods received for storage from the schooner *Maria* consisted of 15 boxes soap, 1 bag coffee, 21 bbls. potatoes, 1 can putty, 2 boxes glass, 2 doors, 2 doz. brooms, 3 cases rifles, etc. On February 24, 1845, Ruben M. Potter, comptroller of customs at Port Lavaca, reported $3,599.90 collected for duties during November of 1844. James Hunter was the deputy customs collector stationed at Port Lavaca in 1845. Rent receipts for the Port Lavaca customshouse were made out for $15 per month. Repairs on the customshouse were noted at $52.92.[22]

With all of the growth taking place in Port Lavaca, some type of organization must have been present. Early records indicate that Capt. John M. Smith laid out the town in 1842. The Upshur map of Port Lavaca in 1842 shows that provisions were made for a church, a cemetery, a public square, and a two-block market place. The map shows the town running eight blocks along the waterfront and extending back ten blocks. Commerce Street, near the water, was very wide. Even before the town was laid out, Ranger Cemetery was being used. One of its occupants was H. Oram Watts, who was killed by the Comanches at Linnville in 1840.

Records on early port activities at Lavaca are meager, consisting mainly of local hand-me-down stories and records in the State Archives dealing with customs activities. These two do not always agree. Cotton was one of the biggest exports and it is thought that the first cotton left Lavaca in 1839. Records show that during the period from March 31, 1839 until January 31, 1846 that a total of 1,110 bales of cotton were shipped from the port of Lavaca. While this seems like a small amount, it must be remembered that a single cotton gin could handle only about 200 bales per year. This is probably an accurate check, since the rich agricultural area around Green Lake which was to help develop Port Lavaca was not settled until 1844–45. An early account of Calhoun County in 1846 is given by Mrs. J. M. Cockran:

> Lavaca, although it had only six residences, two of them hotels, was the seaport for all that part of the state and San Antonio de Bexar. All the goods which were brought from New Orleans, came in sailing vessels to Lavaca and thence were carried on Mexican carts to the interior towns. The trade with Mexico was carried on in the same way to San Antonio and proved so remu-

nerative that the wealthy merchants of that place had long trains of carts on the road constantly to and from Lavaca. . . .

Not long after we went to Lavaca, the Mexican War began and Lavaca became the landing place for General Worth's corps on their way to the Rio Grande Valley.

When the settlers of Green Lake first arrived in Calhoun County, Lavaca was a flourishing town, according to an account by historian James Hatch. Boats were loaded and unloaded by shallow draft lighters and it soon became apparent that a wharf to deeper water was a necessity. The planters of Green Lake and the merchants of Lavaca pooled together in order to construct such a wharf. The merchants furnished the lumber and material and planters furnished the slave labor necessary to build such a wharf.[23]

This would indicate that the first major wharf was built at Port Lavaca in 1846 or 1847. Since troops destined for Gen. Zachary Taylor's army came through the city, it is likely that the wharf was built in the hopes that the U.S. Army would pick Port Lavaca as a permanent military depot. After extensive investigation, Indianola was designated as the gulf coast military depot in 1849. Gen. W. J. Worth, who lived in Port Lavaca for a short time after landing there with his troops, had a hand in the selection of a port on Matagorda Bay. Corpus Christi campaigned hard for the designation.[24] No doubt one or more smaller piers were constructed at Lavaca much earlier than this.

Cotton was the largest export, selling in the range of ten to fifteen cents per pound. Fresh, salted cattle hides, the next important product, brought about six cents per pound. Animal skins of all sorts brought from ten to twenty-five cents, with buffalo robes going for as much as $2. Pecans were present in the export lists, bringing from three to seven cents per pound. Miscellaneous items included: moss, two cents per barrel; tallow, $5 per barrel; cotton seed, $1 per bushel; wool, seven cents a pound; wild rye seed, $2 bushel; mesquite grass seed, $6 barrel; beeswax, twenty-five cents pound. Customs records indicate that the bulk of the exports went to New Orleans, some to Mobile, Alabama, with a few ships going as far as New York.[25]

With the population of the Lavaca Bay area growing steadily, a move was mounted to create a new county for the region. When the first legislature after annexation met on April 3, 1846, a commission was named to create a new county — Calhoun. Addison White, Henry Kitchens, H. Beck, James Cummins, and Thomas

Duke went to work and carved a new county out of Victoria, Jackson, and Matagorda counties and named Lavaca as the county seat.[26] The first meeting of the newly commissioned members of the Calhoun County government was held on September 22, 1846, in the home of H. C. Kitchens in Lavaca. Members of the new county government were: Theodore Miller, chief justice; Sylvanus Hatch and Hermann Telapapa, commissioners; Isaac Brugh, county clerk; Joshua H. Davis, district clerk; Richard West, sheriff; A. Hamilton Cook, justice of the peace; Hiram G. H. Davis, constable. Later, Samuel T. Watts was named assessor-collector and Timothy R. Threlkeld became treasurer.[27]

When the population shifted away from Port Lavaca, a movement developed to remove the county seat to Indianola. The drive was successful in 1852. The county seat remained at Indianola until after the storm of 1886, then returned to Port Lavaca.[28]

During the early 1840s Port Lavaca grew into a prosperous port with a number of trading and forwarding companies making their headquarters in the city. Coastal schooners docked at the seven wharves daily. The continued growth of the city seemed assured when in 1847 the New Orleans-based Harris and Morgan Steamship Line opened offices in Port Lavaca. The largest shipper in the gulf coast waters, Harris and Morgan had a range of vessels from the bay schooner type to the large steamships that sailed into the bay on a regular basis. The port was busy with carts and wagon trains leaving daily for the interior. Trade was excellent. Raw materials from South Texas and Mexico were loaded on boats at Lavaca, and supplies that were arriving from the United States increased as more and more ships docked.

Faced with the high cost of recent improvements to their port, officials at Lavaca made a fatal mistake in 1849 when they drastically increased the dockage fees. The management of the Harris and Morgan Steamship Line reacted quickly. They took advantage of depth soundings that they made over the entire bay several years previously and built their own warehouse and wharf, reaching a half mile into the bay from a spot about three miles below Indianola on Powderhorn Bayou. A new city, Indian Point, came into being. A customshouse was already located at Powderhorn Bayou.[29]

Lavaca's trade dominance did not vanish overnight. The turning point came when a great number of Lavaca merchants, shippers, tradesmen, and home owners began to move to the booming Indianola. Then a gale struck the bay in 1851, venting its most de-

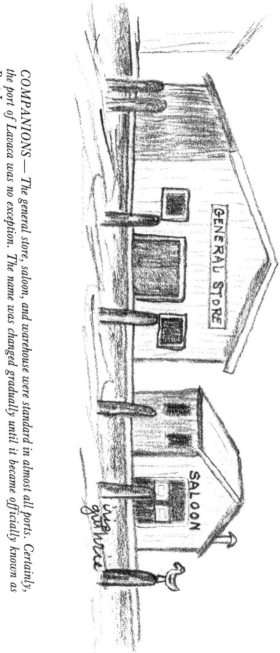

COMPANIONS — *The general store, saloon, and warehouse were standard in almost all ports. Certainly, the port of Lavaca was no exception. The name was changed gradually until it became officially known as Port Lavaca.*

structive force on Port Lavaca. Every wharf in the place was carried away by the fury of the storm. The large storehouse belonging to Mrs. Ross and several other buildings were blown down.[30]

The rift between the merchants in Lavaca and Harris and Morgan became tenuous when several of the company's larger ships were damaged while trying to approach the docks at Port Lavaca. Merchants of Lavaca insisted that the captains were at fault and that there was plenty of depth over the bar. The first captain to damage his ship was fired and the second met the same fate when he too went aground. As a result, Harris and Morgan pulled their larger vessels out of the Port Lavaca trade and sent in smaller ships with less draft. The smaller lighters caused higher expense to Port Lavaca merchants, thus putting them at a disadvantage against their competitors at Indianola. Lavaca suffered more when Victor Bracht published a *History of Texas* that dealt with the bays up and down the coast. He pointed out: "The bay, called Lavaca Inlet, is found a quite difficult channel, with less water than the one at Indian Point." Those fighting words added fuel to the bitter fight.[31]

Port Lavaca did not turn over and die without a fight. The damage done by the 1851 storm was repaired and the merchants who were left actively pursued customers. In 1856, after years of anticipation, the San Antonio & Mexican Gulf Railroad finally started work on the line from Port Lavaca to Victoria, with five miles built by 1858. Although the line was not complete, it had an impact on Port Lavaca's business. The state engineer, in his report, had this to say:

> The remarkable fact may be stated that this five miles of road, terminating in the open prairie at a point remote from any settlement or public highway, has not only been of vast service to the people of Texas, but has actually overpaid running expenses. I witnessed myself the tremendous business it was doing; the noise and bustle; the hundreds of wagons and teams and teamsters drawn to its present terminus or station in the prairie.[32]

Unfortunately, the road was not completed until 1861, at a time when the cloud of the Civil War cast its shadow over all business. In the meantime, Port Lavaca was pictured as fighting back. Jacob De Cordova, writing in 1858, had kind things to say about Lavaca in its trade battle with Indianola. He pointed out that "teamsters can save 12 miles of bad road in rainy weather by stopping at Lavaca." In 1852 the *Indianola Bulletin* claimed that 12,000 bales of cotton were shipped from Port Lavaca and Indianola that year. Knowing that the large plantations and gins were closer to Lavaca, it is likely that a substantial part of this cotton went out of Port Lavaca.[33]

Port Lavaca had several newspapers to espouse their cause during this period. H. Beaumont brought out the *Lavaca Journal* in the summer of 1847. One of the few remaining copies reported that David Foster and E. Donaldson opened a ferry across the Guadalupe River on a direct route from Lavaca to Goliad and San Antonio, reducing the distance by twenty miles. In 1848 the *Journal* entered into the war of the two cities with an editorial that was critical of several of Indian Point's outstanding merchants and leaders, accusing them of misrepresenting facts about Lavaca. His motto on the masthead read "Come and Take One." The *Journal* faded, and W. Ogden bought out the *Commercial* in 1850. Practically one entire issue of the paper was devoted to Governor Bell's message, which the editor characterized as "well-written, able and statesmanlike." The *Lavaca Herald* made its appearance in 1855 under the guidance of James C. Rowan. On April 3, 1857, he reported: "The Poindexter Ice Co. will have a good supply of ice all summer. Neighboring towns can depend on it." The ice was cut in New England in the winter, packed in sawdust and shipped by boat to Texas, where it was stored in double-wall, wooden houses with sawdust in between the walls. The *Port Lavacan* came out from 1892 to 1900, and the *Calhoun Citizen* served for several years until 1970. The *Port Lavaca Wave* is nearing its 100th anniversary.[34]

Before the Civil War, newspapers in Port Lavaca and Indianola devoted much space to promoting their town and castigating the opponents. It was not uncommon for one of the papers to headline a yellow fever or cholera epidemic in the opposing city, warning their readers to stay out of the town. However, credit should go to the *Indianola Bulletin* and editor John Brown for promoting the Indianola Proposal, which espoused cooperation between the rival towns — "As long as we are divided into small rival towns, no one place can furnish proper facility." [35] Nothing ever came of the campaign.

Traces of schools in the early days of Lavaca are nonexistent. In about 1846, after the arrival of Presbyterian minister Stephen Frederick Cocke, a movement was started to raise money for a building to be used for school purposes, except on Sunday when it would be used for church. A list of thirty-four pledges to this enterprise is filed in the Calhoun County clerk's office. Names on the list include Edwin Belden, Samuel A. White, Edward Clegg, Henry C. Kitchen, William G. Ewing, George Parr, James Ross, Cesar Monod, Timothy Threlkeld, Franklin Beaumont, John D. Brower, Thomas Haynes, Col. J. H. Davis, and Dr. Willaim Dallam. The building was built on a lot donated by Hamlett Ferguson. The church-school was located on a lot now occupied by the courthouse annex, library, and old jail. In 1854 the county school system was organized and the county divided into four precincts, Lavaca being in the first. A building for all grades was built in 1897 on a lot where Stanley's Store is now located on Main Street.[36]

Without a doubt the people, especially the merchants, of Port Lavaca did not have time for the Civil War. Economic conditions were on the upswing. The San Antonio & Mexican Gulf Railroad from Port Lavaca to Victoria was completed in April of 1861. However, men from Calhoun County rushed to join local Home Guard units. The commissioners court on July 3, 1861, appropriated $1,500 for general defense of the county to buy ammunition. Military committees were appointed by county court to issue warrants of $25 each, with the ammunition to be distributed to military companies in the county. Storage of the ammunition was to be in a powder magazine at Port Lavaca. Having second thoughts, the court in May of 1862 proclaimed that the store of powder, lead, and caps was "useless for county defenses" and ordered it sold to the highest bidder.[37]

Confederate forces were stationed at Caney, Lavaca, Fort Esperanza, and Indianola, with reserve units in other communities. The main units were Company A, or Van Dorn Guards (commanded by Dan Shea as captain), and Company B, formerly Shea's 4th Battalion Artillery, also known as Indianola Guards. Federal ships applied a blockade in the early days of the war, but blockade runners fared well. War became real when Captain Renshaw sailed his two Federal warships into Matagorda Bay. On October 31, 1862, he appeared off Port Lavaca and demanded capitulation. When Major Shea refused, the Union commander allowed only ninety minutes to clear the town of women and children, after which he began a bombardment. Shea's guns, under Vernon and Reuss, returned an effective crossfire, forcing the Union ships to withdraw out of range of the shore guns. The bombardment continued on November 1, but no attempts were made to seize the town.[38]

Major Shea, commanding officer of the Confederate forces in the Matagorda area, with headquarters in Port Lavaca, anticipated the Federal troops mounting a campaign in the area and on December 28, 1862, he issued orders to destroy bridges, ferries, and wharves in the Matagorda Bay area. The order was issued to Capt. S. C. Breckenridge, commanding cavalry, at Indianola. Orders were also given to put the torch to all buildings in Saluria and blow up the lighthouse.[39]

After the Union forces took Fort Esperanza, with an attack from the rear while shelling it from the sea, they left Saluria on December 23, 1863, and occupied Indianola after some street fighting at Norris Bridge. Port Lavaca was occupied December 26.[40] Union forces occupied the city for over a year. The fact that the occupying soldiers were Negroes did not make an easy transition.

An election was held on April 11, 1864, to elect officials who had taken the oath of allegiance to the United States of America. The election was held at Port Lavaca and not in other parts of the county. For practical purposes, Port Lavaca was now the county seat and remained such until September of 1865, when it returned to Indianola. The county as a whole was poverty-stricken after the war. Bridges, wharves, railroads, and roads were destroyed or were in disrepair.[41]

Recovery came swiftly as soon as the port facilities were repaired and trade was resumed. The Morgan Line began running boats regularly into the bay. The population of the county doubled to about 4,000.[42]

Storms of 1875 and 1886 swept over Matagorda Bay. Indianola was devastated in 1875, but managed to rebuild; however, it never regained its title as a trade port rivaling Galveston. After the storm and tidal wave of 1886, Indianola was abandoned. The few remaining buildings were torn down and moved away.[43]

A special election was held in the county on November 9, 1886, to move the courthouse back to Port Lavaca. The vote was 148-0 in favor of the move. A new courthouse building was built by E. L. Miller and later was accepted by the county on September 1, 1887. No cost is shown in the records; however, it was insured for $5,000. Falls City Construction Company got the bid in the amount of $44,000 for the next courthouse, accepted May 10, 1911. The present courthouse was built by D. W. Marshall Construction Company on a bid of $1,045,993 and dedicated on July 3, 1959.[44]

Port Lavaca was never able to capture the shipping glory that was Indianola's in the booming days before the Civil War. Even with Indianola gone, it was soon apparent that shipping habits were changing. No longer was merchandise brought into coastal ports and carried inland by ox carts and wagon trains. Railroads had taken over the bulk of this once lucrative trade. By 1890 the population of the county had dwindled to 815, but this appeared to be the low point. Through the years it has steadily climbed. Today Calhoun County is a modern industrial complex with a population of 19,574.

Port Lavaca's port now is modern and serves the marine interests as well as the oil and chemical industries which are located in the county. The Corps of Engineers built the Intracoastal Canal and cut through the old reefs that snagged many a schooner as they tried to beat their way into Lavaca's protected port. Many things have changed, but the old Ranger Cemetery that sits on the twenty-foot bluff overlooking the port is a silent reminder that some things never change.

Indianola
Port of Entry for the West

A giant wave rolls shoreward with a might that is awe-inspiring. One second it is magnificent as it moves forward; it crests, and suddenly, its power gone, it fades onto the beach.

The new Texas port of Indianola grew at a magnificent rate, but it also crested and vanished on the beach. As it peaked, it was powerful, breathtaking — the answer to its promoters' wildest dreams.

Indianola's founders envisioned great things for their new port city. Culling through earlier names — Karlshafen, Indian Point, Powderhorn Lake, Old Town, New Town, La Salle, Miller's Point — they chose "Indian," to give it strong name appeal, and added "ola," which means wave in Spanish. Thus, the name Indianola was born. They envisioned a wave of supplies and people spreading from their new port on Matagorda Bay flowing westward — all the way to the west coast.

Actually, the idea for a port city on Matagorda Bay was born in Germany, where a movement was under way in 1842 to send thousands of immigrants to Texas to found a new German state. Prince Karl zu Solms-Braunfels was appointed commissioner general for the project in 1844. Arriving in Texas, he quickly narrowed his choice of an entry port to Matagorda Bay. He struck a deal with

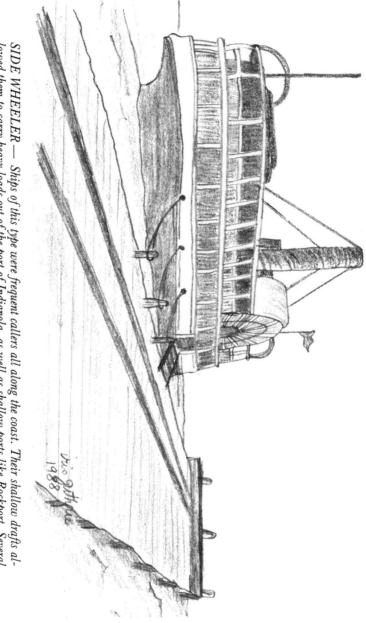

SIDE WHEELER — *Ships of this type were frequent callers all along the coast. Their shallow drafts allowed them to carry heavy loads out of the port of Indianola, as well as shallow ports like Rockport. Several of the wharves at this old port had rail lines laid from the warehouses to the end of the wharf in order to facilitate the loading and unloading of supplies. The cars were pulled out to the ship with mules. Where no rails were laid, the wagons and ox carts moved onto the wharf to load. Indianola did not have railroad service until about 1870.*

Samuel Addison White for permission to land immigrants on his headright certificate No. 37, located on Indian Point.

Prince Karl rented a storehouse for the company's property on Powderhorn Lake, about three miles south of Indian Point, and erected a two-story frame house as an office. He called his settlement Karlshafen. Starting in December, the first of many thousands of German immigrants came ashore at Indian Point, but there were no facilities to house them. Due to poor planning and organization, this first group of immigrants were forced to camp on the beach in tents for several months, waiting for arrangements to be made to transport them to their new homesites. Some of the families became disgusted with the delay and sought homesites in the area, which started the trend for a growing percentage of the German immigrants to settle in the Matagorda Bay area. By January of 1846, more than 3,000 immigrants had landed at Indian Point. Through the next three decades, this tide of settlers grew to the point that one or more ships from Germany were constantly tied up at one of the wharves.[1]

Lavaca, about ten miles northwest, was the center of most shipping activity during this period. Johann Schwarts moved his family to Indian Point in 1844 and bought a small acreage, building the first home after receiving lumber from Galveston. When the Robert B. Moore family moved to Indian Point in 1849, there were three or four other homes in the area. Two of these settlers, Charles Huck and a Mr. Slondier, built the first warehouse. The initial village wharf was in place in 1848. Capt. H. E. Boehner lightered freight to Indian Point on the steamer *Portland* for Baldridge, Sparks and Company.

Life in Indian Point was not that of a modern-day beach dweller. Mosquitoes caused fear at times. Since the homes did not have screens, Mrs. Moore tacked mosquito netting over the bedroom windows. In the living room she had a mosquito bar stretched over a little work table and chair where she sat and sewed. In rainy weather the mosquitoes were especially bad. Smoke had to be made to keep the pests out of homes and to protect cattle at night. Mosquitoes brought yellow fever in epidemic proportions until the early 1900s.

In the late 1840s, the beaches were packed with immigrants. Living conditions were hopeless, sanitation was nonexistent, and mosquitoes were so thick they could be seen as clouds. There were epidemics of typhoid, cholera, and yellow fever. Mass graves were needed to take care of the deaths that have been estimated as high as 2,000. Panic gripped the community and people set out on foot trying to reach the German settlements in Central Texas. More than 200 are thought to have perished trying to reach their objectives. Those who did reach the inland German settlements brought diseases with them.

There were also pluses to the Indian Point area. Powderhorn Lake abounded with oysters; several gallons could be gathered in a few minutes. In the winter the lake was covered with geese and ducks, providing countless meals. In the summer flamingos and cranes turned the lake into a pink and white paradise. Game was plentiful on the surrounding prairies.

In these early days, fresh water was not available, except for rainwater caught and stored in barrels, tubs, and above-ground cisterns. As the community grew, almost every home had not only cisterns above the ground, but large underground cisterns made of shell-crete.[2]

Gradually, more and more families moved to Indian Point and a few business houses were started. Henry Runge opened his banking house and mercantile business in 1845, which would grow into a statewide concern that included shipping, wagon trains, railroads, and mercantile establishments. The South Texas city of Runge is named after him. As businesses moved to town, and more ships called at Indian Point, the complexion of the town began to change. Regular coastal schooners sailed between Lavaca, Matagorda, and Indian Point. Passengers arrived once a week on steamers out of Galveston. With more people coming and going through the port, boardinghouses began to appear in 1847. Edward Clegg opened The Planter's House, Mrs. Angelina Belle Eberly opened a hotel, and C. H. Vanderveer was another hotel owner.

Progress on several fronts came about in 1846. First, Calhoun County was formed, named after John C. Calhoun, American statesman. Equally as important, the city of Indian Point was laid out and the sale of lots was started. Samuel A. White and William M. Cook were the promoters, hiring George Thielepape to do the surveying. On February 7, 1853, Indianola was incorporated by an act of the state legislature. A taxing ordinance set forth nine methods of raising money, ranging from one-fourth cent per $100 value to $20 tax on bowling alleys. A regular garbage and trash pickup on

Saturdays was proposed to include a "slop bucket" hung on the fence for table scraps. This slop was used to feed hogs.

Commission houses, operating out of large warehouses and wharves, began to appear on the waterfront. Theodore Miller, Samuel A. White, and William M. Cook joined H. Runge and Co. As more and more immigrants poured through the port, business increased at the same pace. Large amounts of lumber, hardware, groceries, farming equipment, and other merchandise were stored in Indian Point warehouses, ready for shipment to the interior. The increased traffic out of the port to the interior made it necessary to build bridges over streams and the many sloughs that cut into the coast. Wagon trains and ox carts headed out for such places as Victoria, Yorktown, New Braunfels, Fredericksburg, Bastrop, and Austin. Military supplies moved regularly to San Antonio.[3]

As Indian Point's star ascended in shipping circles, Lavaca's faded, causing bitter words between the shippers and merchants of the two towns. In 1849 Lavaca "shot themselves in the foot" when they decided to raise the fees charged shippers for docking at their wharves. They had just completed new wharves and wanted to get their money back. Harris & Morgan Steamship Company, the largest company in the area, decided that they would build their own wharf below Indian Point rather than pay the increased fees. The decision was a blow to Lavaca, but it was the big shove that the new port needed to catapult it into big time. Once Morgan began operation, primarily out of their new port at Powderhorn, merchants and warehousemen from Lavaca began to join the party. Soon the bulk of shipping was out of Indian Point and Powerhorn.

With growth stretching for several miles up and down the coast at Indian Point, the matter of a single name became important. Debate was vocal, but finally Mrs. John Henry (Mary) Brown came up with the name of Indianola. She and her husband were firmly convinced that the wave of the future would sweep out of Matagorda Bay to all parts of Texas. So, beginning in 1849, all of the previous names were dropped, and Indianola rode high on the crest of the wave.[4]

During this same period still another entry into the growing list of communities blossomed below Indianola. Levi Jones, a merchant in Lavaca, saw the great potential at Indianola and decided to get into the act. After purchasing 5,000 acres six miles below Indianola, he projected the town of La Salle. He constructed a large wharf with a warehouse and laid off a city, offering the lots for sale. Despite the fact that his sale of lots went poorly, he was able to bring a substantial amount of business into his port.

By August of 1850, most of the vessels which were regularly calling at the other Matagorda ports were also stopping at La Salle. In September of 1850 Jones succeeded in getting the United States Customshouse moved from Saluria to La Salle and himself appointed as the collector of customs for the District of Saluria. D. M. Stapp took over in 1857 as collector. The district had been expanded by that time to include ports of delivery at Lavaca, Matagorda, Aransas, Copano, Corpus Christi, San Antonio, and Eagle Pass. Jones's city was never able to take over the role as the leading port. Within a few years the name La Salle had been dropped, and the entire stretch of coast from La Salle to Indian Point was known officially as Indianola.[5]

Among the principal products shipped out of early Texas ports were hides, tallow, and bones derived by slaughtering large herds of cattle. The meat was thrown away as a useless by-product. Experiments were made in salting meat, but the taste was a drawback. The days of the big trail drives came later. In the early 1840s shippers began to experiment with taking live cattle to market in New Orleans by boat. The first known shipment of cattle out of Indianola was on September 24, 1848, when the schooner *Louise Antoinette* loaded 120 head consigned to New Orleans. Solomon G. Cunningham became one of the largest buyers and shippers of live cattle out of the port by 1850, buying out the cattle pens built by J. M. Foster several years earlier. The flavor of these shipments was captured by an early writer:

> I can still see great droves of longhorns transversing the main street of the town, headed for the pens and chutes at the docks. Some of the old steers, 3 to 5 or 6 years old, were of enormous size and paraded a startling growth of horns. They were so wild that many of them had never been branded. Whenever an animal broke from the herd, three cowboys galloped after it, roped it and brought it back, even if they had to drag it.[6]

S. A. White opened a beef canning plant on the outskirts of Indian Point. Evidently, their procedures were not perfect, as spoiled meat was just about as common as good.

Probably the biggest boost to the future of Indianola came in 1850, when the U.S. Army selected the port as the depot for the

Quartermaster and Subsistence Departments. To add substance to
the directive, the army built a 250-foot wharf, known as the Government Wharf. It was complete with a narrow-gauge rail track,
which ran to the warehouse on shore to facilitate the loading and
unloading of goods. In 1851 large amounts of stores for the army
were shipped out of Baltimore and New Orleans to Indianola.
Traffic out of the port was impressive. Army goods moved out in
special trains which contained as many as 150 wagons, each pulled
by six mules. Usually the trains headed to San Antonio and then to
El Paso. It took about a week to make the trip to San Antonio and
another three hard weeks to move on to El Paso.

Prestige was added to the city when the U.S. Boundary Commission arrived in August of 1850. They were headed west to survey the boundary between Mexico and the United States. The 1848
Treaty of Hidalgo, which ended the Mexican War, left many un-
answered problems concerning the border between the two nations.
It was up to John Russell Bartlett to work out the details. He had
105 men in the first party which arrived at Government Wharf.
Local people were so impressed that they took one of John Henry
Brown's large warehouses and staged a Texas-style supper to
which army and local dignitaries were invited. The commission's
first base of operations was in El Paso, but their supplies continued
to come through Indianola. As the commission moved westward,
and supplies continued to follow them through Indianola, travelers
started taking the same route to the west coast. Thus, a considerable amount of traffic that did not want to risk the trip around
Cape Horn by ship landed at Indianola and joined wagon trains
heading west.[7]

During this period the growth of the city was rapid, especially
in rooming houses and hotels that accommodated the ever-increas-
ing number of people moving through the city. It was not uncommon to have as many as 550 to 600 wagons or Mexican carts
camped on the outskirts of town awaiting their turn to move into
the dock area to receive their load.

Trade with northern Mexico began in earnest. The most glam-
orous part of this trade came out of the silver mines in Chihuahua.
Wells Fargo had the contract to move silver bullion from the mines
to Indianola, where it was loaded aboard ship for the trip to the
United States mint in New Orleans. The specially constructed,
high-wheel wagons were drawn by sixteen mules, four abreast.

Local tradition paints a romantic picture of the wagons with bright blue wheels and the harness and wagons decorated with flashing silver. A large number of guards rode shotgun to make sure that bandits did not make a withdrawal. On the trail, the train would carry a large number of spare mules so that fresh teams were always available.[8]

News about Indianola up to this time had largely been carried by the *Victoria Texian Advocate,* but in January of 1852 John Henry Brown established the *Indianola Bulletin,* which was to become widely read and respected throughout the country as the voice of Indianola. Editor Brown, and the others who came after him, did a good job of preserving the unique history of Indianola.

During the height of a yellow fever epidemic, the *Bulletin* carried a story on October 19, 1853, saying that sickness had materially retarded business. He reported that the weekly death toll was twelve, mostly German. At Lavaca the disease was even worse, with 126 cases and twenty-six deaths.

Activity in the port was always top news — six ships reported arriving, four departing, eleven in the bay, and four expected. Another story told about the increase of cotton into the port for shipment. The editor featured a story about the schooner *Martha* from Philadelphia, which was starting a regular run.

The acute shortage of drinking water was brought home to *Bulletin* readers on April 26, 1855, when editor A. Marschalk reported on the prolonged dry spell. It was so dry that the hoops holding the wooden cisterns together dropped as much as eight inches. Cattle were also suffering, since groundwater ponds were dry. But the editor dropped in a note on the bright side with the report of large quantities of red fish and trout being caught daily.

On May 24, 1855, activity in the port was running strong, with cotton exports reaching the largest in history. Weather was always important, but this time rainfall was heavy enough that the editor speculated that all the cisterns would fill. A story proclaimed that 1,500 German immigrants were expected shortly and that a large number of wagons was congregated in the vicinity to take the new arrivals into the interior. Prominently displayed was a small story noting that several wolves were seen prowling the streets on Thursday night. To balance off the news for the week, the editor duly reported that the city council had passed an ordinance making it unlawful for any person to keep a house of ill-fame within the city.

Editors always like to find something new. Marschalk wrote on July 6, 1855, that the Indianola beach was the only point on the Texas coast where wagons could meet ocean steamers. Then on the lighter side, he detailed a brutal affair which occurred between two boatmen, a Sicilian and an Irishman, in the barroom of the Casimir House. The Sicilian, using a slingshot to the head of his opponent, left him apparently dead. However, the editor reassured his readers: "He is alive and kicking." Also held the same night (July 4) was a cotillion, which was a "delightful affair" attended by a delegation from neighboring cities on the bay. This, too, was held at the Casimir House, which could accommodate up to 150 guests overnight. It was Indianola's finest.

The next week the editor announced that he would start on a four-week trip into West Texas to all places accessible by Risher's fine line of stages to look up all of the *Bulletin*'s subscribers and advertisers and to extol the advantages of the paper. Since newspapers of this day had to depend on correspondents in faraway places for news and advertisements, this was a must trip. Another story reflecting the growth of the entire area told of a ship that was unloading 50,000 feet of lumber at the Powderhorn Wharf. Customs and business records of the 1850s reveal that hundreds of shiploads of Florida cypress and long-leaf pine from Louisiana were unloaded at Indianola, destined to fill the building needs of hundreds of communities in the interior.

The editor could not resist giving Indianola a chamber of commerce boost in the August 24, 1855, edition:

> Indianola: On shell-white beach between White and Powderhorn bayous. Population about 1,500, is county seat and principal receiving depot of the government for large supplies and for troops on western frontier. Well supplied in merchants, one of the finest hotels in Western Texas, vessels of largest size can approach its wharves and connect directly with wagons from interior without lighters. It also is anchorage and depot for Harris and Morgan steamships.

The first post office was established September 7, 1847, with John W. Pope as postmaster. Harris and Morgan mail boats arrived in Matagorda Bay weekly. The Saltmarsh Stage Line had a mail contract for a route that ran from Indianola by way of Lavaca to Victoria. The schedule was tied to ship arrivals and departures. Captains Theodore and Charlie Johnson operated a mail stage out of Indianola which went to Saluria by ferry and then proceeded down Matagorda Island, crossing over to St. Joseph Island by ferry, and stopping at the stage station named St. Joseph (directly across from present-day Rockport). Mail and passengers were then taken by boat to Lamar, St. Mary's, Copano, and Corpus Christi. Mail service improved as the ships began calling twice a week and better roads were built, especially close to Indianola where several sloughs and marshes had to be crossed.

The county seat of Calhoun County remained at Lavaca until the commissioners court ordered the move to Indianola on August 17, 1852, after a special election. Records were moved on August 21. Due to a dispute over where the Indianola courthouse would be located, the new building was not started until 1857 and not completed until 1860. The building cost $15,000 and was made of concrete blocks. The county seat remained in Indianola until the town was destroyed in 1886. On November 2 an election was held and the county seat returned to Lavaca.[9]

Schooling in Indianola was probably carried on by parents in their own homes in the first years after the community was settled. The first mention of a private school came in 1848, with August Winburg as the first teacher, and was held in a small building facing Front Street. Hez Woodward was also an early teacher. A private school for females was established in the Presbyterian church about the same time. The Indianola Male and Female School came into being in 1854 and was operated by R. W. Yates in the house of B. F. Yates on Main Street. Instruction was offered for $2 to $5 per month. Eudora Moore, in her writings, remembered starting to a private school in 1855 with Miss Smith as a teacher, followed by Mr. Yates and Mr. Cleveland. Tuition was $2.50 per month. Later in Moore's schooling, Mrs. Ocie Willis was the teacher, living and teaching in the Baldridge house. Singing was her specialty and her fee was $5 per month. Private schools included Indianola Male & Female School, 1854, R. W. Yates; Colston Private School; School for Boys and Girls, 1859, H. B. Cleveland; and St. Mary's Institute, operated by French and Irish nuns.

Texas enacted a public school education law in 1854, to which the county commissioners complied by dividing the county into four precincts. Whether there was cooperation between the private schools and public schools is not known; however, it appears likely, since a graduation for Indianola High School was held in the Methodist church in 1854. In 1859 public schools were firmly established, judging from an entry in county commissioners court records in 1859 approving teacher salaries as follows: Mrs. C. A. Ring, $220.90; Mrs. A. F. Threlkeld, $15.20; Frederick Goepfert, $229.80; J. M. Bickford, $111.70; H. B. Cleveland, $27.50; and Fred Dietzel, $376.90. Schools appeared to be still in session during the Civil War, but barely. Miss Moore taught school in a small building behind their home after the war. The school building was destroyed by the storm of 1875.[10]

With all of the German immigrants pouring through Indianola, it is understandable that the first church services were held at Karlshafen in a tent under a large oak tree. The Lord's Supper was celebrated on December 23, 1844. It was not until 1854 that a Lutheran church was organized.

The Indianola Presbyterian congregation built a church in May of 1851. Since it was the only church, contributions toward the building were made by all religious groups, with the provision that a like sum would be returned to each group when they built a building. This was done.

The Methodist church came into being shortly afterward. In the yellow fever epidemic of 1858 the Methodist pastor, William F. Hubert, was a victim. Hubert had also served the Lavaca church. He was followed by Robert N. Drake.

Mr. Elder's warehouse is credited as being the scene of the first church service at Indian Point. The Reverend Orr and James Howerton, Sr., a layman, conducted this first meeting and organized a Baptist Sunday School in 1846.

The Catholic congregation was in a formative stage in 1848 and was headed by Reverend John A. Jacobs, who was credited with work among the yellow fever victims in 1858.[11]

Indianola was a busy port. Products from all over the world came into its warehouses and were loaded onto wagon trains for the interior. Cargoes were handled in a matter-of-fact method; that is, until the *Supply* crossed the bar at Decrow's Point on April 29, 1856. Not until the next day, when Maj. Henry C. Wayne, U.S. Army, came ashore, did folks at Indianola know that history was about to be made with the introduction of camels into the United States. The animals were to be used by the army to carry loads over the arid western plains. The *Supply* was unable to come up to the wharves due to its draft, so the lighter *Fashion* was sent out to receive the camels for transfer to the wharves. Due to heavy seas it was impossible to unload the animals. Finally, the *Supply* sailed to calm waters of the mouth of the Mississippi River, where the transfer to lighters was made. The camels were unloaded at Indianola on May 14.

While the army's experiment with camels was a failure, Indianola, as the home port for the camels, became famous all over the United States. A number of other shipments of camels came through Indianola until the sight of camels parading down Main Street was commonplace.[12] The Civil War disrupted the experiment and the project was dropped, the camels being sold or turned loose. The big problem with the camels turned out to be sore feet — they were accustomed to soft desert sand, not the rough terrain of the West.

By the mid-1850s Indianola was poised to become one of the leading ports in Texas. In less than ten years, the shipping business in America recognized the Matagorda port as one of the best funnels for goods to be directed into the growing western part of Texas and the nation. Merchants in Indianola sensed that they were on the threshold of an explosion in the shipping business and took steps to meet the need. In October of 1856 a group of businessmen organized the Western Texas Wharf Company, whose main purpose was to build better wharf facilities. Henry Runge headed the organization of local stockholders, with Southern Steamship Company as the largest stockholder. A new, longer pier was built near Powderhorn Bayou, primarily for Southern Steamship, the new name of Harris and Morgan line. Business boomed and real estate brought premium prices. Records show lots selling for as much as $4,000.[13]

Indianola businessmen approached the state legislature in 1858 for another railroad charter, which was granted under the name of Indianola Railroad Company. Earlier, the Powderhorn, Victoria, and Gonzales railroad failed to gain enough support to function. Local opinion disagrees as to whether or not this rail line was built before the Civil War; however, it was definitely in operation in 1871, running from Indianola to Lavaca Junction, a distance of about eleven miles. A roundhouse existed in Indianola.

Charles Morgan, chief stockholder in the Harris and Morgan Steamship Line, played a dominant role in the final building plans of the Indianola Railroad. Morgan had secured an interest in the San Antonio and Mexican Gulf Railroad and was most anxious to see a rail line into Indianola where his shipping interests were at stake. Morgan purchased lots and received grants from the city to bring the rail line to his improved wharf near Powderhorn. When completed, goods off of Morgan ships could be loaded directly into boxcars on the wharf for shipment to the interior.[14]

Editor William T. Yancey, who replaced the *Indianolian* in 1858 with the *Indianola Courier and Commercial Bulletin,* was extremely upbeat on his presentation of news and emphasized week after week the growth on all fronts in Indianola. In May of 1859 a Mr. Rooke erected a bath house for use by the public. It had compartments, all fitted in good style. The editor added his touch: "It has long been needed." News for the week mainly dealt with the port where the three-masted schooners *Union* and *Mary Turbell* arrived with a cargo of lumber. Several more ships were listed as soon to arrive with more lumber. The schooner *Independence* came up the "inside route" with hides and wool for shipment on an oceangoing ship out of Indianola. Several ships were loading cargoes not listed in the paper.

Newspapers of this era were dependent upon the ship captains to bring them news and newspapers from their ports of call. Editors made constant mention of the newspaper being delayed because ships were late docking with out-of-state newspapers. On July 30 editor Yancey of the *Indianola Courier* passed on this bit of information: "Fifty yellow fever cases in Brownsville. . . . one out of three have died." A story noted that the retail market was good and even gave the readers a shopper's guide: "Chickens, $2.50 to $3, doz.; ducks, 50¢ to 75¢, pair; butter, 25¢ to 30¢, lb.; eggs, 25¢, doz.; beef, 4 to 5¢, lb.; mutton, 8 to 10¢, lb." Yancey dropped in this gem: "It is better to love a person you cannot marry than to marry a person you cannot love."

A mass meeting on November, 24, 1860, was attended by 132 people requesting the governor to call the legislature into session to facilitate the sovereignty of Texas. Copies of the resolution were to be mailed to every county in Texas.

In November of 1860 it was announced that Southern Steamship Company planned to put on a number of new steamers from Indianola to New Orleans to take care of the increased trade. The tone of the times was reflected in the editor's comment on politics: "Hon. Jeff Davis thinks secession is the only thing if Lincoln chosen." No doubt a later ship brought additional news about the political situation: "Lincoln probably elected." The death of Dr. Joseph H. Barnard, made famous at the massacre of Col. James Fannin's men in Goliad, was reported at age sixty-six.

The sentiment in favor of secession permeated through every issue of the *Courier*. On December 1, a company of minutemen was enrolled in Indianola and another in Lavaca. But the editor kept his wit as he dropped in a choice filler: "A live abolitionist was in town last week, but he took passage on the first steamer. It is rather tropical here for birds of that feather."

The January 5, 1861, edition brought the news that Sam Houston had called the legislature into session for the twenty-first. The election date was also announced for Calhoun County to elect delegates to this convention. But despite the fact that war appeared imminent, business in the port continued to grow. The steamships *Matagorda* and *Orizaba* landed 2,150 head of sheep, together with a lot of trained shepherd dogs and three Durham bulls, from Ohio destined to go to the San Antonio area.

With the Civil War under way, the *Courier* on May 6, 1861, reported that Matagorda Bay was listed among southern ports to be blockaded by the federal government. Another sobering note was included in a story which told about four pieces of artillery that were headed from Fort Clark to Indianola. But the editor still was able to find the light side: "D. H. Todd, brother-in-law of President Lincoln, appointed lieutenant in Confederate army." [15]

Conditions changed radically in the next few months. The long-threatened blockade by the Federal navy was now real, and the backlog of ships stacked up in the Indianola harbor vanished. The long lines of wagons waiting for freight were also gone. Business in Indianola had virtually dropped to zero. An occasional ship got past the blockade and made it into port, but these were rare. Trade up and down the coast inside the barrier islands continued, but this did not bring in the needed goods from the outside. The exception was trade with Mexico, which expanded rapidly. Cotton from Matagorda plantations now took the long, tortuous Cotton Road to the Rio Grande and then across into Mexico. Much-needed supplies came back up the trail.

The commissioners court appropriated $1,500 for general defense, and two Home Guard units were organized in Indianola. Company A was under Capt. D. E. Crosland and Company B was under Capt. Leon Rouff. The Indianola Artillery Company was under the command of Capt. George Thielepape. An eight-man military committee was organized, with two men from each precinct in the county. On May 20, 1862, the committee got the commissioners court to levy a twenty-five-cent tax on each $100 of taxable value to pay for relief to families of soldiers who were without funds.

Brig. Gen. D. M. Stapp, 24th Brigade, Texas Militia, had headquarters in Indianola. Maj. Dan Shea's command played a big role in plans around Indianola in the frantic effort made by the Confederate command to beef up defenses in anticipation of a Federal attack by land and sea. Gen. David E. Twiggs, commander of Federal troops in Texas at the start of the war, surrendered his troops to the Texas militia with the provision that they be sent home via Indianola. The first contingent sailed on the *Daniel Webster,* but before a second batch could leave on the *Star of the West,* the Confederate *Mohawk* captured the *Star* in a midnight venture in the gulf just off of Pass Cavallo.

Union gunboats appeared off the pass on October 25, 1862, and subjected Fort Esperanza with such heavy fire that the defenders abandoned their guns and retreated to Indianola. The Federal ships, under the command of Capt. William B. Renshaw, entered the bay and anchored offshore at Indianola. The next day the *Westfield* approached a wharf under a flag of truce, asking to meet with representatives of the city. H. B. Cleveland, T. D. Woodward, and Capt. Henry Sheppard went aboard the ship and listened to Renshaw's demands, which they turned down. A fierce bombardment on Indianola followed, in which one resident was killed. The Federal troops came ashore and looted extensively. Several days after the bombardment and looting, the Federal ships all withdrew from Matagorda Bay.

Confederate forces tried to use the lull to beef up their defenses. John Bankhead Magruder was assigned this job. His idea was to wreck the port cities in Matagorda Bay. Believing that the bay was the key to the Mexican trade, he issued orders to Major Shea to destroy wharves, warehouses, bridges, lighthouses, and railroads in the bay area. He wanted to deprive the Federal forces from the use of these facilities if they were successful in their invasion. Naturally, these orders were bitterly resisted by locals. However, on January 15, 1863, Major Shea reported to Magruder that the destruction had been carried out. After the war, shipping interests in Indianola were longer getting back into full swing, due to the destruction. Galveston, where no docks were destroyed, got a big jump in the race for port supremacy.

Gen. Nathaniel P. Banks of the Union army brought the chill of steel to Indianola. Federal forces quickly moved up the coast from Brownsville to Corpus Christi, crushing opposition. By November of 1863 Fort Esperanza was outflanked and outgunned. The defenders spiked their guns, blew up ammunition supplies, and retreated for the second time to Indianola. As soon as the Federal troops consolidated their positions, they crossed over to the mainland and took Indianola for the second time. This time the Federals fortified their positions and made the city their headquarters. The residents in Indianola remained virtual prisoners in their homes until March of 1864, when a change in plans called for the withdrawal of troops from Indianola. Life slowly returned to normal as the people tried to clean up the mess left by the occupation. Homes and businesses were fixed up the best way possible without any new materials. The commissioners court began functioning again, but as long as the naval blockade continued, life could not return to normal.

After the Confederacy collapsed, Federal troops again occupied Indianola. Company B of the 35th United States Infantry took over an area on A and B streets about eleven blocks from the courthouse and remained there until all Federal troops were removed from the South. The occupation force was generally well behaved, although Eudora Moore, in her recollections, told stories of the Negro occupation troops firing off guns and causing some trouble.[16]

Just as soon as the Federal blockade was lifted on June 24, 1865, vessels started returning to Indianola. Some of the first lumber which arrived at the port went to rebuild the wharves and warehouses. Charles Morgan had been busy in Washington before the war ended, and as soon as the treaty was signed he began getting his remaining ships back into operation.

Within a short time ships were coming into the bay at a steady pace. The charter of Indianola Railroad was renewed in October of 1866. Work began in 1865 on the reconstruction of the San Antonio and Mexican Gulf Railroad from Victoria to Lavaca. Trade with Mexico was resumed, bringing back the lines of wagons and Mexican carts. Stage lines resumed regular schedules and, until the Indianola Railroad was completed in the early 1870s, remained the only transportation in and out of Indianola.

By 1867 the face of Indianola had been largely repaired, with a number of new buildings added. A serious fire in January wiped out a large part of the business section, including the customshouse and several stores. But this was not the only disaster to hit in 1867. Yellow fever broke out and swept through the entire town, including the Federal army of occupation. Dr. Joseph Martin Reuss estimated that there were no less than 550 to 600 cases out of a population of about 2,000. Oran Warder Nolen told the story in *Frontier Times* about people not being able to dig graves fast enough to take care of the deaths. Finally, the city resorted to burying the dead in trenches. As a result of this epidemic the Fifth Military District issued an order setting up quarantine stations on the gulf coast.

Indianola appeared to feed on adversity. Epidemics, storms, and fires beset the city, but with each passing month more cargo was moving through the port and more people were making the port their home. Indianola had long been one of the biggest shippers of live cattle, and in 1869 Francis Stabler put in a packing plant that refrigerated the sides of beef and delivered them to one of Morgan's steamers which was equipped with refrigeration. The event got a big play in the New Orleans *Picayune* on July 13. The days of butchering cattle for hides, tallow, and horns were just about past.[17]

The railroad, predicted as "just around the corner" for over two decades, appeared now to be a reality. Editor Ogsbury wrote on April 25, 1871, in the *Indianola Weekly Bulletin* that a party of dignitaries had boarded special cars and traveled as far as Victoria, returning the following day. After years of waiting, Indianola finally was connected with the outside world by rail.

The growth of the city could be read in between the lines in the *Bulletin*. Three doctors were now practicing in the city, and they also took care of the countryside, as an ad proclaimed: "Rates for country practice, one dollar per mile. The parties calling, paying transportation. Necessary attention, charged extra." The editor freely predicted that many new buildings would be erected as a result of the railroad.

Progress was also apparent when a story noted that many of the city streets were blocked during the day by teams waiting to get to the docks. Ads in the papers reflected the progress as well, since there were three restaurants and several oyster saloons offering their menus. But bad luck was always present, as was shown in a story that detailed how the schooner *Planet*, loaded with lumber

bound for Corpus Christi, went aground fifteen miles above Decrow's Point. The vessel was a total loss, but part of the cargo was
saved.

The *Texana*, a vessel built in a shipyard of Indianola, highlighted
a new industry. The April 25 *Bulletin* listed eight ship arrivals and four
clearances. Fifteen companies were listed under a heading "Receipts
of Produce." The products varied from 595 bales of cotton to 25 pigs
of copper. Shipments of metals from the mines in northern Mexico
were arriving regularly. On June 20 the editor noted that lumber sales
were high, with one yard loading out forty wagons in one day. Ox
teams traveled up to 200 miles for lumber.

Editor John Henry Brown was not bashful when it came to editorial comment. On August 15, 1871, he blasted corruption:
"Never was there a more corrupt government than that of Texas as
administered by Davis and his faction." A community meeting was
held in Temperance Hall to protest to legislators.

Growth brings problems, as illustrated in a report on the city
council. It was pointed out that several privies stood on corners of
two streets, to the great annoyance of persons passing. The city
acted. They passed an ordinance stating that privies could not be
within ten feet of a street. A story called attention to the fact that
new buildings were going up due to increased trade. For the first
time, brick buildings were being built.

The *Bulletin* reported that two or three trains a day hardly suf-
ficed to carry the enormous load of merchandise to the interior. But
then the railroad had its problems, as seen in a note that the loco-
motive on the Victoria run hit a cow while crossing a bridge near
town. On May 8, 1872, the news of a contract for transportation of
government freight to San Antonio was given out via Indianola.

Population increased as more and more ships called at the
dozens of wharves. Downtown Indianola took on the marks of a
city, with an abundance of stores, shops, and professional offices.
Modern hotels took care of the hundreds of transients who arrived
daily. Casimir House, Indianola's finest, boasted splendid furnish-
ings and light by chandeliers. Churches and schools, private and
public, were well attended.

Indianola had lived through a number of storms, so when the
weather turned bad on Wednesday, September 15, 1875, no one
was alarmed. Rain came down in torrents and the bay level started
rising. The wind continued at gale force all night. By daylight on

Thursday, the eastern side of town was underwater and water was breaking over Main Street in a number of places. By noon the water was pouring through the cross streets in an angry torrent. Boats were loaded with women and children and drawn by ropes down Main Street toward the upper part of town, which was thought to be the safest area. Nightfall found the water running five feet deep through town. Buildings along the bayfront were being swept away.

Thursday night was described by survivors as a "Night of Horror." By midnight the wind changed to the northwest and increased in violence. For over eighteen hours the wind had been forcing the bay water across the reef that was Indianola. As the wind changed, and the vortex of the storm crashed down on the huddled victims, the water came back with immense power. Friday dawned cold and dreary, but finally the depth of the flood was diminishing and by 6:00 A.M. the streets were free of water.

What had been a thriving town of well over 2,000 now lay shattered, with bodies to be found everywhere. At least 270 people lost their lives. Many others were unaccounted for, and some probably moved away without leaving a forwarding address. Hundreds of buildings were washed completely away; most of the remaining ones were damaged to some extent.

The brave souls who remained faced the challenge of rebuilding their city. A plan surfaced to move the city to the north shore of Powderhorn Lake to a higher elevation that would forestall future flooding. The backing of Charles Morgan was sought for the project. When it was not forthcoming, a number of merchants chose to pack up and leave. One of the men leaving was C. A. Ogsbury, publisher of the *Indianola Bulletin*. The editor took a job in Cuero and wrote at length about the narrow-minded outlook of the Morgan interests.

Indianola made a valiant effort to rebuild, and to some extent life did return to normal. But the enthusiasm that had marked the growth of the early 1870s was gone. With shipping turning to other avenues, some of the businessmen attempted to turn the focus to tourist trade. This proved successful to a limited extent.

The end came on August 20, 1886. The utter destruction of the city can best be told by a story published on August 28 in the *Victoria Advocate:*

The terrific force of the storm is nowhere more apparent than at

Indianola. Buildings which stoutly withstood the great cyclone of 1875, went down as if made of pasteboard. To the eastward of the railroad track nothing remains but a large safe belonging to H. J. Huck and Co., which marks the spot where the office of the Huck Lumber Yard once stood. Proceeding up the street, on the right stood the customshouse, badly shattered but still erect, as is also the adjoining building. The block on the opposite side suffered badly, and the street is filled with shattered buildings. . . .

The storm struck at about 5:00 A.M. on August 20. Sometime during the morning a fire broke out, destroying every building on Main Street from the signal office to Villeneuve corner. Destruction was complete. For the next few days people gathered around shattered piles to salvage what they could. Any building, even partially left intact, was dismantled and moved away. On September 20 the commissioners court called a special election regarding moving the county seat back to Lavaca. The vote was overwhelming for the move. A fire in April of 1887 wiped out buildings that had been patched together. The post office was closed on October 4, 1887. Indianola, "Queen City of the West," was no more.

Today the remains of an underground cistern and a historical marker help guide tourists to the site of the once great port. A cemetery a mile distant tells the final story.

Saluria
Deepwater Port

Pass Cavallo leads from the Gulf of Mexico into Matagorda Bay. The treacherous, swift currents that swirl around its reefs have proved the death of literally dozens of sailing vessels. But despite its many drawbacks, early settlers sought to conquer nature's forces and establish port cities on either side of the pass.

Tom Decrow established Decrow's Point on the north side of the pass and built a long wharf out to ten feet of water. Judge H. W. Hawes helped build Saluria on the south side of the pass, and his wharf reached eleven feet of water and was able to accommodate any ship that could enter the bay. Port Cavallo and Fort Cavallo both enjoyed a brief moment in history on the north side of the pass on Matagorda Peninsula. Fort Cavallo was at its height during the Civil War, with as many as 4,000 troops committed to the defense

WHARF TO DEEP WATER — Ships with drafts of seven to nine feet could pull into the wharf at Saluria, which ran from Resaca Street out to deep water. Both the deepwater ships and the coastal lighters used the port, which was on the left side of Paso Caballo on the bay side of Matagorda Island.

of the Confederacy. Port Cavallo was at one time the temporary port of entry for the customs district.[1]

On the south side of the pass was Calhoun, sometimes called Calhoun City, the official city of the Republic of Texas, and Saluria. Calhoun City was home of most of the port pilots who boarded inbound vessels to guide them to interior ports and check their cargo for customs purposes.

In the early days of the Texas Republic land speculation was rampant. Dozens of promoters sought to establish the port that would serve as the entry port to the west. The first customs District of Matagorda was established on June 12, 1837. The District of Calhoun came into existence on January 21, 1841, and on December 14, 1842, Alexander Somervell was appointed as head of the district.[2]

Texas got into the town promotion business on January 21, 1839, when Congress passed an act setting aside 640 acres on the east end of Matagorda Island, near the pass, for the townsite of Calhoun. Not only did Congress set up the town, but they decreed that the lots be sold on the first Monday in June of 1841 and continue until one-fourth were sold.[3] The complete history of Calhoun is well hidden.

Evidently, little interest was shown in the official port of the state of Texas, even though the state created the customs District of Calhoun and named Calhoun as the port of entry. However, at the same time they established Port Cavallo on the pass as a temporary port of entry until customs facilities could be built at Calhoun. George Collinsworth was named collector for the District of Calhoun. He was replaced by Thomas Marshall Duke, who served until he was replaced by Alexander Somervell. The customs District of Saluria crept into the records in 1842, with Somervell still in office. In fact, he served until 1854, when he died under strange circumstances.

The collector had left Lavaca alone in a small boat, carrying with him a large sum of money. Later his body was found tied to the boat and the money missing. His career had been colorful. He was in the mercantile business in San Felipe, had served in the army at Bexar and San Jacinto and, for a short time, was secretary of war under President David G. Burnet. He was also a senator, an Indian fighter, and commander of a brigade of militia that pursued General Woll to Laredo. The cause of his death was never determined.[4]

History fails to give the exact location of Calhoun; however, on Arrowsmith's map it is located southeast of the bulge of the island of Matagorda just after entering Pass Cavallo. Edward Linn, brother of John of Linnville fame, did the surveying. A total of 173 lots were laid out, with one each set aside for the Methodist, Catholic, and Presbyterian churches. Two squares were reserved for public use, another for a fish market, and another for male and female academies. Provision was made for a fort, later to be called Fort Washington. At a later date Congress set aside $1,000 for this fort. Saluria was at the northeastern bulge of the island, with its wharf reaching out into McHenry's Bayou. This was almost directly across from Alligator Head on the mainland and the point of departure for ferries headed for Matagorda Island.

Matagorda Island was among the many parcels of premium land that Empresarios James Power and James Hewetson received in direct purchases at the time they received their grant from the Mexican government to bring colonists to Texas. Colonel Power apparently did not challenge the State of Texas when it attempted to establish Calhoun on his land. However, just as soon as the project was abandoned, he projected his own city for the area — Saluria. Interested in the project with him were Gen. Alexander Somervell and Judge Milford P. Norton. Later, on March 17, 1847, Colonel Power made a contract with Somervell, John Washington Rose, and J. W. Denison whereby 640 acres of the Saluria townsite were deeded to Somervell as the land agent and trustee. The agreement called for one-fourth of the lots to be conveyed to Power and the remainder sold, with the proceeds divided four ways. In 1856 the legislature passed a law confirming the title to the land, thus clearing up any cloud that might be over the property.

Over 300 lots were laid out in the townsite. Resaca Street paralleled McHenry's Bayou, and at the end of this street a wharf reached out to water eleven feet deep. A large warehouse was at the corner of Buena Vista and Resaca streets serving the wharf which was operated by Judge A. W. Hawes.[5]

Hawes became the driving force in the growth of Saluria through his wharf and warehouse. Practically all of Morgan's ships called at Saluria, as well as many others. Saluria's wharf extended into water deep enough to take any ship that could enter the pass. As a result, a lot of goods destined for other locations were brought into the Hawes wharf and unloaded to be reshipped by lighters, which made regular trips between the Matagorda Bay ports and ports to the south. Most of the oceangoing ships used Saluria as one of their principal bases.

As Saluria grew, so did the population of Matagorda Island. More and more people bought acreage on the island and made their permanent home just behind the sand dunes. Cattle ranches provided the main income for fifty to sixty families. The growth of Saluria and Matagorda Island brought about the introduction of stagecoach service from Indianola to Saluria, down Matagorda Island to Cedar Bayou, where a ferry took the stage across, and finally to St. Joseph, where mail and passengers transferred to a ship to complete the journey. Two sea captains, Charlie Johnson and Peter Johnson, ran the stages, ferries, and ships linking dozens of communities.

The decade of the 1850s was the one of most growth for Saluria. The good wharf facilities caused the *Kate Ward,* one of the river steamers owned by Capt. Jesse Obadiah Wheeler, to move from crowded facilities at Indianola to Saluria. By 1850 mail boats went on a weekly basis to Matagorda Bay ports, including Saluria. But despite the fact that Saluria was growing, it was evident that political clout rested elsewhere. This was seen when Dr. Levi Jones was successful in moving the customshouse from Saluria to his new town of La Salle.

One of the drawbacks of Saluria was the powerful Pass Cavallo currents that ships had to face in making the sharp turn to dock at Saluria. On January 9, 1851, the steamship *Palmetto* was caught in these crosscurrents and went aground. Everything but the mail was a total loss. The Morgan Lines, owner of the ship, decided against their ships calling at Saluria. This was a blow to Hawes and to other shipping interests in Saluria. In June a severe storm raked Saluria, causing severe wind and water damage.

In late 1852 Hawes appeared before the commissioners court and received permission to operate ferries from Alligator Head to Saluria. Ferries had existed in the past, but on a hit-and-miss basis. Hawes proposed a regular schedule, which the court approved. Toll for a wagon and six oxen or horses was set at $1, or a wagon with four horses only seventy-five cents. Clearly, Hawes was working to open up commerce by land for Saluria. In 1859 George Heald took over the operation of the ferry.

Records of schools and churches at Saluria are scant. A note in the *Lavaca Herald* on December 5, 1857, tells that Hugh W. Hawes opened a school in Saluria. Tuition ran from $3 to $5 per month. J. M. Bickford was the principal. In 1860 Episcopal Bishop Alexander Gregg made a sweep through the area and baptized two children in Saluria.[6]

Saluria's destiny was linked with Fort Esperanza at Pass Cavallo. Fort Washington, with earthen embankments, was authorized during the days of the Republic to protect Pass Cavallo. Three cannons were supposed to have been installed. When it became evident that the pass would have to be protected against Federal forces in the Civil War, Fort Esperanza (meaning hope in Spanish) was constructed slightly up the island from Fort Washington. The new position was considered easier to defend.

Slave labor was brought in to assist the three companies of soldiers who were assigned to the fort. The earthen walls were 20 feet thick and 200 yards long. Shell and concrete were used to bind logs from the Colorado River logjam into the walls. The fort was put to the test in October of 1863, when the Federal fleet drew up at the pass and concentrated such a mass of cannon fire that the defenders spiked their guns and retreated to Indianola. A good number of Saluria residents did likewise. The fleet did not remain in Matagorda Bay. After it left, Confederate forces returned to the fort and strengthened the fortifications. They also constructed fortifications to protect the rear of the fort from forces coming up the island by land.

Union forces did a great deal of damage up and down Matagorda Island, but the biggest damage to Saluria came at the hands of the Confederate forces. Acting on orders from above, Maj. Dan Shea ordered Capt. S. T. Breckenridge in December of 1862 to proceed to Saluria, drive off all of the cattle, set fire to the buildings, blow up the lighthouse, and destroy the wharf. This was done to keep the facilities from falling into the hands of the Union forces.

The few remaining residents of Saluria had a few weeks of respite when the Union forces pulled out. Federal forces hit Corpus Christi on November 16, 1863, then moved rapidly toward Matagorda Bay. Aransas Pass fell on November 17, and the Union forces moved up St. Joseph Island, encountering some opposition at Cedar Bayou. By November 27 Union forces under Brig. Gen. T. C. G. Ransom had advanced to the outer earthen works that had been thrown up to protect Fort Esperanza's rear. Outnumbered and outflanked, the Confederate forces at the fort once again

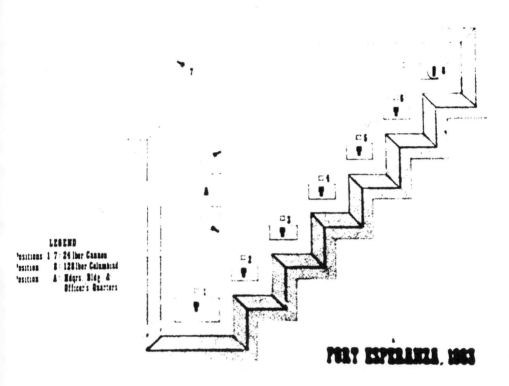

LEGEND
Positions 1 7: 24 lber Cannon
Position   8: 128 lber Columbiad
Position   A: Hdqrs. Bldg &
                 Officer's Quarters

FORT ESPERANZA, 1863

FORT ESPERANZA — This old fort overlooking Paso Caballo from Matagorda Island was designed to keep Yankee invaders out of Matagorda Bay. Beset from sea, and threatened from the rear by a force under the command of N. P. Banks, the Confederates retreated to the mainland before the Federal troops overwhelmed them. Caleb G. Forshey commanded a battalion of Confederate artillery at the fort. The drawing was made by Enos Reed, Company K, 34th Iowa. Fort Washington was also in the same location, and Saluria was just a short distance away.

retreated across the bay to Indianola. The Federal forces occupied Fort Esperanza, while Saluria was used as a campsite for the bulk of the army. When they finally left, little was left of the town.[7]

After the war there was nothing to come home to in Saluria. Recognizing that Matagorda Island was depopulated, the commissioners court on October 7, 1864, did away with precinct four, which included Saluria. After the war, on April 5, 1869, the court recognized that people had returned to Saluria, so they redrew the precinct lines, with Saluria and Matagorda Island being precinct five. A check of deed transfers shows that there were only two conveyances in 1869, one a sheriff's sale and the other a purchase by H. W. Hawes, Sr. After this, the only deed transfers were from Hawes, Sr., to relatives.[8]

Saluria suffered several blows that made its rebuilding next to impossible. First, the Confederate forces had put the torch to the wharf and warehouses. During the Union occupation, property was seized and a few standing buildings were torn down for the lumber. After the war, reconstruction realities made it difficult to get the necessary capital to rebuild the seaport facilities. For almost a decade a few people held on at Saluria, probably hoping for a change that would allow the old port to recapture the magic of the 1850s. Before this could happen, the storm of 1875 virtually destroyed all vestiges of the rebuilt community, but it still refused to die. A few homes were built and a semblance of a community existed until the storm of 1886, in which three lives were lost and at least a dozen homes were destroyed. The end is told by Judge Hawes:

> [addressed to] D. Lewis, Indianola, or any merchant if he is not there.
> SALURIA, Aug. 20 — Please send me five barrels of flour. We have nothing to eat on the island except meat. All people on the island saved except Betty Mead (colored) and her two children. All houses except the life saving station at the upper end of the island washed away or destroyed, and people left with only the clothes they had on their back. Nearly all the cattle and sheep were drowned, and the balance will die for want of water. E. Hawes, Sr.

Perhaps it is fitting that Judge Hawes wrote the final epitaph to Saluria. Hawes was a major landholder on Matagorda Island from the beginning and the biggest booster of Saluria. After the storm of 1886, he recovered and continued to operate a ranch on the island. He and his heirs survived all of nature's adversities, but they could not cope with Uncle Sam. First, the United States government purchased for $1 a fifty-foot square block of land on the north bank of McHenry Bayou, opposite the old town of Saluria and fronting the store of Captain Baker. On that spot they located a short wooden tower, calling it Saluria Light. Eighty years after getting this foothold, the government took all of the Hawes land during World War II and used it as a range for bomber target practice. Hawes heirs waited patiently for the promised return of their land when the war was over. The government blocked all efforts of the Hawes heirs to reclaim their land.[9] They found that politicians were harder to predict than a hurricane — and a lot more powerful.

River Ports
(Texana, Tidehaven, Point Palacios, Caney Creek)

Water transportation was possibly the best way that early Texans had to move their produce to market. As a result a number of real estate promotions involving river ports sprang up. Some prospered and others died on the vine.

Texana,[1] located near the junction of the Lavaca and Navidad rivers, was one of the first of these river ports. Established in 1832 by Dr. F. F. Wells, and a sister-in-law, Pamelia McNutt Porter, it quickly became an important community with the Texas army using it as an early staging point. Boats could move easily from Lavaca Bay, up the Lavaca River to Texana. In smaller boats goods were taken to the interior up the Lavaca and Navidad rivers, with produce returned to Texana for shipment.

Texana was the county seat of Jackson County, with regular weekly steamboat service and overland stagecoaches. In 1880 Texana was the center of distribution for mail to other towns for many miles around. It had a prosperous business community and as many as fifteen to twenty ships called weekly. In 1882 *The Clarion* was published in the city. In 1883 the railroad missed Texana and went through Edna. Within a year, most of the people followed and in 1884 an election moved the county seat to Edna. After a few years, the once-prosperous port was a ghost town.[2]

Tidehaven, located on the Tres Palacios River (about four miles east of the present city of Blessing), was founded in the early 1830s by Pumphrey Burnett. One of Austin's Old Three Hundred,

Burnett also had visions of establishing a flourishing port on the navigable Tres Palacios River. The name came from the fact that the tidewaters came within a short distance of the port. By the mid-1830s steamers were coming up the river to Tidehaven, discharging goods destined for the interior and taking on produce from nearby farms and ranches. Evidently, the operators of Tidehaven had warehouses at other ports, since the port of Tidehaven does not appear in the early Republic customs records.

The foundations of the wharf that reached out into the river can still be found on the banks of the Tres Palacios River. In later years a slaughterhouse for cattle was built at the wharf. The bricks from this old building, as well as its foundations, are still to be found on the site.

In 1858 John E. Pierce and Abel Head Pierce arrived in Texas and purchased extensive landholdings in the Tidehaven area. They began shipping cattle out of the expanded port facilities. At one time they had a contract with Spain to furnish cattle for their army during their struggle to hold Cuba.

Tidehaven grew and prospered, with hotels, stores, and other businesses. A post office was established in 1856 and operated until 1904.

About the only vestiges of proof that Tidehaven existed are a few physical remains, plus the fact that several nearby cemeteries mark the last resting places of these pioneers.[3]

Point Palacios was actually on the bay and was not a river port. However, it received its commerce from the system of creeks and rivers that fed into Tres Palacios Bay. Founded in 1838 by R. R. Royall and John Duncan, the new town was located on Half Moon Point, where the Matagorda and Tres Palacios bays come together. The city was never a big success; however, warehouses and wharves built to serve the river trade did prosper.

Several plantation owners perfected an overland route to get their cotton to Point Palacios. One was Capt. John Duncan, who had a plantation on Caney Creek. He hauled his cotton overland to Elliott's Ferry on the Colorado River and then continued overland to the deep Wilson Creek. Flat-bottomed boats were poled up the creek to receive the cotton which was then taken down the creek to Tres Palacios Creek and then on to Palacios Point for shipment.

A map made by Silas Dinsmore in 1844 shows how farmers from the upper reaches of the Colorado got their cotton to Point Pa-

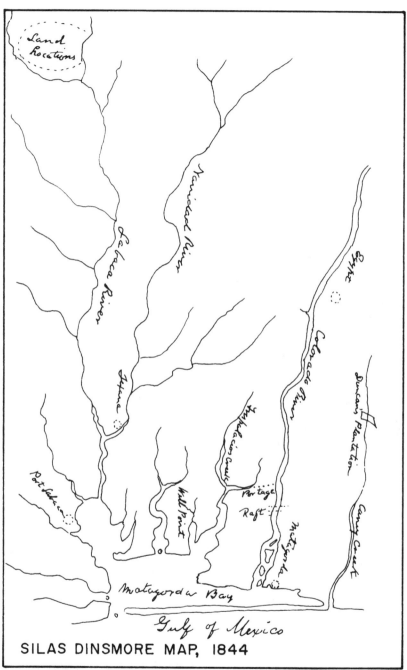

SILAS DINSMORE MAP, 1844

RIVER PORTS — *Shippers from the upper Colorado River got around the logjam by making a portage to Wilson Creek, which was navigable and ran into Tres Palacios Bay. This map was drawn in 1844 by Silas Dinsmore.* (Courtesy of Matagorda Historical Commission; original in Barker Texas History Center) lacios. His map clearly shows a portage between the Colorado River, just above the raft that blocked the river, and Wilson Creek, which was navigable to the bay.[4]

Caney Creek was deep enough for river steamers to reach thirty or more miles upstream. There were numerous warehouses along the banks where ships could tie up and receive cotton.

Notes

CORPUS CHRISTI BAY /ARANSAS BAY

1. Carlos Castañeda, *Our Catholic Heritage in Texas* (Austin: Von Boeck-mann-Jones Co., 1936), 1:7–15.
2. Hobart Huson, *History of Refugio County* (Houston: Guardsman Publishing Co., 1956), 1:67.
3. Castañeda, *Catholic Heritage*, 1:300–350.
4. *Ibid.*, 1:308.
5. William M. Carroll, *Beranger's Discovery of Aransas Pass*, edited and anno-tated by Frank Wagner (Friends of the Corpus Christi Museum: 1983), 21–22.
6. Castañeda, *Catholic Heritage*, 1:311.
7. Huson, *Refugio*, 1:72.
8. Castañeda, *Catholic Heritage*, 4:215–221.
9. Keith Guthrie, *History of San Patricio County* (Austin: Nortex Press, 1986), 6.
10. *Ibid.*, 7.

El Copano

1. William H. Oberste, *History of Refugio Mission* (*Refugio Timely Remarks*, 1942), 12, 13; Hobart Huson, *History of Refugio County* (Houston: Guardsman Pub-lishing Co., 1956), 1:89.
2. Albert Samuel Gatschet, *The Karankawa Indians* (New York: Kraus Re-print Corp., 1967), 43, 44.
3. Oberste, *Mission*, 16.
4. *Ibid.*, 29.
5. Carlos E. Castañeda, *Our Catholic Heritage in Texas* (Austin: Von Boeck-mann-Jones Co., 1936), 5:91.
6. Oberste, *Mission*, 136.
7. Huson, *Refugio*, 1:85–98; Oberste, *Mission*, 146–158; Carlos E. Casta-ñeda, *The Mexican Side of the Texas Revolution, 1836* (Dallas: P. L. Turner Co., 1928), 158.
8. Huson, *Refugio*, 1:89.
9. *Ibid.*, 1:91.
10. *Ibid.*
11. John Henry Brown, *History of Texas from 1685 to 1892* (St. Louis: L. E. Daniell, 1892), 1:33.

12. Huson, *Refugio*, 1:73.

13. Charles Wilson Hackett, *Pichardo's Treatise on the Limits of Louisiana and Texas* (Austin: University of Texas Press, 1931), 1:352, 420–422, 441, 442.

14. *Ibid.*, 1:350.

15. Hobart Huson, *El Copano (Refugio Timely Remarks*, ca. 1920s), 6.

16. *Ibid.*, 1.

17. Henderson Yoakum, *History of Texas* (New York: Redfield, 1856), 1:109.

18. Huson, *Refugio*, 1:177.

19. Yoakum, 1:127.

20. Huson, *El Copano*, 6.

21. Dudley Wooten, *Comprehensive History of Texas* (Dallas: Wm. G. Scarff, 1898), 1:168.

22. Keith Guthrie, *History of San Patricio County* (Austin: Nortex Press, 1986), 8.

23. Huson, *El Copano*, 15, 16.

24. Camp Ezell, *Historical Story of Bee County* (Beeville: Beeville Publishing Co., 1973), 9, 10.

25. Huson, *El Copano*, 9.

26. William Kennedy, *Texas: the Rise, Progress and Prospects of the Republic of Texas* (Clifton: Augustus M. Kelley, 1841, reprint 1974), 392–394.

27. *Ibid.*, 432–443; Huson, *El Copano*, 17.

28. John H. Jenkins, ed., *The Papers of the Texas Revolution 1835–1836* (Austin: Presidial Press, 1973), item 1526.

29. Henry Stuart Foote, *Texas and the Texans* (Philadelphia: Thomas Cowperthwait & Co., 1841), 2:104.

30. "Military Problems of the Goliad Campaign," *Southwestern Historical Quarterly*, 43:8.

31. Jenkins, ed., *Papers*, item 221.

32. *Ibid.*, item 593.

33. *Ibid.*, item 1625.

34. *Ibid.*, items 1487, 1510, 1532, 1547, 1563, 1625, 1658.

35. *Ibid.*, item 1936.

36. Huson, *El Copano*, 26.

37. *Ibid.*, 27.

38. Jenkins, ed., *Papers*, items 2131 and 2478.

39. Huson, *Refugio*, 1:389.

40. Castañeda, *Mexican Side*, 234.

41. Yoakum, 2:180; Huson, *El Copano*, 33–34.

42. Huson, *Refugio*, 1:394, 395.

43. Republic of Texas Customs Records, Texas State Archives, box 4–26/7: Secretary of Treasury to Duke, July 17, 1837; Secretary to Duke, August 11, 1837; Jenkins, ed., *Papers*, item 1510.

44. Customs Records, box 4–26/34: *Southern*, manifests, letters, September 11 and October 11, 1837.

45. *Ibid.*: Letters, January 28 and February 4, 1838; September 10 and December 3, 1839; January 20 and January 23, 1840.

46. Huson, *El Copano*, 34, 35. Shell-crete is made by burning oyster shell until the shell is reduced to lime. The lime is then used as a bonding agent, mixed with

crushed shell and sand, then poured into forms that have been set in place. The great advantage of shell-crete was that the material was in abundance at no cost, and the thick walls offered insulation from the heat in summer and from the cold in winter. The roofs were made of slate imported from Ireland.

47. Mirabeau B. Lamar, *Papers of Mirabeau B. Lamar* (Austin and New York: Pemberton Press, 1968): Plummer to Lamar, March 12, 1839, 5:261, No. 1128; Plummer to Lamar, May 17, 1840, 3:392, No. 1804.

48. Customs Records, box 4–26/34: Manifest, September 11, 1837.

49. Huson, *Refugio,* 1:417.

50. Huson, *El Copano,* 45.

51. Turner Papers from the Harwood Collection, Mrs. H. H. Rugeley, custodian (Alguna, December 1852).

52. Huson, *El Copano,* 39, 40.

53. Refugio County Commissioners Court records, 1:30.

54. Huson, *El Copano,* 40, 41.

55. Huson, *Refugio,* 1:441; Huson, *El Copano,* 44, 45.

56. Huson, *Refugio,* 1:559, 560.

57. Huson, *El Copano,* 42–45.

58. Peter A. Johnson, "Two Sea Captains," unpublished manuscript, compiled and edited by Hobart Huson, 22.

59. J. Frank Dobie, *A Vaquero of the Brush Country* (Austin: University of Texas Press, 1957), 21.

Aransas City

1. William H. Oberste, *Texas Irish Empresarios and Their Colonies* (Austin: Von Boeckmann-Jones Co., 1953), 86; Power Papers, unpublished.

2. Keith Guthrie, *History of San Patricio County* (Austin: Nortex Press, 1986), 14, 15.

3. Oberste, *Irish Empresarios,* 231.

4. *Ibid.,* 231, 232.

5. Hobart Huson, *History of Refugio County* (Houston: Guardsman Publishing Co., 1956), 1:417.

6. *Ibid.,* 1:422, 423.

7. *Ibid.,* 1:423, 438–449.

8. Hobart Huson, *El Copano* (Refugio Timely Remarks, ca. 1920s), 34.

9. Customs Records of the Republic of Texas, Texas State Archives, box 4–26/6: Secretary of treasury to Duke, dated July 17, 1837.

10. *Ibid.,* box 4–26/34: Manifest of schooner *Southern,* dated September 11, 1837.

11. *Ibid.,* box 4–26/6: Duke to Smith, October 11, 1837; Smith to Duke, January 28, 1838; secretary to Duke, February 4, 1838.

12. *Ibid.,* box 4–26/31: Fulton's quarterly report dated December 31, 1838; Huson, *Refugio,* 1:420, 421.

13. Mirabeau B. Lamar, *Papers of Mirabeau B. Lamar* (Austin and New York: Pemberton Press, 1968), 2:item 1240.

14. *Ibid.,* 3:item 1341.

15. H. P. N. Gammel, ed., *Laws of Texas* (Austin: The Gammel Book Co., 1898), 10.

16. Customs Records, box 4–26/6: Letters dated May 1 and October 1, 1843.

17. *Ibid.*, box 4–26/31: Annual report of 1839.

18. Oberste, *Irish Empresarios,* 233, 234; Huson, *Refugio,* 1:52.

19. Lamar, *Papers,* 2:item 585; Huson, *Refugio,* 1:52.

20. Huson, *Refugio,* 1:433, 434.

21. Henderson Yoakum, *History of Texas* (New York: Redfield, 1856), 2:355; Huson, *Refugio,* 1:469, 470.

22. Oberste, *Irish Empresarios,* 236; Huson, *Refugio,* 1:423.

23. Huson, *Refugio,* 1:421.

24. *Ibid.,* 1:439, 441.

25. Refugio County Commissioners Court records, 1:80; Huson, *Refugio,* 1:411.

26. Gammel, ed., *Laws of Texas,* 2:99.

St. Mary's

1. The material covering the legal battle between Smith and Power comes from many sources, chiefly: "St. Mary's of Aransas," printed in the *Refugio Timely Remarks* over a number of years and written by Hobart Huson (unpublished work in possession of Keith Guthrie); Hobart Huson, *History of Refugio County;* court and commissioners court records of Refugio County and Aransas County; Gammel's *Laws of Texas;* letters in the Turner Papers from the Harwood Collection, Mrs. H. H. Rugeley, custodian; vertical files of Corpus Christi Public Library, Victoria Public Library, and Rockport Public Library; Byrne Papers, Barker Texas History Center, University of Texas at Austin; customs records and letters, Texas State Archives, Austin; and St. Mary's Cemetery records.

2. Hobart Huson, *History of Refugio County* (Houston: Guardsman Publishing Co., 1956), 1:567.

3. Refugio Commissioners Court records, 1:186.

4. "St. Mary's of Aransas," *Refugio Timely Remarks,* Chapter 5. Perhaps it was a quirk of fate, or perhaps some kind of retribution, but later it was found that Joseph Smith's house was built on the wrong survey and he lost title to it, much in the same way that Colonel Power had lost his home on Live Oak Peninsula.

5. Huson, *Refugio,* 1:571.

6. Keith Guthrie, *History of San Patricio County* (Austin: Nortex Press, 1986), 154.

7. "St. Mary's," Chapter 5.

8. Refugio Commissioners Court records, 1:194, 195, 248.

9. Huson, *Refugio,* 1:573.

10. *Ibid.*

11. Byrne Papers, Barker Texas History Center, University of Texas at Austin, 2.

12. Huson, *Refugio,* 1:573.

13. *Ibid.,* 1:574.

14. *Ibid.,* 1:201, 202.

15. Turner Papers from Harwood Collection, Mrs. H. H. Rugeley, custodian.

16. Huson, *Refugio*, 1:569.
17. Turner Papers.
18. "St. Mary's," Chapter 11.
19. Refugio Commissioners Court records, 1:282, 285, 294.
20. Huson, *Refugio*, 2:139.
21. *Ibid.*, 2:85–86.
22. *The Vaquero*, copies in Barker Texas History Center, University of Texas at Austin.
23. Gammel, ed., *Laws of Texas*, 7:207.
24. "St. Mary's," Chapter 10.
25. Huson, *Refugio*, 2:152.
26. *Ibid.*, 2:142.
27. *Ibid.*, 2:148, 149.
28. *Ibid.*, 2:151.
29. *Ibid.*, 2:154, 155.
30. Old St. Mary's Cemetery located one mile northeast of Bayside.

Lamar

1. Hobart Huson, *History of Refugio County* (Houston: Guardsman Publishing Co., 1956), 1:385, 399.
2. William H. Oberste, *Texas Irish Empresarios and Their Colonies* (Austin: Von Boeckmann-Jones Co., 1953), 236.
3. *Ibid.*
4. Huson, *Refugio*, 1:417, 425.
5. H. P. N. Gammel, ed., *Laws of Texas* (Austin: The Gammel Book Co., 1898), 1:1315.
6. Republic of Texas Customs Records, Texas State Archives, box 4–26/7: Secretary of Treasury to Duke, July 17, 1837, Secretary to Duke, August 11, 1837; John H. Jenkins, ed., *Papers of the Texas Revolution, 1835–1836* (Austin: Presidial Press, 1973), 2:item 1510.
7. Mirabeau B. Lamar, *Papers of Mirabeau B. Lamar* (Austin and New York: Pemberton Press, 1968), 5:555.
8. Gammel, ed., *Laws of Texas*, 2:195. The *Journal of the Sixth Congress* reported that in 1842 another attempt was made to return the customshouse to Lamar, but it failed; Customs Records of the Republic of Texas, quarterly report dated March 30, 1839, noted rent paid for two quarters on customshouse in Aransas City for $120, with receipt showing money paid to George W. Fulton. The next entry was a request to pay James Gourlay $66 for three-months' rent of customshouse at Lamar, payable to James W. Byrne.
9. Customs Records, box 4–26/31: Quarterly reports for 1839.
10. Customs Records, box 4–26/34: Manifest of schooner *Caroline*, February 25, 1840.
11. Huson, *Refugio*, 1:529; Peter A. Johnson, "Two Sea Captains," unpublished manuscript edited by Hobart Huson, 2.
12. Huson, *Refugio*, 1:556.
13. Refugio County deed records, D:47–49, 233.
14. Byrne Papers, Barker Texas History Center, University of Texas at Austin, handwritten circular by Pryor Lea.

15. Huson, *Refugio*, 1:562.

16. *Ibid.*, 1:563; Refugio deed records, E:133–136.

17. Harry Traylor, "Famous Colt Six Shooter Originated in Workshop of Colt Brothers at Lamar," *Rockport Pilot*, October 15, 1942.

18. Huson, *Refugio*, 1:564.

19. B. Edwards, *The Story of Colt's Revolver* (Harrisburg, PA: Stackpole Co., 1953), 97–102.

20. *Ibid.*, 92, 94, 215.

21. Chris Emmett, *Texas Camel Tales* (San Antonio: Naylor, 1932), 14–16.

22. Mrs. Ella McRae Clay, "History of Lamar," unpublished manuscript, 4–5.

23. *Ibid.*, 3, 4.

24. *Ibid.*, 2–3. Frequently there were no saloons in early communities. Liquor was regularly carried in barrels at grocery stores and general merchandise establishments. Capt. Phillip C. Paul operated this type of store in Lamar; Huson, *Refugio*, 1:199.

25. Johnson, "Two Sea Captains," 7, 8. (Peter A. Johnson was sheriff of Refugio County, 1905–1916.)

26. Clay, "History of Lamar," 6.

27. *Ibid.*, 9.

28. Unpublished interview made by Mrs. Clarence Kerlagen with Carrie Little, niece of Mrs. O'Connor, in November 1938.

29. Johnson, "Two Sea Captains," 13; Huson, *Refugio*, 1:595, 596.

30. Johnson, "Two Sea Captains," 2, 3; Huson, *Refugio*, 1:83, 123.

31. Huson, *Refugio*, 1:505.

32. Johnson, "Two Sea Captains," 1–3, 8; Huson, *Refugio*, 2:44.

33. Huson, *Refugio*, 2:9, 38, 39.

34. *Ibid.*, 2:53, 54.

35. Johnson, "Two Sea Captains," 5.

36. Huson, *Refugio*, 2:83, 84.

37. Johnson, "Two Sea Captains," 8.

38. Clay, "History of Lamar," 7.

Port Preston

1. Hobart Huson, *History of Refugio County* (Houston: Guardsman Publishing Co., 1956), 1:424. Perry is one of the more colorful characters in a period that produced outstanding men. Born in England, he came to the United States with immigrants from England and Ireland. He soon became an avid promoter of Texas and was involved with a group who set out to establish a colony in Texas, but after an accident, he ended up in New Orleans in banking. Still a fervent backer of the Texas cause, he advanced money for supplies and kept a ship in New Orleans for use by Texans. After San Jacinto, the legislature passed a bill acknowledging that Texas owed him $38,053.23. It is not clear whether he was ever paid. (*Lamar Papers* 2:220, 221; H. P. N. Gammel, ed., *Laws of Texas* (Austin: The Gammel Book Co., 1898), 2:118; Refugio County deed records, D:508, E:120, 121, 205; Refugio County Commissioners Court minutes, 1:33)

Black Point

1. Hobart Huson, *History of Refugio County* (Houston: Guardsman Publishing Co., 1956), 1:13.
2. Keith Guthrie, *History of San Patricio County* (Austin: Nortex Press, 1986), 55.
3. Joseph Milton Nance, *Attack and Counterattack* (Austin: University of Texas Press, 1964), 86.
4. Eugenia Reynolds Briscoe, *City by the Sea: A History of Corpus Christi, Texas, 1519–1875* (New York: Vantage Press, 1985), 45, 69.
5. Huson, *Refugio*, 1:13.
6. *Ibid.*, 1:497–498, 568, 578.

Corpus Christi

1. Carlos E. Castañeda, *Our Catholic Heritage in Texas* (Austin: Von Boeckmann-Jones Co., 1936), 1:7–14; Hobart Huson, *History of Refugio County* (Houston: Guardsman Publishing Co., 1956), 1:60.
2. Eugenia Reynolds Briscoe, *City by the Sea: A History of Corpus Christi, Texas 1519–1875* (New York: Vantage Press, 1985), 23–28.
3. Joseph Milton Nance, *After San Jacinto* (Austin: University of Texas Press, 1963), 42.
4. H. P. N. Gammel, ed., *Laws of Texas* (Austin: The Gammel Book Co., 1898), 1:1334, 1335.
5. *Ibid.*, 1:1480–1481.
6. Coleman McCampbell, *Texas Seaport* (New York: Exposition Press, 1952), 23.
7. *Corpus Christi, A History and Guide,* compiled by writers for Works Progress Administration (Corpus Christi: Caller-Times Publishing Co., 1942), 49. Another version of Kinney's early life finds him involved in a scandal with another man's wife, forcing him to leave home. Settling in Peru, Illinois, he became a land promoter and built a paper fortune that was wiped out in a financial panic. Facing bankruptcy, he headed for Texas.
8. Mary A. Sutherland, *The Story of Corpus Christi* (Houston: Rein & Sons, 1916), 104, 105; Briscoe, 282, 283.
9. Refugio Commissioners Court records, 1:441; Huson, *Refugio,* 1:441; Mirabeau B. Lamar, *Papers of Mirabeau B. Lamar* (Austin: Pemberton Press, 1968), 5:item 555.
10. Huson, *Refugio,* 1:442.
11. Lamar, *Papers,* 4:213. *The Handbook of Texas* gives date of first post office as 1850; Hortense Ward used 1844.
12. Briscoe, 37.
13. McCampbell, 26; Briscoe, 37.
14. Nance, *After San Jacinto,* 445–469. Residents of San Patricio petitioned for the removal of Ferguson from office.
15. Briscoe, 84–92, 103, 104.
16. E. A. Hitchcock, *Diary,* edited by W. A. Croffut (New York: Books for Libraries Press), 193.
17. *Corpus Christi: A History,* 71, 72.

18. Hitchcock, *Diary,* 197, 198.

19. *Corpus Christi: A History,* 77.

20. *Corpus Christi Caller-Times,* June 18, 1959.

21. Briscoe, 113, 115, 116. The city was reincorporated by the fourth legislature in April 1852.

22. *Ibid.,* 116, 117.

23. *Corpus Christi: A History,* 85, 86; Briscoe, 122, 123, 124; McCampbell, 30.

24. *Corpus Christi: A History,* 90–91; Briscoe, 149.

25. Hortense Warner Ward, "Kinney's Trading Post," unpublished manuscript, Corpus Christi Public Library. Kinney's wife was the daughter of James Webb, former secretary of state for the Republic of Texas. The divorce was for "abandonment." Kinney served as senator in the first four sessions of the Texas legislature after annexation and one term as representative in the eighth session. He tried unsuccessfully to get President Lincoln to appoint him minister to Nicaragua and later urged that the president give him a post either in Spain or Mexico. Sam Houston agreed to endorse him as a possible choice for minister to Mexico. Finally, Kinney wrote desperate letters to President Jefferson Davis offering his services as an undercover informant in Spain or Mexico under the Confederacy.

26. "Scrapbook," newspaper clippings in Dan Kilgore Collection, Corpus Christi State University Library.

27. *Corpus Christi Caller,* September 22, 1974.

28. Lynn M. Alperin, *Custodians of the Coast* (Corps of Engineers Publications: 1977), 133.

29. U.S. House of Representatives, 67th Congress, 2d session, document no. 321.

30. Briscoe, 210, 211.

31. McCampbell, 45.

32. *Corpus Christi: A History,* 102–121.

33. Mary A. Sutherland, *The Story of Corpus Christi* (Houston: Rein & Sons Co., 1916), 32–34.

34. Briscoe, 255, 257, 262; *Corpus Christi: A History,* 131.

35. Ruth Dodson, "The Noakes Raid," *Frontier Times* 23 (October 1945), 175–187.

36. *Corpus Christi: A History,* 145, 154.

Sharpsburg

1. Keith Guthrie, *History of San Patricio County* (Austin: Nortex Press, 1986), 45, 253; *San Patricio County News,* anniversary edition, September 10, 1926; Mary Frances Hunter, speech, copy in possession of Keith Guthrie; *Odem-Edroy Times,* May 29, 1958; *Texas State Gazetteer and Business Directory;* invoices, Barker Texas History Center, University of Texas at Austin; San Patricio County deed records, Vol. A, B, C.

Aransas Pass / Harbor City

1. *Aransas Pass Progress,* November 19, 1909. Other sources list 1854 as the date for the beginning of work by Central Transit. It appears that the project was conceived in 1854 and work actually got started by 1858.

2. Hobart Huson, *History of Refugio County* (Houston: Guardsman Publishing Co., 1956), 2:287.

3. Dorothy Louise Nims, "A History of the Village of Rockport" (master's thesis, Southwest Texas State Teachers College, 1939), 68, 69, 70, 74.

4. Walter P. Webb, et al., eds., *Handbook of Texas* (Austin: Texas State Historical Association, 1952), 2:747–748.

5. Lynn M. Alperin, *Custodians of the Coast* (Corps of Engineers Publications: 1977), 126–127.

6. *Ibid.*, 126–128.

7. Charter No. 4520, filed in office of Secretary of State of Texas.

8. Keith Guthrie, *History of San Patricio County* (Austin: Nortex Press, 1986), 189–190.

9. *Aransas Harbor Herald,* April 23, 1893; *Aransas Pass Progress,* November 19, 1909.

10. F. A. Schmidt, "Rails Across the Bay," pamphlet, in possession of Keith Guthrie.

11. Alperin, 129.

12. Guthrie, 191, 192; Alperin, 132.

13. San Patricio County deed records, Vol. 29:6, 7.

14. W. H. Vernor, *A Rugged American, Aransas Pass Progress* (n.p., 1955), 21.

15. Charter No. 20353, Secretary of State of Texas.

16. Guthrie, 194–197.

17. *Aransas Pass Progress,* September 26, 1919.

18. Alperin, 133.

19. Tom Lea, *The King Ranch* (Toronto, Boston: Little, Brown & Co., 1957), 2:601.

20. Alperin, 134.

21. Files of *Aransas Pass Progress* and *San Patricio County News,* for 1919, 1920, 1921, 1922, 1923.

Rockport

1. Alpha Kennedy Wood, *Texas Coastal Bend* (second printing by Kathryn Holmes Wood, 1979), 84.

2. Hobart Huson, *History of Refugio County* (Houston: Guardsman Publishing Co., 1956), 2:157.

3. Refugio County Commissioners Court records, Vol. G: 357, 406; A. Ray Stephens, *The Taft Ranch* (Austin: University of Texas Press, 1964), 10.

4. Keith Guthrie, *History of San Patricio County* (Austin: Nortex Press, 1986), 32, 33.

5. Turner Letters from the Harwood Collection, Mrs. H. H. Rugeley, custodian (copy of letters in possession of Keith Guthrie and Corpus Christi Public Library). Marcellus Turner to Amasa Turner, August 1859, from Chicago. Marcellus had left Texas with a herd of cattle and headed for Missouri in 1859. Finding no market there, he pushed on to Chicago, where he sold part of the herd and was forced to slaughter and pickle the rest. The barreled beef was sent to New York, where Tom Coleman was able to sell the hams for $14 per barrel but was not able to sell the remainder. Over 1,200 barrels of beef were left with a broker and finally sold months later for barely enough to get the Star Company out of debt.

6. J. Frank Dobie, *A Vaquero of the Brush Country* (Austin: University of Texas Press, 1957), 23.

7. *Texas Almanac, 1871,* 144.

8. Coleman-Fulton Papers, Barker Texas History Center, University of Texas at Austin, director's minutes of 1873 and 1874.

9. *Victoria Advocate,* 88th anniversary edition (1934); Dorothy Louise Nims, "A History of the Village of Rockport" (master's thesis, Southwest Texas State Teachers College, 1939), 37, 38, 40, 46.

10. Nims, 42.

11. *Ibid.,* 44.

12. *San Antonio Express,* September 19, 1915.

13. *Ibid.,* May 12, 1912.

14. Nims, 43.

15. Huson, *Refugio,* 2:157–160.

16. *Ibid.,* 2:141, 167–170.

17. Coleman-Fulton Papers, letter G. S. Whitney, Rincon Ranch, to Tom M. Coleman; Stephens, 36.

18. Refugio County Commissioners Court minutes, 1:393–408.

19. Huson, *Refugio,* 2:190.

20. Aransas County Commissioners Court minutes, 1:25.

21. Stephens, 74.

22. Nims, 51.

23. *Rockport Pilot,* 70th anniversary special, August 31, 1939; Nims, 43, 44.

24. *Corpus Christi Caller,* August 19, 1957.

25. Nims, 72.

Portland

1. Keith Guthrie, *History of San Patricio County* (Austin: Nortex Press, 1986), 172–178, 274–275; *Corpus Christi Caller-Times,* May 9, June 23, October 13, 1911; Coleman-Fulton Pasture Company, directors' minutes (1910–1916, 1919), Barker Texas History Center, University of Texas at Austin.

SAN ANTONIO BAY /ESPIRITU BAY

1. Hobart Huson, *History of Refugio County* (Houston: Guardsman Publishing Co., 1956), 1:101–106.

Mesquite Landing

1. Hobart Huson, *History of Refugio County* (Houston: Guardsman Publishing Co., 1956), 1:5, 73.

2. *Ibid.,* 1:78.

3. *Ibid.,* 1:108, 109.

4. *Ibid.,* 1:123.

5. *Ibid.,* 1:561.

6. *History of Refugio County* (Refugio County Historical Commission: 1987), 152.

7. Huson, *Refugio*, 1:235.
8. *History of Refugio County*, 169.

MATAGORDA BAY /SAN BERNARDO BAY

1. Brownson Malsch, "Historic Landing at Matagorda Bay," *Victoria Advocate,* January 24, 1985.
2. Matagorda County Historical Commission, *Historic Matagorda County* (Houston: D. Armstrong Co., 1986), 16.
3. Carlos E. Castañeda, *Our Catholic Heritage in Texas* (Austin: Von Boeckmann-Jones Co., 1936), 1:300–350; Keith Guthrie, *History of San Patricio County* (Austin: Nortex Press, 1986), 5.
4. Hobart Huson, *History of Refugio County* (Houston: Guardsman Publishing Co., 1956), 1:68.
5. William M. Carroll, *Beranger's Discovery of Aransas Pass,* edited and annotated by Frank Wagner (Friends of the Corpus Christi Museum: 1983), 7–12.
6. Bexar Archives, 1:133. Translation Series 2:36.
7. *Ibid.,* 133:40, 41.
8. *Ibid.,* 133:47.
9. Walter P. Webb, et al., eds., *Handbook of Texas* (Austin: Texas State Historical Association, 1952), 2:548.
10. Bexar Archives, 133:12.
11. *Ibid.,* 11:523, 526.
12. *Ibid.,* 11:219.
13. *Ibid.,* 10:4.
14. *Ibid.,* 12:216.

Matagorda

1. Eugene C. Barker, *Austin Papers* (Austin: University of Texas Press, 1927), 1:28, letter, Austin to J. E. B. Austin, April 8, 1821.
2. Eugene C. Barker, *The Life of Stephen F. Austin* (Austin: Texas State Historical Association, 1949), 23, 24, 25.
3. *Ibid.,* 32, 33, 34.
4. *Ibid.,* 39.
5. Lester G. Bugbee, "What Became of the Lively," *Southwestern Historical Quarterly,* 3:141–148.
6. Barker, *Life of Stephen F. Austin,* 40.
7. James R. Yeamans, Sr., unpublished notes on Matagorda, 19, 20–25.
8. Barker, *Life of Stephen F. Austin,* 87, 88.
9. *Ibid.,* 91, 92.
10. *Ibid.,* 117.
11. *Ibid.,* 143.
12. Yeamans, notes on Matagorda, 26.
13. Lorraine Bruce Jeter, *Matagorda Early History* (Baltimore: Gateway Press, Inc., 1974), 9.
14. *Ibid.,* 9, 10; Walter P. Webb, et al., eds., *Handbook of Texas* (Austin:

Texas State Historical Association, 1952), 2:908; Yeamans, notes on Matagorda, 29, 30, 44.

15. Ed Killman, *Cannibal Coast* (San Antonio: Naylor Co., 1959), 203–206, 208, 209.

16. Mary S. Wightman Helm, *Scraps of Early Texas History* (Austin: Eakin Press, 1987), 9. The *Little Zoe* was supposed to have drawn only four and one-half feet of water, according to Yeamans, whose grandfather was one of the passengers.

17. Jeter, 10; Yeamans, notes on Matagorda, 49.

18. Yeamans, notes on Matagorda, 10. In 1833 Wilbarger and four friends were hunting near Bastrop when they were jumped by a party of Comanches. Two of the men got away, but Wilbarger and another were shot down and left for dead — minus their scalps. The next day when his companions returned to the scene to bury him, they discovered Wilbarger soaked with blood but still alive. He lived twelve years longer.

19. *Ibid.*, 33.

20. *Ibid.*, 52, 67, 68. Benjamin and Esther Wightman became the first to be buried in the Matagorda Cemetery, she on June 20, 1830, and he six weeks later.

21. *Ibid.*, 55.

22. Barker, *Austin Letters,* petition asking permission to start a town at mouth of Colorado River (2:1426); Yeamans, notes on Matagorda, 36–40, 54. James Yeamans, in his unpublished notes, tells that a channel about six feet deep and forty feet wide was actually dredged through Dog Island by the proprietors of the town to allow shallow-draft vessels to approach Matagorda in the mid-1830s. "It was no unusual sight to see 10 or 12 foreign vessels lying at anchorage in the bay below Dog Island." (D. E. E. Braman unpublished notes dated 1858.)

23. James Yeamans, Sr., unpublished notes on *Mary's Bayou,* 1.

24. Jeter, 12; Matagorda County Historical Commission, *Historic Matagorda County* (Houston: D. Armstrong Co., 1986), 1:32, 33; Yeaman's notes on Matagorda, 54.

25. Yeamans, notes on Matagorda, 111, 113; Jeter, 11; *Historic Matagorda,* 1:143.

26. Yeamans, notes on Matagorda, 118, 122, 124.

27. *Historic Matagorda,* 1:148.

28. Jeter, 12–14; Yeamans, notes on Matagorda, 1.

29. *Southwestern Historical Quarterly,* 40:232, 233.

30. Jeter, 18; John Columbus Marr, "History of Matagorda County" (master's thesis, University of Texas, 1928), 119.

31. Barker, *Life of Stephen F. Austin,* 263.

32. *Ibid.*, 348, 360, 366, 392, 410, 414; Jeter, 19, 20, 21, 24.

33. Hobart Huson, *History of Refugio County* (Houston: Guardsman Publishing Co., 1956), 1:212, 214, 215.

34. *Ibid.*, 1:212, 215, 216, 217; Yeamans, notes on Matagorda, 162.

35. Huson, *Refugio,* 1:217, 220, 237, 241, 242. Members of Collinsworth's expedition from Matagorda included: George Collinsworth, captain; D. C. Collinsworth, second lieutenant; James W. Moore, first lieutenant; Ira Ingram, Spirce Dooley, R. S. Reding, Thomas Anderson, James Rawls, R. O. Graves, J. W. Baylor, B. J. White, Benjamin White, T. M. Blake, J. P. Borden, B. Rawls, G. W. Paine, R. Stevenson, R. R. Erwin, H. T. Davis, H. F. Armstrong, Thomas Reed,

A. Scott, J. B. Barton, D. George, N. B. Williams, R. Mercer, W. Carleton, L. McCullough, John Duncan, W. Cummins, J. L. Osborn, Samuel Wildy, John Hall, M. Hicks, Thos. Thompson, Philip Dimmitt, A. Constanta, John Bowman, W. New, T. C. Hamilton, James Duncan, M. Carbahall, J. A. Padilla, D. Martindale, A. H. Jones, W. J. Lightfoot, and John Flick (Jeter, 22, 23, 24).

36. Yeamans, notes on Matagorda, 178, 181, 186.

37. Lewis W. Newton, *History of Texas* (Dallas: Southwest Press, 1932), 181; Louis J. Wortham, *History of Texas* (Fort Worth: Wortham-Molyneaux Co., 1924), 2:22; Almonte Report in Yeamans, notes on Matagorda, 143.

38. Yeamans, 162, 168, 170, 172.

39. John H. Jenkins, ed., *Papers of the Texas Revolution, 1835–1836* (Austin: Presidial Press, 1973), 1:items 667, 704, 1448, 1470, 1507.

40. *Historic Matagorda*, 131–140; Marr, "History of Matagorda," 119–124.

41. *Historic Matagorda*, 38; Yeamans, notes on Matagorda, 221.

42. Marr, "History of Matagorda," 93–94; Yeamans, notes on Matagorda, 110.

43. Marilyn McAdams Sibley, *Lone Stars and State Gazettes* (College Station: A&M Press, 1983), 90, 91; Richard King, *Printing in the Republic of Texas* (Texana: 1968), 349, 350.

44. Yeamans, notes on Matagorda, 84; Webb, et al., eds., *Handbook of Texas*, 2:157. D. E. E. Braman in his manuscript "Information About Texas in the Year 1858" put it this way: "The Hurricane of Sept. 18, 1854 prostrated nearly all the buildings in the town, and destroyed much personal property." Don Egbert Braman came to Texas in 1837, fought with Gen. Sam Houston, served as a customs officer at Matagorda in 1847, was appointed clerk of the First Judicial District, and studied law while holding that office. He was admitted to the bar in 1853 and served as mayor of Matagorda for several years before being appointed county judge by Governor Elisha M. Pease. He began writing for early newspapers and in 1854 published his book, which gives some insights on economic conditions in the pre-Civil War days. A number of his writings have been preserved. His writings also state: "The public buildings of Matagorda are the courthouse, jail, Odd Fellows Hall, Episcopal Church, and a very large and superior public school house." Evidently the courthouse was rebuilt immediately, since it is apparent that legal transactions were not hindered.

45. *Southwestern Historical Quarterly*, 59:173.

46. *Historic Matagorda*, 1:212.

47. H. P. N. Gammel, ed., *Laws of Texas* (Austin: Gammel Book Co., 1898), 1:1315, 2:77, 512; "Customs Administration," *SWHQ*, 21:20–33; *Historic Matagorda*, 1:421, 422.

48. Customs Records, Texas State Archives: Letters, receipts, checks, box 4–26/23.

49. Robert Lee Crane, Jr., "Customs Service of the Republic of Texas" (master's thesis, University of Texas, 1939), 92–100.

50. Customs Records, box 4–26/23: Bill of lading for schooner *Aurdra*, January 10, 1836.

51. Customs Records, box 4–26/21: Note asking warehouseman to collect money from Thomas W. Mather, July 28, 1837.

52. Customs Records, box 4–26/25: Listing of captains and boats working out of Matagorda in 1837.

53. *Historic Matagorda,* 1:119, 120.

54. Yeamans, notes on Matagorda, 262, 324.

55. *Southwestern Historical Quarterly,* 61:255–269.

56. Jeter, 5, 6, 8, 62, 79; Yeamans, notes on Matagorda, 157, 261, 262; *Historic Matagorda,* 1:31, 321, 325, 344; Webb, et al., eds., *Handbook,* 2:157, 158; *Southwestern Historical Quarterly,* 61: 255–269.

57. Yeamans, notes on Matagorda, 156–160.

58. Arda Talbot Allen, *Miss Ella* (San Antonio: The Naylor Co., 1951), 5–16; Yeamans, notes on Matagorda, 328, 329.

59. *Historic Matagorda,* 1:356; Yeamans, notes on Matagorda, 61; Allen, 5–16.

60. Yeamans, notes on Matagorda, 274, 277–287, 348–365.

61. *Ibid.,* 265–268.

62. Annie Webb Blanton, "Military Records of Wharton and Matagorda Counties," unpublished, Barker Texas History Center, University of Texas at Austin; *Historic Matagorda,* 1:165–166.

63. Huson, *Refugio,* 2:78, 79; *Historic Matagorda,* 164.

Linnville

1. John J. Linn, *Reminiscences of Fifty Years in Texas* (Austin: Steck Company, 1935), 10–28. Walter P. Webb, et al., eds., *Handbook of Texas* (Austin: Texas State Historical Association, 1952), 2:60.

2. John H. Jenkins, ed., *Papers of the Texas Revolution* (Austin: Presidial Press, 1973), letter, Johnstone to *Louisville Daily Journal,* 7:item 4022.

3. Linn, 249–251.

4. Customs Records of the Republic of Texas, Texas State Archives, boxes 4–26/27, 4–26/11, 4–26/12, 4–26/53: Letter, Collinsworth to Watts, July 7, 1837; letter to all collectors, secretary to Collinsworth, June 8, 1838. George Fred Rhodes, "Historically Speaking," *Port Lavaca Wave,* October 25, November 1, November 18, 1985.

5. Linn, 338–344.

6. E. W. Winkler, ed., *Secret Journals of the Senate,* December 24, 1840, 191; Customs Records, boxes 4–26/27, 4–26/11, 4–26/12, 4–26/53, 4–26/20: Kleppenburg to Chalmers, May 3, 1841; letter, Collinsworth to Watts, February 24, 1841; letter, George Earlee to Thomas M. Duke, April 16, 1841, District of Calhoun, Port of Cavallo. Also, Robert Edward Lee Crane, Jr., "Administration of Customs Service of the Republic of Texas" (master's thesis, University of Texas, 1939), 92–114.

Cox's Point / Dimmitt's Landing

1. Walter P. Webb, et al., eds., *Handbook of Texas* (Austin: Texas State Historical Association, 1952), 1:503, 504; Paul Freier, "Looking Back," *Port Lavaca Wave,* February 20, 1974; William Kennedy, *Texas: The Rise, Progress and Prospects of the Republic of Texas* (Clifton: Augustus M. Kelly, 1974), 787; Customs Records,

Texas State Archives, box 4–46/25 (receipt to O. Balfour dated September 20, 1838); *Southwestern Historical Quarterly,* 43:2104.

    2. *Southwestern Historical Quarterly,* 43:10, 20, 1305, 2351; Webb, et al., eds., *Handbook,* 1:430.

Lavaca

    1. *Houston Post,* November 10, 1963 (article by O. W. Nolen).

    2. Mirabeau Buonaparte Lamar, *Papers of Mirabeau B. Lamar* (Austin and New York: Pemberton Press, 1968), 1:125–128.

    3. *Ibid.,* 3:265.

    4. *Southwestern Historical Quarterly,* 48:216, 217.

    5. *Ibid.,* 48:535; Eugene C. Barker, *Austin Papers* (Austin: University of Texas Press, 1927), 2:758–761.

    6. John J. Linn, *Reminiscences of Fifty Years in Texas* (Austin: Steck Company, 1935), 13, 14, 24.

    7. *Southwestern Historical Quarterly,* 65:26.

    8. *Ibid.,* 43:10.

    9. *Ibid.,* 43:20.

    10. Lamar, *Papers,* 2:item 2351.

    11. "Journal of Gideon Lincecum's Travels in Texas 1835," edited by A. L. Bradford and T. N. Campbell, *Southwestern Historical Quarterly,* 53:198, 199; Mary Austin Holley, *Texas* (Austin: Steck Company, 1935), 55.

    12. Hubert Howe Bancroft, interview with George Washington Trahern, *Southwestern Historical Quarterly,* 58:101.

    13. H. P. N. Gammel, ed., *Laws of Texas* (Austin: The Gammel Book Co., 1898), 1:1315.

    14. E. W. Winkler, ed., *Secret Journals of the Senate of Texas,* May 23, 1837, 55.

    15. Customs Records of the Republic of Texas, Texas State Archives, box 4–26/23: Letters from secretary to Lavaca District; signatures on manifests, pay vouchers.

    16. *Ibid.:* Letters to Collinsworth, June 8, 1838.

    17. Gammel, ed., *Laws of Texas,* 2:77; Customs Records, box 4–26/23: Letter to Watts from secretary of state, January 26, 1839.

    18. Customs Records, box 4–26/11: Letter, Kleppenburg to Chalmers, May 3, 1841. The move is confirmed to "a port two miles below Linnville" where the Watts Brothers had a two-story warehouse. The letter does not identify the new town as Lavaca. Ships were still being cleared to the port of Linnville as late as July 1841.

    19. Gammel, ed., *Laws of Texas,* 2:512.

    20. Customs records, box 4–26/20: Entry logs of ships to Port Lavaca, 1837–41.

    21. Paul Freier, "Looking Back," *Port Lavaca Wave,* 8, 71; Customs Records, box 8–26/10: Entry logs of ships to Port Lavaca, 1838, 1839.

    22. Customs Records, box 4–26/12: Undated sketches of Port Lavaca customs office; box 8–26/10: Manifests for schooner *Maria,* duty collections for 1844, 1845.

    23. Mrs. J. M. Cockran, "Reminiscence of an Old Texas Pioneer," unpub-

lished manuscript serialized in *Port Lavaca Wave* by George Fred Rhodes, chairman, Calhoun County Historical Commission. Mrs. Cockran arrived in Calhoun County in 1846 with her parents, Rev. and Mrs. S. F. Cocke, after an overland trip in a wagon train that left Virginia in 1844.

24. Eugenia Reynolds Briscoe, *City by the Sea* (New York: Vantage Press, 1985), 122, 123; [Corpus Christi] *Star,* December 16, 1848, March 17, 1884; *Corpus Christi Caller-Times,* August 29, 1965.

25. Robert Edward Lee Crane, Jr., "Customs Service of Texas" (master's thesis, University of Texas, 1939), 117–120.

26. Gammel, ed., *Laws of Texas,* 2:1347.

27. Calhoun County Court Journal, minutes of commissioners court, Vol. A:1–9.

28. Calhoun County Historical Commission, *Shifting Sands of Calhoun County* (1981), 20, 21.

29. Calhoun County, *Shifting Sands,* 6, 7, 60, 61; *Southwestern Historical Quarterly,* 76:167; Fretelliere, "San Antonio," *Texas Magazine* (March 1912), 55.

30. *Colorado Tribune,* July 7, 1851.

31. George Fred Rhodes, "Historically Speaking," *Port Lavaca Wave,* September 19, 1986.

32. Calhoun County, *Inventory,* prepared by Works Progress Administration, University of Texas sponsor, 1941 (published by Calhoun County), 10.

33. Jacob de Cordova, *Texas* (Philadelphia: E. Crozet, Co., 1858), 288; *Southwestern Historical Quarterly,* 76:167; Calhoun County, *Inventory,* 10.

34. Existing copies of old papers in Barker Texas History Center, Austin; George Fred Rhodes, September 19, 1986.

35. Calhoun County, *Shifting Sands,* 61; *Indianola Bulletin,* October 19, 1853.

36. Calhoun County, *Shifting Sands,* 28, 31, 47; Calhoun County Commissioners Court records, Vol. A:143.

37. Calhoun County Commissioners Court records, Vol. B:8, 12, 13, 15, 16–70; Calhoun County, *Inventory,* 10, 11.

38. *Southwestern Historical Quarterly,* 65:14.

39. Hobart Huson, *History of Refugio County* (Houston: Guardsman Publishing Co., 1956), 2:46; Calhoun County Commissioners Court records, Vol. G:174 ff.

40. Huson, *Refugio,* 2:82.

41. Calhoun County Commissioners Court records, Vol. B:21–50, 40, 41, 42–58, 60, 66.

42. *Texas Almanac, 1871,* 98, 287.

43. "History of Indianola," by Lelia Seeligson, *Indianola Scrap Book* (Austin: Jenkins, 1974), 35, 36, 37.

44. Calhoun County, *Shifting Sands,* 20, 21; Calhoun County Commissioners Court records, C:198, D:44.

Indianola

1. George Fred Rhodes, "Historically Speaking," *Port Lavaca Wave,* April 18, 1986, 2B; May 2, 1986, 2B. Brownson Malsch, *Indianola, The Mother of Western Texas* (Austin: Shoal Creek Publishers, Inc., 1977), 6, 7.

2. Eudora Moore, "Recollections of Indianola," *Indianola Scrap Book* (Aus-

tin: Jenkins, 1974), 94, 95, 97; Lelia Seeligson, "History of Indianola," 24, in *Scrapbook.*

3. Walter P. Webb, et al., eds., *Handbook of Texas* (Austin: Texas State Historical Association, 1952), 2:515; George Fred Rhodes, September 12, 1986, 2B, September 19, 1986, 2B, September 26, 1986, 2B; Malsch, 15, 17.

4. George Fred Rhodes, October 17, 1986, 2B, October 24, 1986, 2B.

5. *Ibid.*

6. Article by W. S. Adair in *Dallas News*, February 2, 1925; Malsch, 37, 38, 56, 188.

7. *Victoria Texian Advocate*, September 6, 1850.

8. George Fred Rhodes, October 24, 1986, 2B; *Southwestern Historical Quarterly*, 51:56, 57.

9. Peter A. Johnson, "Two Sea Captains," unpublished manuscript, 1, 2; Malsch, 19, 55, 63; George Fred Rhodes, November 7, 1986; Calhoun County, *Shifting Sands of Calhoun County* (1981), 21.

10. George Fred Rhodes, February 20, 1987; Malsch, 31, 119; *Indianola Scrap Book*, 26, 33; Calhoun County, *Shifting Sands*, 28.

11. Malsch, 46, 63, 115; *Indianola Scrap Book*, 26; Violet Bierman Thurman, *Old Town Indianola* (San Antonio: Standard Printing, 1952), 45.

12. Chris Emmett, *Texas Camel Tales* (San Antonio: Naylor, 1932), 1–19; George Fred Rhodes, March 27, April 3, April 10, 1987.

13. Calhoun County deed records; Commissioners Court proceedings for years 1855–60; Malsch, 108.

14. Calhoun County deed records; S. G. Reed, *A History of Texas Railroads* (Kingsport, TN: Kingsport Press, 1941), 90; *Indianola Bulletin*, April 30, September 5, November 21, 1871.

15. *Indianola Courier*, scattered copies in Barker Texas History Center, University of Texas at Austin.

16. Hobart Huson, *History of Refugio County* (Houston: Guardsman Publishing Co., 1956), 2:38, 40, 45, 46, 63, 78, 82, 86; Malsch, 145, 154, 155, 162–180; Calhoun County Commissioners Court records, 1861–1865; *Indianola Scrap Book*, 31, 32, 33.

17. Malsch, 185, 191, 194, 202, 203; George Fred Rhodes, March 3, 1987.

Saluria

1. Matagorda County Historical Commission, *Historic Matagorda County* (Houston: D. Armstrong Co., 1986), 1:386; Calhoun County Historical Commission, *Shifting Sands of Calhoun County* (1981), 61.

2. H. P. N. Gammel, ed., *Laws of Texas* (Austin: The Gammel Book Co., 1898), 1:1315, 2:512; E. W. Winkler, ed., *Secret Journals of the Senate*, December 14, 1842, 232.

3. Gammel, ed., *Laws of Texas*, 2:511–513; William Kennedy, *Texas: the Rise, Progress and Prospects of Republic of Texas* (Clifton: Augustus M. Kelley, 1841), 784; Hobart Huson, *History of Refugio County* (Houston: Guardsman Publishing Co., 1956), 1:502.

4. Robert Edward Lee Crane, Jr., "Administration of Customs Service of Republic of Texas" (master's thesis, University of Texas, 1939), 106, 107.

5. Huson, *Refugio,* 1:502–505; *Indianola Scrap Book* (Austin: Jenkins, 1974), 193–195; Brownson Malsch, *Indianola, The Mother of Western Texas* (Austin: Shoal Creek Publishers, 1977), 3.

6. Malsch, 51, 57–59, 61–65, 83, 108, 117, 140; *Indianola Scrap Book,* 193–195; George Fred Rhodes, "Historically Speaking," *Port Lavaca Wave,* December 13 and December 27, 1985.

7. Calhoun County, *Shifting Sands,* 66; Malsch, 151, 163, 180–181; Huson, *Refugio,* 2:59, 60, 61, 63, 65, 77, 82.

8. Malsch, 181, 199; *Indianola Scrap Book,* 195.

9. *Indianola Scrap Book,* 138.

River Ports

1. Texana was originally called Santa Anna in honor of the Mexican general. When the general became unpopular in Texas, the name was changed by a vote of the people with 84 voting for Texana, submitted by John S. Menefee, and 19 for Pulaski, offered by Major Kerr.

2. I. T. Taylor, *The Calvacade of Jackson County* (San Antonio: Naylor Co., 1938), 58–63, 89–93; Walter P. Webb, et al., eds., *Handbook of Texas* (Austin: Texas State Historical Association, 1952), 2:730.

3. Personal interviews with Mr. and Mrs. Abel Pierce; Matagorda County Historical Commission, *Historic Matagorda County* (Houston: D. Armstrong Co., 1986), 2:110, 225, 404.

4. *Matagorda County Tribune,* Century of Progress edition (1937); *Historic Matagorda,* 110, 111, 385.

Bibliography

Books

Allen, Arda Talbot. *Miss Ella*. San Antonio: The Naylor Co., 1951.

Alperin, Lynn M. *Custodians of the Coast*. Corps of Engineers Publications: 1977.

Barker, Eugene C. *Austin Papers*. 3 vols. Austin: University of Texas Press, 1927.

————. *The Life of Stephen F. Austin*. Austin: Texas State Historical Association, 1949.

Briscoe, Eugenia Reynolds. *City by the Sea: A History of Corpus Christi, Texas, 1519–1875*. New York: Vantage Press, 1985.

Brown, John Henry. *History of Texas from 1685 to 1892*. 2 vols. St. Louis: L. E.Daniell, 1892.

Calhoun County Historical Commission. *Shifting Sands of Calhoun County*. 1981.

Calhoun County. *Inventory*. Prepared by Works Progress Administration, University of Texas sponsor, 1941. Published by Calhoun County, Texas.

Carroll, William M. *Béranger's Discovery of Aransas Pass*. Edited and annotated by Frank Wagner. Friends of the Corpus Christi Museum: 1983.

Castañeda, Carlos E. *The Mexican Side of the Texas Revolution, 1836*. Dallas: P. L. Turner Co., 1928.

————. *Our Catholic Heritage in Texas*. 6 vols. Austin: Von Boeckmann-Jones Co., 1936.

Corpus Christi, A History and Guide. Compiled by writers for Works Progress Administration. Corpus Christi: Caller-Times Publishing Co., 1942.

De Cordova, Jacob. *Texas*. Philadelphia: E. Crozet Co., 1858.

Dobie, J. Frank. *A Vaquero of the Brush Country*. Austin: University of Texas Press, 1957.

Edwards, William B. *The Story of Colt's Revolver*. Harrisburg, PA: Stackpole Co., 1953.

Emmett, Chris. *Texas Camel Tales*. San Antonio: Naylor, 1932.

Ezell, Camp. *Historical Story of Bee County*. Beeville: Beeville Publishing Co., 1973.

Foote, Henry Stuart. *Texas and the Texans*. 2 vols. Philadelphia: Thomas, Cowperthwait & Co., 1841.

Gammel, H. P. N., ed. *Laws of Texas*. 10 vols. Austin: The Gammel Book Co., 1898.

Gatschet, Albert Samuel. *The Karankawa Indians*. New York: Kraus Reprint Corp., 1967.

Guthrie, Keith. *History of San Patricio County*. Austin: Nortex Press, 1986.

Hackett, Charles Wilson. *Pichardo's Treatise on the Limits of Louisiana and Texas.* 3 vols. Austin: University of Texas Press, 1931.

Helm, Mary S. Wightman. *Scraps of Early Texas History.* Austin: Eakin Press, 1987 (first published in 1884).

Hitchcock, E. A. *Diary.* Edited by W. A. Croffut. New York: Books for Libraries Press.

Holley, Mary Austin. *Texas.* Austin: Steck Company, 1935. Facsimile of original, Lexington, KY: J. Clarke & Co., 1836.

Huson, Hobart. *El Copano. Refugio Timely Remarks,* ca. 1920s (printed in the *Refugio Timely Remarks* and later in a paperback).

———. *History of Refugio County.* 2 vols. Houston: Guardsman Publishing Co., 1956.

Indianola Scrap Book. Austin: Jenkins Publishing Company, 1974. Facsimile reproduction of first edition compiled and published by the *Victoria Advocate,* 1936. Reprinted 1974 by Calhoun County Historical Survey Committee.

Jenkins, John H., ed. *The Papers of the Texas Revolution, 1835–1836.* 10 vols. Austin: Presidial Press, 1973.

Jeter, Lorraine Bruce. *Matagorda Early History.* Baltimore: Gateway Press, Inc., 1974.

Kennedy, William. *Texas: the Rise, Progress and Prospects of the Republic of Texas.* Clifton: Augustus M. Kelley, 1841. Reprint 1974.

Killman, Ed. *Cannibal Coast.* San Antonio: Naylor Co., 1959.

King, Richard. *Printing in the Republic of Texas.* Texana: 1968.

Lamar, Mirabeau B. *Papers of Mirabeau Buonaparte Lamar.* 10 vols. Edited from original papers in Texas State Archives. Austin and New York: Pemberton Press, 1968.

Lea, Tom. *The King Ranch.* 2 vols. Toronto, Boston: Little, Brown & Co., 1957.

Linn, John J. *Reminiscences of Fifty Years in Texas.* Austin: Steck Company, 1935.

Malsch, Brownson. *Indianola, The Mother of Western Texas.* Austin: Shoal Creek Publishers, 1977.

Matagorda County Historical Commission. *Historic Matagorda County.* 2 vols. Houston: D. Armstrong Co., 1986.

McCampbell, Coleman. *Texas Seaport.* New York: Exposition Press, 1952.

Nance, Joseph Milton. *After San Jacinto.* Austin: University of Texas Press, 1963.

———. *Attack and Counterattack.* Austin: University of Texas Press, 1964.

Newton, Lewis W. *History of Texas.* Dallas: Southwest Press, 1932.

Oberste, William H. *History of Refugio Mission. Refugio Timely Remarks:* 1942.

———. *Texas Irish Empresarios and Their Colonies.* Austin: Von Boeckmann-Jones Co., 1953.

Reed, S. G. *A History of Texas Railroads.* Kingsport, TN: Kingsport Press, 1941.

Refugio County Historical Commission. *History of Refugio County.* 1987.

Sibley, Marilyn McAdams. *Lone Stars and State Gazettes.* Reprint. College Station: A&M Press, 1983.

Stephens, A. Ray. *The Taft Ranch.* Austin: University of Texas Press, 1964.

Sutherland, Mary A. *The Story of Corpus Christi.* Houston: Rein & Sons Co., for Corpus Christi Chapter of Daughters of the Confederacy, 1916.

Taylor, I.T. *The Calvacade of Jackson County.* San Antonio: Naylor Co., 1938.

Texas Almanac. 1871.

Thurman, Violet Bierman. *Old Town Indianola.* San Antonio: Standard Printing, 1952.

Vernor, W. H. *A Rugged American, Aransas Pass Progress.* N.p., 1955.

Webb, Walter P., et al., eds. *Handbook of Texas.* 2 vols. Austin: Texas State Historical Association, 1952.

Wood, Alpha Kennedy. *Texas Coastal Bend.* Second printing by Kathryn Holmes Wood, 1979.

Wooten, Dudley. *Comprehensive History of Texas.* 3 vols. Dallas: Wm. G. Scarff, 1898.

Wortham, Louis J. *History of Texas.* 2 vols. Fort Worth: Wortham-Molyneaux Co., 1924.

Yoakum, Henderson. *History of Texas.* 2 vols. New York: Redfield, 1856.

Public Records

Aransas County Commissioners Court records
Aransas County deed records
Calhoun County Commissioners Court records
Calhoun County deed records
Calhoun Commissioners Court proceedings for years 1855–1860
Refugio County Commissioners Court records
Refugio County deed records
Refugio County Court records
St. Mary's Cemetery records
San Patricio County deed records
U.S. House of Representatives. 67th Cong., 2d session. Document no. 321.

Archival Materials

Bexar Archives. Barker Texas History Center, University of Texas at Austin.

Byrne Papers. Barker Texas History Center, University of Texas at Austin.

Coleman-Fulton Papers. Barker Texas History Center, University of Texas at Austin. Directors' minutes of 1873, 1874, 1910–1916, 1919.

Republic of Texas Customs Records. Texas State Archives, Austin.

Turner Papers. Harwood Collection, Corpus Christi Public Library. Mrs. H. H. Rugeley, custodian. Copy in possession of Keith Guthrie.

Winkler, E. W., ed. *Secret Journals of the Senate.* December 24, 1840, May 23, 1837, December 14, 1842.

Newspapers

Aransas Harbor Herald, April 23, 1893.
Aransas Pass Progress, November 19, 1909, September 26, 1919.
Colorado Tribune, July 7, 1851.
Corpus Christi Caller-Times, May 9, June 23, October 13, 1911, August 29, 1965.
Corpus Christi Caller, August 19, 1957, September 22, 1974.
[Corpus Christi] *Star,* December 16, 1848, March 17, 1884.
Dallas News, February 2, 1925.
Houston Post, November 10, 1963.
Indianola Bulletin, April 30, September 5, November 21, 1871.

Indianola Courier, scattered copies in Barker Texas History Center, University of Texas at Austin.
Matagorda County Tribune, Century of Progress edition, 1937.
Odem-Edroy Times, May 29, 1958.
Port Lavaca Wave, February 20, 1974.
Rockport Pilot, 70th anniversary special, August 31, 1939.
San Antonio Express, May 12, 1912, September 19, 1915.
San Patricio County News, anniversary edition, September 10, 1926 (also copies from 1919, 1920, 1921, 1922, 1923).
Vaquero (copies in Barker Texas History Center).
Victoria Advocate, 88th anniversary edition (1934) and January 24, 1985.
Victoria Texian Advocate, September 6, 1850.

Periodicals and Journals

Dodson, Ruth. "The Noakes Raid." *Frontier Times,* Vol. 23, (October 1945).
Southwestern Historical Quarterly, published by Texas State Historical Society, Austin.
Fretelliere, "San Antonio," *Texas Magazine,* March 1912.

Unpublished Material

Blanton, Annie Webb. "Military Records of Wharton and Matagorda Counties," unpublished. Barker Texas History Center, University of Texas at Austin.
Clay, Mrs. Ella McRae. "History of Lamar." Unpublished manuscript, copy in possession of Keith Guthrie.
Huson, Hobart. *St. Mary's of Aransas,* printed in serial form in *Refugio Timely Remarks* over a number of years. Copy in possession of Keith Guthrie.
Johnson, Peter A. "The Two Sea Captains." Unpublished manuscript, compiled and edited by Hobart Huson. Copy in possession of Keith Guthrie.
Power Papers, unpublished.
"Scrapbook," a collection of clippings from Corpus Christi newspapers in Dan Kilgore Collection, Corpus Christi State University Library.
Ward, Hortense Warner. "Kinney's Trading Post." Unpublished manuscript, Corpus Christi Public Library, Local History Room.
Yeamans, James R., Sr. Unpublished handwritten notes on Matagorda compiled over his lifetime. Copy in possession of Keith Guthrie.
————. Unpublished handwritten notes on *Mary's Bayou.* Copy in possession of Keith Guthrie.

Theses

Crane, Robert Edward Lee, Jr. "Administration of Customs Service of the Republic of Texas." Master's thesis, University of Texas, 1939.
Marr, John Columbus. "History of Matagorda County." Master's thesis, University of Texas, 1928.
Nims, Dorothy Louise. "A History of the Village of Rockport." Master's thesis, Southwest Texas State Teachers College, 1939.

Pamphlets, Speeches, and Interviews

Hunter, Mary Frances. Speech, copy in possession of Keith Guthrie.
Little, Carrie. Personal interview with Mrs. Clarence Kerlagen, November 1938.
Pierce, Mr. and Mrs. Abel. Personal interview.
Schmidt, F. A. "Rails Across the Bay." Pamphlet, copy in possession of Keith Guthrie.

Index

Harrison, Russell B., 85
  William Henry, 85
Hart, E., 31
Hart's Lake, 82
Hatch, James, 163
  Sylvanus, 164
Haupt, Lewis M., 85
Hawes, H. W., 189, 192, 193, 196–
    197
  Hugh W., 194
Hawkins, Commodore, 157
  James B., 140, 141–142
  Joseph, 118
Hawkinsville, 136, 140, 141
Hay, Wm. J., 54
Hayes, G., 119
  John, 152
Haynes, Arthur, 45
  Thomas, 168
Hays's Rangers, 59
Heald, George, 193
Heard, A. J., 51
  Holmes, 51
  T. C., 51
Hearn, Robert Patrick, 67
Helm, ———, 123
  George, 119
  Mary, 125
  Meredith, 125
Henry, 161
Henry, James C., 161
Herring, J. C., 98
Herrlich, Aug., 161
Hewes, 94
Hewes, James, 56
  Samuel, 20, 30, 31
Hewetson, James, 11, 28, 38, 40, 54,
    95, 192
Hill, Robert, 145
Hines, A. D., 147
  R. H., 161
History of Texas, 166
Hitchcock, Major General, 74, 79
Hobby, Alfred Marmaduke, 46, 78
  Barney, 46
  Bill, 46
  Edwin, 46
  William P., 46
Hodges, Galen, 137, 138, 144
Hogan, Andrew J., 98

Hogg, James Stephen, 99
Hoit, J. Q., 132
Holmes, Edward L., 135
Holtz, Helmuth, 144
Holzinger, J. J., 131–132, 151
Hord, Jesse, 145
Horton, Albert C., 130
Houston, Sam, 16, 18, 29, 31, 32, 69,
    128, 131, 149, 151, 155, 159, 183
Howard, Charles, 135
Howe, A. P., 31
Howell, J. N., 147
Howerton, James, Sr., 180
Hoyt Hotel, 85
Hubert, William F., 180
Huck, Charles, 172
Huck Lumber Yard, 189
Hudson, 94
Hughes, Charles, 51
  J., 62
  Robert, 24
Hull, George Robert, 39, 54
Hunter, James, 162
Hurd, Captain, 132
  W. W., 157
hurricanes: (1854) 126, 145; (1875)
    136; (1916) 88, 100; (1919) 89,
    101 (*see also* storms)
Huson, Hobart, 7, 23, 34, 44, 52, 104,
    107
Hutchinson, 94
Hynes, J. H., 98
  John, 108
  Peter, 108
Hynes Spring, 7, 21, 25

I
Independence, 157, 182
Indianola, 60, 70, 76, 110–111, 139,
    164, 166, 168, 169, 170–189
Indianola Artillery Company, 183–
    184
Indianola Bulletin, 167, 177–178
Indianola Guards, 168
Indianola High School, 179–180
Indianola Male and Female School,
    179
Indianola Proposal, 167
Indianola Railroad Company, 181–
    182, 185
Indian Point, 164, 166, 167, 172–174

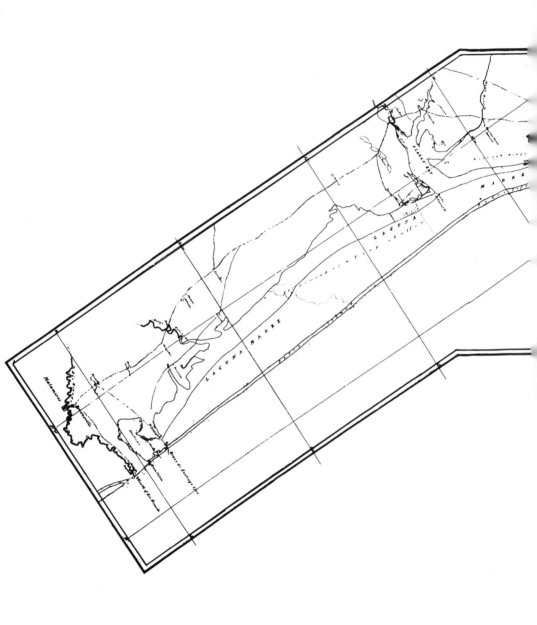